SELECTIVE EXPOSURE TO COMMUNICATION

COMMUNICATION

A series of volumes edited by:
Dolf Zillmann and Jennings Bryant

"SELECTIVE EXPOSURE TO COMMUNICATION"

Edited by

Dolf Zillmann
Indiana University
and
Jennings Bryant
University of Houston

LEA LAWRENCE ERLBAUM ASSOCIATES, PUBLISHERS
1985   Hillsdale, New Jersey   London

Lawrence Erlbaum Associates, Inc., Publishers
365 Broadway
Hillsdale, New Jersey 07642

Library of Congress Cataloging in Publication Data
Main entry under title:

Selective exposure to communication.

(Communication)
Includes indexes.
1. Mass media—Psychological aspects. 2. Mass media—
Audiences. I. Zillmann, Dolf. II. Bryant, Jennings.
III. Series: Communication (Hillsdale, N.J.)
P96.P75S47 1985   302.2'34   85-6727
ISBN 0-89859-585-1

Printed in the United States of America
10 9 8 7 6 5 4 3 2 1

Contents

List of Contributors

Charles K. Atkin, Department of Communication, Michigan State University

Jennings Bryant, School of Communications, University of Houston – University Park

John L. Cotton, School of Management, Purdue University

Allan Fenigstein, Department of Psychology, Kenyon College

Bradley Greenberg, Department of Communication, Michigan State University

Barrie Gunter, Independent Broadcasting Authority, England

Carrie Heeter, Department of Communication, Michigan State University

Ronald G. Heyduk, Department of Psychology, Hartwick College

Percy H. Tannenbaum, Survey Research Center, University of California

Jacob Wakshlag, Department of Telecommunications, Indiana University

James G. Webster, Department of Communication, University of Maryland

Dolf Zillmann, Institute for Communication Research, Indiana University

Preface

Research into what is usually referred to as "mass communication" has concentrated on the societal impact of the media. The ways in which these media influence people and affect their behavior have been at issue. For the most part, undesirable effects were pondered and documented. Only a few desirable effects received similar attention and scrutiny. The research preoccupation with impact has been so pronounced that, comparatively speaking, next to no attention has been paid to questions such as why people enjoy whatever they elect to watch or hear, and more fundamentally, why they elect to watch or hear, in the first place, whatever it is that they elect to watch or hear.

The commercial media institutions have in all probability collected a considerable amount of data in grappling with these "money questions." But the findings are, for the most part, not available to the academic community, and it is doubtful whether they would appreciably contribute to a general understanding of the principles that govern exposure behavior. Basic research on these questions seems to have been hampered by a number of factors, but mainly by academic prejudice. First and foremost, empirical-minded investigators have been most reluctant to tackle an issue as "frivolous" as entertainment. The news and persuasion of any kind were bona fide research topics. Research on the appeal of drama, sitcoms, soaps, and sporting events apparently lacked a sufficient degree of dignity. The fact that those in the humanities who generated proposals pertaining to the enjoyment of entertainment often failed to articulate them in such a way that they could be subjected to empirical verification—whereas specific, testable hypotheses were advanced in persuasion research—did not help matters. Additionally, techniques to study impact and even selective exposure to informative messages were fully developed, but procedures to deal with selective-exposure behavior in the realm of entertainment were not. Whatever it may have been in particular that hampered progress in research, eventually it became clear that the so-called mass media are primarily entertainment media (despite much wishful thinking to the contrary) and that it is dignified and important, if not imperative, to explore and comprehend the "hows" and "whys" of the consumption of mass media entertainment.

Research on the selection of informative and entertaining messages for consumption has been done eclectically by various investigators at various institutions. Although considerable progress has been achieved by different parties, these parties had little, if any, contact with one another, and their efforts have never been integrated. To our knowledge, there has never been a symposium on research into selective exposure to informative and entertaining messages. Nor has there ever been a publication that brought together the recent research in this area. This volume was put together in an effort to end this dilemma and to put selective-exposure research on the map as a significant research venture.

We have been most fortunate in attaining the collaboration of investigators who have made notable contributions to the study of selective-exposure phenomena. Their work spans a great variety of manifestations of selective-exposure behavior and approaches to studying it. The fact that the contributors are about evenly divided between psychology and communication departments, and that some have dual affiliations, attests to the interdisciplinary character of theory and research in this emerging domain of inquiry. The various contributions are introduced at the end of chapter 1. This opening chapter serves as a general introduction to selective-exposure research for the noninitiated reader.

We are most grateful to all contributors for making this volume possible. We are grateful, too, to our graduate students who helped in one capacity or another in putting things together. Finally, we owe a debt of gratitude to our spouses and children for granting all that time for unmitigated selective exposure to the tasks at hand.

Dolf Zillmann
Jennings Bryant

1 Selective-Exposure Phenomena

Dolf Zillmann
Indiana University

Jennings Bryant
University of Houston

At any moment, an enormity of stimuli impinges on the living organism. The organism neither is equipped to handle this stimulus onslaught, nor would it be meaningful in terms of self- and species-preservation to accomplish such a task. Survival, it seems, is well served by the neglect of most potential information. Or to put it more positively, survival is well served by a *selective reduction of information,* that is, a reduction to behaviorally significant cues to which the organism can respond in an adaptive fashion.

The selection of information is controlled, first of all, by the build of the organism—specifically, the build of the sensory organs. Potential information (i.e., any physical process) that fails to stimulate these organs is obviously immaterial to the behavior of the organism. However, the "physical" reception of information by no means guarantees that the information is of any behavioral consequence. The organism focuses its perceptual efforts in unique ways, and it tends to utilize its limited capacity for processing received information in particular ways also. Focusing attention implies, of course, that not all available information can be given equal attention and that some information might not receive any attention. Focusing, then, implies selection. And as not all perceived information can be processed (i.e., behaviorally utilized or stored for later retrieval and behavioral utilization), processing also entails selection. But whereas sensory selection is fixed with the build of the organism, perceptual focus and selective processing are behavioral processes that are characterized by considerable plasticity. Although many of these selective processes are automatic and mechanical, many others are under volitional control and deliberate.

The various processes under consideration are perhaps best illustrated by considering early humans. Cave dwellers, for instance, were probably often

1

surrounded by signals from numerous animals. They were ill equipped for visual perception in dim light and in the dark, and they missed out on much of the barely audible and inaudible vocalizations of creatures such as bats. They were equipped, however, to respond quickly to sudden noises produced in their immediate vicinity and to vivid peripherally received visual events. The automatic reaction was one of spatial adjustment for the purpose of attaining superior perceptual control of the sources of information. This reaction is known as the orienting response, and its obvious survival value lies in the creation of a readiness for fight and flight. The reflexive adjustment was likely to be followed by selective attention, such as to a threatening animal's teeth and claws rather than its tail and fur condition. The processing of an encounter of this sort was then equally "idiosyncratic." Generally speaking, whatever made the biggest impression (e.g., the pain from a bite and all the cues associated with that experience) was likely to be focused on in rehearsal and memory. This, of course, is just another way of saying that some happenings received disproportionate, selective attention in rehearsal and memory. The selective commission of perceived events to memory—at the expense of many other simultaneously occurring events of less significance—ultimately gave impetus to paying attention *deliberately:* An animal that was recognized as dangerous, for instance, had to be tracked perceptually in preparation for fight or flight. The survival value of such attentional behavior is again quite obvious. Needless to say, perceptual tracking is not specific to fight–flight reactions. It applies to all essentials in life, such as the attainment of food, shelter, and mate.

What, in this illustration, could and should be considered selective exposure? Not the sensory constitution of the organism with its implications for selective access to the physical world. Not the transitory checking out of an event as a result of orienting and defensive responses. Not the reflexively controlled focusing on certain events in the sensory field that characterizes selective attention. And not the screening for salient elements in the processing of the percepts that is usually referred to as rehearsal or selective rehearsal, nor the implications thereof for selective recall. Selective exposure, instead, designates *behavior that is deliberately performed to attain and sustain perceptual control of particular stimulus events.*

According to this definition, selective exposure subsumes anything from closely watching a poisonous snake in the grass, following the flight of a bumblebee, listening to a birdcall, watching the road and other cars as we travel down the highway, reading the newspaper, listening to records in solitude or while keeping an eye on the children, and watching television intently or while doing the dishes.

Selective exposure can be accomplished with little effort, or it may require great energy expenditure. Reading a book, for instance, is comparatively nonstrenuous physically. Watching a car race from the pits, in contrast, demands rapid head and body adjustments that can be strenuous. Differences in energy expenditure in the service of the act of perception per se might be considered trivial, however, when compared with expenditures engendered in the attainment and maintenance of perceptual control that relies on locomotor pursuit. Watching one's children play baseball in the backyard, for instance, is selective exposure that might require stepping out of the house. Going to Shea Stadium to see the Mets play calls for a somewhat greater effort. Visiting Europe is more effortful yet, despite the fact that most of the movement necessary is accomplished while sitting in a cushioned seat. However, such energy expenditure reduces to insignificance when one compares it to self-powered locomotion to places and events to which exposure is sought. Hunting deer in the mountains, for instance, entails selective exposure that is highly energy consuming.

These rather obvious considerations of energy expenditure associated with the attainment and maintenance of selective exposure prepare us for a look at the cultural evolution of such exposure. Like other animals, humans were at first limited to selective exposure by self-powered locomotion. Irrespective of motives for exposure, persons could elect to pursue perceptually what was happening "here and now." To the extent that this was possible, they could walk, swim, ride, or paddle to places where events occurred to which they sought exposure. They could also forgo direct exposure and content themselves with verbal accounts of these events or with poor iconic representations (e.g., drawings of athletic events). Only rather recently has it become technically and economically feasible for large numbers of people to ship their bodies with reasonable speed to the places to which they seek exposure. Almost all Americans now can see the Grand Canyon in person, and uncounted Japanese can enjoy direct exposure to Salzburg and Mozart's home. In principle, people move themselves and are being moved to locales of interest, so that they can see, hear, touch, smell, and taste the events to which they seek unmitigated perceptual access; and technology has greatly facilitated this process. At the same time, however, technology has accomplished the reverse as well: It has found ways to move events of interest to the people. Specifically, technology has provided means to represent physical events visually and auditorily (or audio-visually) with great fidelity, to store these representations, and to revive them at any later time. And whereas little progress has been made in the iconic conservation and manipulation over time of tactile and olfactory stimuli, audio-visual representation often exhibits "hyperfidelity" by furnishing visual and auditory access to events that goes beyond the capabilities of the unarmed eye and ear. Through screen and speaker, then, the world at large can be audio-visually accessed. Selective exposure to potentially all existing audio-visual environments can be accomplished with the flick of a dial or the push of a button.

Selective exposure to an ever increasing number of environments has become low-energy armchair behavior. By pushing hand-held remote controls, any number of events can be accessed; and access can just as readily be abandoned in favor of exposure to other events. Television viewers can effortlessly jump from exposure to news events in China to a soccer match in Italy, and from a nature film about Norwegian reindeer to a domestic comedy show or dramatic street violence. Whatever tickles their fancy, for whatever reason, may be consumed—and abandoned upon a moment's dissatisfaction. The selection of particular programs may be thought out and planned. But it may also be spontaneous and rather mindless, even mechanically determined. And as viewers might go back and forth between programs in efforts to catch most of the significant events in two or more, so can they alternate exposure to representations on the screen and their immediate environment. Selective exposure, then, need not be construed as a continual, uninterrupted effort at sustaining perceptual control. Especially if a particular set of events is information-poor such that perceptual control can be maintained with intermittent attention, exposure is likely to be divided between two or more environmental settings. Someone cooking a meal, for instance, might well be able to keep an eye on pots and pans while peeking in on the news. And a child may watch Mister Rogers and, in a dull moment, continue to play with her toys—only to look back at the set when the trolley bell rings for the trip to the Land of Make Believe. It seems that visual attention to the screen is often unnecessary for exposure to occur, as continued auditory attention suffices for message comprehension and also cues the necessary return of visual attention.

Notwithstanding these complications, the choice situations for selective exposure to television are quite clear. The elementary choice is between no exposure and exposure. The characteristic choice presupposes this elementary decision and is among a finite number of available offerings (i.e., broadcasts and programs off cable, disk, tape, etc.). Although it is assumed that these choices are made for the purpose of attaining and sustaining perceptual control of the selected programs, exposure cannot be expected to be complete. Visual and auditory attention are likely to be drawn away from the represented events. This nonattention, usually the result of happenings in the immediate environment, can be visual, auditory, or both; and it can be momentary or extensive. A mother, for instance, might be inclined to watch her favorite soap, but be forced to attend to her child for much of the time. Her selective exposure obviously will have alternated between show and child. She exposed herself to both sets of events. This may have been in succession. But it is also conceivable that her auditory attention, unlike her visual attention, was never critically disrupted. The answer to questions such as "Was she selectively exposed to the *entire* program?" can only be arbitrary. Selective exposure in mixed or multiple media consumption leads to similarly indefinite assessments. How is exposure that fluctuates between a simultaneously consumed radio concert and a sitcom on television or between various athletic contests on different monitors to be apportioned? The simplest empirical approach appears to lie in determining the time periods during which behavioral efforts at attaining and sustaining perceptual control of particular representations were immediately evident to an observer.

However, for all practical purposes, the discussed difficulties in deciding on what was and what was not selective exposure to a particular program or program segment can be circumvented by determining *whether or not exposure to the program or the segment was intended and/or was the primary perceptual activity during the time course of the program or segment.* Such conceptualization accommodates esoteric practices of mixed and multiple media consumption. But more important, it handles the characteristic exposure condition: one set, with one person in charge of selecting programs, one at a time—granted distractions and social influences on the choice.

The fact that the new communication technology allows the manipulation of audio-visual environments with enormous ease and provides an abundance of program choices at all times undoubtedly will have significant behavioral and social effects. Some effects are obtrusive. The sheer amount of television viewing in whatever form (i.e., broadcasts, off cable, disk, tape, etc.) attests that exposure to the environments presented on the monitor is more engaging and presumably more enjoyable than many alternative, immediate environments. There are few social circumstances and emotional conditions that are consistently preferred over the environments on the screen. The television environment outshines and outglamours the common home, and the actions it entails outdo the daily dread by a wide margin. At a most basal level, once the monitor runs and fills the home with flashes of color and brightness, with rapid motion, and with drastic sound-level changes, it is difficult to resist paying attention to it. The active television screen is, so to speak, the last thing in the house to which its inhabitant will perceptually habituate.

The stimulus wealth of television, sometimes referred to as rapid-fire exposition, has been met with some concern. However, the great issues of social concern have been content related. The ubiquity of violent crime in drama, in particular, has been thought to promote crime and violence in society as well as a fear of becoming a victim of crime or violence. In so-called effects research, an enormous number of investigations have probed this issue and its ramifications. The determination of ill effects of exposure to whatever is abundantly present in media fare has altogether dominated mass communication research. Why people enjoy whatever they enjoy and why they seek exposure to whatever they seek exposure to are questions that have been met with surprising indifference. This is not to say that enjoyment of entertaining television fare has received no attention at all. Nor is it to deny that meticulous counts of exactly who consumes what how often and so forth have been compiled routinely, along with the answers to some questions as to why viewers liked this and not that. It is to say, however, that compared to effects research the study of why people elect to consume some messages and not others has been greatly neglected. Selective-exposure research has been scarce, sporadic, and eclectic. It is this volume's mission to correct this situation by bringing together the widely dispersed, conceptually and methodologically diverse approaches to the phenomenon of selective exposure, and it is hoped that such integration and focusing will highlight the phenomenon and its significance and stimulate exploratory interest.

The issues for selective-exposure research are manifold. What stable selective tendencies, or message-consumption preferences, or tastes as traits exist in what kind of person? How and why were they formed? What is their fate, and how can they be altered? What consequence have moods and emotions for message selection? What about states of general excitedness and states of boredom and fatigue? What are the implications for message selection of holding particular beliefs and convictions? Why do some people take a strong interest in public-affairs information, whereas others resort to fiction? Why do some people turn to comedy, others to serious drama? Why to comedy or drama under particular circumstances? What attracts some to tragedy? Why do some yearn for horror movies and others, or the same people at different times, for musicals? What is it about sports that draws people to the screen? And what is it that makes people go fishing and turn their backs to the screen, at least temporarily?

The common element in all these questions is the following dependent variable: the effect *on* message selection for consumption. Not the effect *of* the consumption of selected messages; nor, as in conventional media-effects research, the effect *of* the consumption of messages that, for the most part, were selected by a party other than the consumer.

Such conceptual focus is not only epistemologically warranted in that it promotes the exploration of choice behavior regarding message consumption, but it also leads to and, in fact, demands reinterpretations and qualifications of much media-effects research. In experimental research, as a rule, exposure to messages is forced. Subjects are randomly assigned to consumption conditions, and the effect of specific assignments is ascertained relative to that of others. This procedure is appropriate as long as it can be assumed that all messages whose effects on a variable of interest are being compared are at least once in a while, by choice and under similar circumstances, consumed by the respondents. Such an assumption is often untenable, however; and if so, qualifications need be placed on any findings. Let us assume, for instance, that it has been demonstrated that exposure to situation comedy reduces the anger and aggressive behavior of angry people. Can it be concluded from this that, given the preponderance of such programs on television, situation comedy helps to curb anger and aggression in society? Not with confidence, as it is conceivable that in acute anger most persons would refrain from exposing themselves to laughter and merriment. Comedy might be consumed mainly in states other than anger, and consumers thus would not attain a potential benefit of exposure to comedy. Consequently, it could be contended that comedy alleviates much anger only if it had been demonstrated that: (a) angry persons' exposure to these materials has an anger-reducing impact *and* (b) angry persons seek or, at least, do not avoid exposure to comedy. Similarly, if it had been demonstrated that exposure to erotica alleviates feelings of depression, it would still have to be shown that depressed persons are drawn to consuming erotica before it could be contended that erotica curb depression under conditions in which consumption is left to the consumers (i.e., they are free, in their particular state, to consume whatever they feel like consuming).

It should be clear that the argument here is not that exposure effects tend to be determined on subjects who, when free to do as they please, would never elect to expose themselves to the materials in question. Studying the effects on enjoyment of replay frequency in boxing telecasts, for instance, with subjects who are professedly opposed to boxing and would definitely not watch such programs obviously has little ecological validity, and the generalization of any effects to avid boxing fans is inadvisable and reckless. It is not such missampling of subjects and the resulting unwarranted conclusions about exposure effects on a population of interest that is at issue, but the possibility that *exposure to communication is situation- and disposition-specific*. It is this possibility that compromises the generalization of many exposure effects. This volume presents a considerable amount of evidence showing that the possibility is more than just that: It is a fact for selective-exposure behavior generally, and future effects research will have to face up to these complicating circumstances.

The selective-exposure conceptualization not only complicates the interpretation of numerous experimental findings, but also troubles much correlational work that seeks to support directional hypotheses. Although such efforts confront insurmountable methodological problems, they are commonly made—perhaps in hopes that they will supplement and complement approaches that are technically more compelling and thus help generate a consistent and coherent effects pattern. *The* directional or "effects" hypothesis that is often deemed supported by correlational data is, of course, the proposal that exposure to particular messages has specific effects on behavior. Irrespective of the possibility that a relationship between exposure and behavior might be the result of extrinsic factors, the directional hypothesis usually can be reversed: Instead of exposure causing behavior, behavioral conditions might cause selective exposure. Selective exposure, then, frequently offers an alternative to the effects hypothesis.

To illustrate this, let us assume that a positive correlation had been observed between the amount of crime-drama consumption and fear of victimization. The effects hypothesis projects that exposure fosters fear, and the findings would be consistent with this projection. But the correlation is equally consistent with the selective-exposure hypothesis projecting the opposite: namely, that fear, for some specifiable reason, makes crime drama attractive and fosters exposure. Similarly, a positive relationship between horror-movie attendance and morbid interests does not secure that the movies created such interests. It is equally possible that these interests lead to attendance. There is no assurance, however, that either the effects hypothesis or the selective-exposure hypothesis provides a better account of the relationship than other factors, which might also have an influence on the related ones.

The selective-exposure approach is thus likely to modify and complement much of the impact research as well as promote more careful and specific interpretations of research findings. But this is only part of the story. The explanation of selective-exposure phenomena is, as stated earlier, important in its own right; and the new communication technology, as it affords an abundance of choices to the message consumer, is bound to produce significant social issues.

On the positive side, consumers will be able to pick from a wealth of informative and entertaining programs. They will be able to satisfy their curiosities about uncounted topics. And they will be able to select materials that best entertain them and therefore best serve to restore their energies for productive action. On the negative side, one might fear overexposure to trivia and an "addiction" to entertainment as "instant gratification." Concerns have been voiced already, and legitimately so. For instance, televised educational efforts seem to require more and more embellishments in order to hold the attention of viewers. This is especially true of programs for children, many of which have become bang-bang presentations that carry far more material to entertain and amuse than to teach. The justification for such programming style is that, were the fireworks and jokes absent, the children would turn to competing (i.e., simultaneously available) programs and then not be exposed to educational information at all. The fact that, before too long, children will be able to skip over undesirable parts of a program in a fast-preview fashion (as with tape and disk) would further complicate matters and is a nightmare for many educators.

The outlook seems equally bleak for informational efforts concerning adults. What, for instance, will happen when news programs compete against abundant entertainment options such as comedy, drama, and sports? Is it unreasonable to expect that large segments of the population will turn to these gratifications rather than resist them for good citizenship? Those who many years ago projected political apathy to grow from massive entertainment consumption get a second chance for being right when the forthcoming abundance of choice will manifest itself. If three national networks and public television plus an independent station or two could not produce sufficient "narcotizing dysfunction," the new communication technology just might manage to drive political apathy to a breaking point for democratic society. But concerns such as these perhaps will prove exaggerated and groundless, and the abundance of choice will amount to an abundance of fireworks turned drab—that is, to a flood of similarly unattractive choices.

Issues like these need not be matters of grand speculation, however. Selective-exposure research has developed techniques to explore all conceivable choice situations and thus is capable of projecting what is likely to happen when particular choices are or become available. The clarification of the big and not-so-big issues is now in the researchers' hands and depends, for the most part, on their ingenuity and persistence.

Turning from what is to be done to what has been done already, this volume comprises a first comprehensive review of past and present theory and research in selective exposure. This chapter was written to introduce the reader who is unfamiliar with selective-exposure research to the phenomenon as such and to its significance. In chapter 2, John L. Cotton discusses the theory of cognitive dissonance and its application to selective exposure. He reviews the considerable body of research that this theory has generated. Until recently, this pioneering research constituted about all the research that was conducted on selective-exposure phenomena. James G. Webster and Jacob Wakshlag, in chapter 3, detail and critically analyze the old and the new, the simplistic and the sophisticated techniques that have been and are being used to measure exposure and selective exposure, especially to television. Chapter 4, by Charles K. Atkin, reviews the research that has been conducted to explore the motives for the consumption of entertaining messages in the perception of the consumers. In contrast to the earlier, narrow focus on persuasion and dissonance reduction as a benefit of exposure, this research projects a multitude of reasons for exposure to a variety of messages. The concentration on more inclusive motivational concepts such as informational utility and gratification led the way in opening up the study of selective exposure to the main course of the mass media—namely, entertainment. In chapter 5, Barrie Gunter further explores consumption choices. His analysis is more strongly focussed on behavior, however. Instead of probing the consumers' perceptions of their own motives, he seeks to infer these motives, especially persisting ones, from assessments of their actual choices. It is undoubtedly useful and important to ascertain people's accounting of why they do what they do. Inferences from the assessment of actual consumption behavior that varies as a function of known message variables are generally considered more compelling, however, as they bypass the distortions that are commonly associated with self-perception and self-reports. Allan Fenigstein and Ronald G. Heyduk continue the behavioral analysis of media exposure in chapter 6. They highlight experimental technique in the study of selective exposure in determining the implications of specific cognitive and behavioral states for the consumption of entertaining messages that feature violent action. Dolf Zillmann and Jacob Wakshlag, in chapter 7, report on similar experimental investigations. However, these investigations address the controversial relationship between exposure to the preponderance of crime in television drama and fear of criminal victimization. The research that is reported seeks to establish that this relationship, in part, is a selective-exposure phenomenon. In chapter 8, Dolf Zillmann and Jennings Bryant deal with the implications of mood states for message choice. Mainly on the basis of experimental investigations, a case is made for the "emotional utility" of the consumption of particular entertaining messages. Jacob Wakshlag examines exposure to educational television in chapter 9. He reports the scarce experimental research in this field of inquiry. In chapter 10, Carrie Heeter and Bradley Greenberg take a look at program selections in cable television, which offers an abundance of choice. They concentrate on the emergence of choice patterns under these conditions and relate these patterns to choice models capable of coping with this new wealth in program access. Finally, in chapter 11, Percy H. Tannenbaum tackles what is easily the most neglected phenomenon in selective exposure: repeated exposure to the same offerings. Repeated exposure is obvious for all purely auditory media. For the visual and audio-visual media, in contrast, it has gone virtually unnoticed, and neither theoretical nor empirical minds have paid much attention to it.

The chapters, taken together, hopefully will remedy the neglect of selective-exposure phenomena and accomplish an awakening of theoretical curiosity about and research interest into the seeking of exposure to novel, informative, and/or entertaining messages from any kind of communication medium.

2 Cognitive Dissonance in Selective Exposure

John L. Cotton
Purdue University

In using information, we are seldom passive absorbers of data; rather, we selectively seek, choose, and screen the information we use. Although this is typically done to avoid irrelevant or useless information, there are often occasions when information is selected on the basis of its agreeable nature, and not its intrinsic value. One explanation for this selective exposure comes from the theory of cognitive dissonance developed by Leon Festinger (1957). This chapter reviews the research on selective exposure to information, focusing on Festinger's theory and the research it generated. From this review, we can determine whether this type of selective exposure occurs and examine other factors that may affect it.

Festinger's (1957) theory states that when a person holds two cognitions that are incompatible or inconsistent, an uncomfortable arousal, or dissonance, is produced. The cognitions can be attitudes, beliefs, and knowledge about one's behavior, or any other knowledge about oneself or the environment. When the person becomes aware that two or more of these cognitions are contradictory, dissonance is created. The magnitude of this dissonance depends on the importance of the cognitions involved. Because the dissonance is uncomfortable, the person will try to reduce it, often by modifying one of the cognitions.

Consider someone who believes he or she is essentially a good and truthful person, but has just lied to someone else (Festinger & Carlsmith, 1959). Dissonance will occur because of the opposing cognitions: (a) "I'm a good, truthful person." (b) "I just lied to this person." The dissonance, or uncomfortable arousal, will motivate the person to do something to reduce it. In this case, the person might rationalize, "I had to lie in order to avoid hurting them; it's just a little white lie."

11

In his theory of cognitive dissonance, Festinger (1957) proposed that one way dissonance can be reduced is through selective exposure, and he suggested three hypotheses. First, if little or no dissonance occurs, there will be no motivation for selective exposure. Second, moderate amounts of dissonance will lead to the seeking of information that would reduce the dissonance and the avoidance of information that would exacerbate it. Third, extremely high levels of dissonance will not increase selective exposure, but could lead the person to seek information increasing the dissonance and to avoid information reducing it (Festinger, 1957, pp. 127–128). This last hypothesis comes from the idea that if dissonance is too great, selective exposure will not be sufficient to reduce the inconsistency. Thus, seeking contrary information may force the person to change one of the contradictory cognitions and reduce dissonance in that manner.

One situation that typically produces dissonance is making an important decision between two equally attractive alternatives. Suppose you are buying a car and have decided on either a Volkswagen or a Honda. Both are equally attractive to you, so it is a difficult decision. You finally choose one (the Honda), and dissonance is produced. You have two inconsistent cognitions. On the one hand, you did not choose the Volkswagen, yet on the other hand, it has many attractive features. How do you reduce this dissonance?

Festinger theorizes that one way the dissonance can be reduced is through selective exposure. After a difficult decision, such as buying a car, the consumer may selectively seek information that supports the decision and avoid conflicting data. In this way, the chosen alternative becomes more attractive and the unchosen alternative less desirable. The dissonance is thereby reduced or eliminated.

Ehrlich, Guttman, Schonbach, and Mills (1957) tested just this type of selective exposure with new car owners. These investigators found that new owners read more advertisements of the model they purchased than ads of cars they considered but did not buy. The selective exposure was much less pronounced with car owners who had purchased their automobiles more than a year earlier.

Dissonance can be produced in ways other than with a difficult decision. Whenever behavior is contrary to a person's attitudes, values, or beliefs, dissonance should occur. For example, the cigarette smoker who believes cigarettes cause lung cancer, but continues to smoke, should experience considerable dissonance. One way this dissonance can be reduced is by changing one's beliefs, for example, thinking that cancer concerns are exaggerated or that everything (including smoking) causes cancer. Selective exposure to information helps support this shift and reduces the dissonance.

The impact of dissonance on selective exposure in cigarette smokers has been examined in several studies, including one by Brock and Balloun (1967). These authors had smokers and nonsmokers listen to tape-recorded messages that either favored or opposed smoking. The messages were interrupted continuously with static, so if subjects wished to hear the message clearly, they had to repeatedly press an antistatic button. Selective exposure was demonstrated, as smokers tended to push the button to eliminate the static more while listening to the prosmoking message. In contrast, nonsmokers pushed the button more while the antismoking message was being played.

Although these two studies give the impression that selective exposure to information is a relatively robust and reliable effect, the research testing this phenomenon has generally produced equivocal findings. Some researchers (e.g., Freedman & Sears, 1965) have concluded that selective exposure does not exist. The next two sections of this chapter review early research on selective exposure and its early dismissal. The third section focuses on possible problems with this early research, arguing that the findings and interpretations are questionable. The fourth section reviews recent research and provides a more positive (and probably more accurate) conclusion concerning selective exposure. The final section focuses on several relatively unexplored issues related to selective exposure to information.

EARLY RESEARCH (1957–1965)

Because his hypotheses are relatively specific in requiring the arousal of cognitive dissonance, Festinger (1957) discussed only one study of selective exposure not intended to test the theory. Originally reported by Lazarfeld (1942), this study concerned the listening audience of a series of educational radio programs. The programs focused, in different installments, on how various national groups have contributed to American culture. Lazarfeld found that the audience for each program was generally the national group being praised in that installment. The program was not effective in teaching tolerance because listeners only selected information that promised to agree with their attitudes. Consistent information (praise for one's nationality) was sought, whereas discrepant information (priase for other nationalities) was avoided.

A laboratory study conducted by Festinger and several of his colleagues is also reviewed in the 1957 volume. In the experiment, subjects chose one of two positions in a game they would play with the experimenter. The subjects were told that one of the positions would be more advantageous than the other and that they should be able to choose the correct position. The game involved gambling, and subjects were to attempt to win as much money as possible. The subjects could change their position at any time, but to do so would cost them a stiff penalty. After playing the game long enough to establish a winning or losing record, the subjects were offered statistical information showing which was the best position.

According to dissonance theory, the subjects who were losing should have experienced dissonance, with the degree of dissonance depending on the amount of their losses. Festinger and his colleagues found that subjects with very high losses and those who were winning tended not to use the information. However, subjects with moderate losses used the information a great deal. In terms of the theory, subjects who had been winning were not experiencing dissonance, and consequently, the information was of little value. For subjects with moderate losses (i.e., moderate dissonance), there was motivation to seek supportive information, and it seemed possible that the information would prove them correct. So these subjects employed the information extensively. For the subjects with high losses (and high dissonance), the information was insufficient to reduce the dissonance, and was therefore ignored.

Cohen, Brehm, and Latane (1959) replicated Festinger's gambling study, also manipulating the publicity of the subject's choice. In the public condition, the subject's choice of position and his or her success in the game would be reported in the school paper. In the private condition, this choice and success would only be known to the subject and the experimenter. The results essentially replicated those of Festinger, with the publicity manipulation enhancing the selective-exposure effects.

The previously discussed study conducted by Ehrlich et al. (1957) also found support for the dissonance predictions. New car owners tended to notice advertisements for their own car more than those for other models. This tendency was much less pronounced for owners who had purchased their cars more than a year earlier.

Mills, Aronson, and Robinson (1959) gave psychology undergraduates the option of taking either a multiple choice or essay final exam. The students were further told that the final exam would either have a major impact (70%) or minor impact (5%) on their grade for the course. After making their decision, the students were offered a choice of six articles they could read concerning exams. The articles focused on either essay or multiple choice exams and were either positive or negative about that type of test. Mills et al. found that students preferred articles about the examination they were to take when the information was positive. When it was negative, however, no differences were found. The authors explained their findings in terms of dissonance theory and also postulated that persons seek more information overall about something they have chosen.

In an attempt to replicate and improve upon Mills et al.'s results, Rosen (1961) also had undergraduates choose either an essay or objective exam, and then offered them information. However, when offering negative information about each type of exam, Rosen did not include negative words in the description (as Mills et al. did). Instead, Rosen described the articles as urging people to switch from one type of exam to the other. Contrary to selective-exposure predictions, a majority of the subjects (67%) preferred articles advocating a switch from the type of exam they had chosen to the other type of exam.

Adams (1961) investigated selective exposure to information concerning hereditary and environmental factors in child development. Mothers were questioned as to whether they thought heredity or environment has the greatest impact. They were then asked to listen to a talk by a fictitious expert arguing the same or the opposite position on the issue. Following the talk, the subjects were asked if they would like to listen to another expert discuss the subject. Subjects were to indicate which of the two speakers (one favoring or one opposing their position) they preferred. The results indicated that subjects who had experienced dissonance (listened to a contrary expert) desired information more than control subjects. However, both the dissonance subjects and the control subjects preferred to hear a talk favoring their side of the issue. Adams attempted to explain this finding by postulating that many of the control subjects may have also been experiencing dissonance. Another explanation, of course, is that dissonance may not have been required for selective exposure to occur.

Selective exposure to information concerning lung cancer by smokers and nonsmokers was first investigated by Feather (1962). He asked college undergraduates to rank how interesting they would find a series of magazine articles. There were two forms of the survey: One form included an article entitled "Smoking Leads to Lung Cancer"; the other included "Smoking Does Not Lead to Lung Cancer." After gathering their information preferences, the investigator administered a survey of their smoking habits. Feather found, contrary to dissonance predictions, that smokers were more interested in the smoking article regardless of whether it was supportive or critical of their smoking habit.

In a replication of this study, Feather (1963) also investigated personality variables, specifically extraversion and neuroticism. He again found that smokers were more interested than nonsmokers in any information concerning smoking. No effects were found for the personality dimensions.

In another study of smokers and nonsmokers, Brock (1965) focused on the impact of the subject's choice. Brock replicated Feather's (1962) study but used an additional manipulation. Subjects were either led to believe that they were simply indicating their preference for information or that they would immediately be reading the information they selected as part of the study. Brock found that the selective exposure occurred only when subjects actually expected they would be reading the information. The results from conditions in which subjects were not expecting to read the articles were comparable to those of Feather.

Jecker (1964) attempted to show that persons experiencing dissonance not only seek out dissonance-reducing information, but also actively avoid dissonance-enhancing information. Although this is part of Festinger's hypothesis, the avoidance of information had been tested much less often. Jecker had undergraduates choose a partner to compete with against another person in an experimental game for a cash prize. After making his choice for a partner, each subject was offered information from personality inventories concerning his partner or his opponent. The information was further divided into favorable and unfavorable information concerning each person. In contrast to dissonance predictions,

Jecker found that subjects spent equal amounts of time reading dissonance-reducing and dissonance-increasing information. A further analysis focusing on subjects' initial scanning of the information did find evidence of selective exposure. However, this latter analysis was of questionable merit, leaving generally negative results.

Cannon (1964) predicted that self-confidence moderates the selective-exposure effects of dissonance. He argued that a confident person will select discrepant information with the intention of refuting it. In fact, the highly confident person may *prefer* discrepant information, because refuting it would be more satisfying than reading information already congruent with one's attitudes. In a study examining this, Cannon had undergraduates read and analyze several cases concerning business policy. After each of the first three cases, the experimenter indicated that the subject's analysis was correct or incorrect and the number of other subjects who made the same analysis. This feedback was randomly manipulated so that half the subjects were told they had successfully analyzed all of the cases correctly, and the rest were told they were only correct on the first case. After completing the fourth case, subjects were told to write an essay concerning their analysis of the case, and they were offered articles about the case for assistance. Cannon also hypothesized that negative information about a solution to the case would be more useful than positive information. Therefore, five articles were offered to the subjects: one neutral article, and one positive and one negative about the two possible solutions to the case.

Cannon found effects for both usefulness and confidence. Subjects generally preferred supportive articles, and this tendency was more pronounced for positive (i.e., less useful) articles. Less confident subjects chose supportive articles overall. However, confident subjects chose dissonance-provoking articles when they were negative about their analysis (i.e., more useful for defending the analysis). Therefore, there are cases (e.g., a confident person with useful information) in which dissonance theory can predict that a person will seek dissonance-enhancing information.

Freedman (1965a) attempted to replicate Cannon's study using essentially the same experimental situation. Although Freedman found similar effects for the usefulness of information (i.e., negative information about a choice was preferred over positive information), he found no effects for confidence. Freedman also found no evidence of selective exposure by low-confidence subjects. That is, these subjects did not prefer information supporting their analysis of the case. Other attempts to replicate Cannon's effects for confidence (Lowin, 1969; Schultz, 1974; Thayer, 1969) have also been unsuccessful.

Employing a judicial situation, Sears (1965), like Feather, found no effects for cognitive dissonance on selective exposure. In Sears' study, psychology undergraduates read synopses of two murder cases. Guilty and innocent versions were developed for both cases. Each subject read one synopsis where the evidence suggested guilt and another where the evidence implied innocence. After reading the synopses and giving a verdict for each case, the subjects were offered further information about the cases (the defense and prosecution summations, and the judge's charge to the jury). In one condition, the students were told they would find this additional material familiar, whereas in the other condition, they were told it would be new and unfamiliar information. Sears found a strong preference overall for information contrary to the initial synopsis (and the subject's verdict). This preference was stronger when the information was expected to be familiar, as opposed to unfamiliar information. Sears argued that these findings clearly challenge the notion of selective exposure.

Freedman (1965c) had subjects listen to an interview designed to make the interviewee sound very qualified or very unqualified. After rating the interviewee, subjects were asked to read another evaluation. Subjects were offered a choice between an evaluation that agreed or disagreed with theirs. Of 18 subjects, 17 chose the contradictory evaluation. Again, the dissonance prediction was not supported.

Mills (1965a) conducted two studies of selective exposure using a marketing situation. Subjects were asked to rank 10 different products according to desirability and then choose between 2 products for a free gift. Some subjects were offered a choice between 2 products they had ranked closely (e.g., second and third), whereas others chose between 2 they had ranked further apart (second and ninth). In addition, Mills varied the revocability of the choice, with some subjects making an irrevocable decision, some making a decision that could be changed only with difficulty, and others making a nonbinding choice. After making the choice, subjects indicated how interested they would be in reading ads about each of the 10 products. The procedure was the same in the second study, except that all subjects chose between the products they had ranked second and third in desirability.

The selective-exposure hypothesis would predict that subjects would prefer to read about the product they had chosen and would not want to read about the product they had declined. This was tested by comparing the actual preferences for information with predicted preferences based on the ratings of the products. For both experiments, desirability of the products predicted how much subjects would like to read about the products. Subjects were more interested in reading about the products they had ranked higher. The results indicated that subjects preferred information on their chosen product more and wanted information on the declined product less than would be predicted. This effect was significant in the second study, but was a nonsignificant trend in the first study. These effects were found only when the decision was irrevocable.

In another marketing study, Mills (1965b) explicitly manipulated certainty about the subjects' choices by having subjects choose between two adjacently ranked items (second and third) or two differently ranked items (second and nineteenth). Mills found that uncertainty (i.e., a difficult decision) increased the desire for information about the chosen alternative, but had no effect on desires for information about the unchosen alternative.

EARLY APPRAISALS OF SELECTIVE EXPOSURE

In the period between the first description of cognitive dissonance in 1957 up through the middle 1960s, a total of 17 studies was conducted investigating selective exposure. Of these, 7 found evidence for the effect, 9 found no evidence, and 1 produced mixed results. At this point, selective exposure definitely did not appear to be a very robust or reliable finding.

Even more disturbing to selective-exposure investigators was the fact that other aspects of Festinger's cognitive dissonance theory were enjoying reliable support. Studies demonstrated that dissonance changes attitudes (Festinger & Carlsmith, 1959), it increases commitment to a behavior (Rabbie, Brehm, & Cohen, 1959), and it affects interpersonal processes (Davis & Jones, 1960). In contrast, selective exposure was proving to be an elusive phenomenon, appearing in one study and then disappearing in the next.

The lack of consistent results in selective-exposure studies led Freedman and Sears (1965), in an influential review, to state categorically that the "evidence does not support the hypothesis that people prefer to be exposed to supportive as opposed to non-supportive information" (p. 94). They went on to suggest that research in the selective-exposure area be abandoned altogether.

In a landmark volume concerning cognitive consistency and cognitive dissonance (Abelson et al., 1968), several authors discussed the state of research concerning selective exposure to information. Reiterating his earlier views, Sears (1968) concluded, "there is no empirical evidence indicating a general preference for supportive information over nonsupportive information" (p. 786).

In sharp contrast to Sears' dismissal, however, Mills (1968) concluded from his review that there was sufficient evidence to suggest the existence of selective exposure. In yet another review, Katz (1968) focused on selective exposure in mass communication. He reviewed research from outside the dissonance paradigm and found considerable positive evidence for selective exposure. In terms of voting studies (e.g., Berelson, Lazarsfeld, & McPhee, 1954), religious communications (e.g., Parker, Barry, & Smythe, 1955), and other forms of mass communication (e.g., Hyman & Sheatsley, 1947), the evidence for selective exposure appeared reliable.

In a summing up of the reviews concerning selective exposure, McGuire (1968) sided quite strongly with Sears. McGuire noted the generally poor record of published results and wondered if there might also be a massive accumulation of unpublished data that was nonsupportive of selective exposure. McGuire then went on to deride the "touching . . . tenacity with which the selective avoidance 'principle' has been asserted" (p.797) and advocated discontinuing any further research on the topic.

The review by Freedman and Sears (1965) and the negative conclusions of Sears (1968) and McGuire (1968) had considerable impact within social psychology. Although researchers continued to investigate selective exposure, the topic moved from a major arena of dissonance theory and research to a minor sidelight. Dissonance theory and its ramifications were the major areas of interest for social psychology during the 1960s, but selective exposure was essentially ignored. More than 10 years after these negative reviews, studies of selective exposure (e.g., Cotton & Hieser, 1980; Frey & Wicklund, 1978) began their theoretical introductions with the possibility that selective exposure was a nonexistent effect.

As the reader may have noticed, some of the earlier studies suffer from a variety of methodological flaws. Although some of these problems might tend to make selective-exposure effects more likely, for the most part they probably act to reduce any effects, or at least to blur the effects. The following section discusses a variety of artifacts, or difficulties, with the research that may have affected the results found in many studies.

PROBLEMS IN SELECTIVE-EXPOSURE RESEARCH

Level of Dissonance

In a methodological review of the selective-exposure literature, Rhine (1967b) argued that inconsistent results in this research may be due to research design problems. Rhine noted that Festinger hypothesized effects for at least three levels of dissonance (low, moderate, and very high). Festinger's theory hypothesizes a curvilinear relationship between selective exposure and dissonance, with the maximum effects at moderate levels, and few or no effects at low and very high levels. However, most tests of these hypotheses included only two levels of dissonance (low and high). If the low dissonance was in fact not very low or if the high dissonance was too high, selective-exposure effects would not have been predicted.

Related to this is the question of whether dissonance was in fact produced by the experimental manipulation. Most studies put subjects in situations where dissonance was *assumed* to occur, yet this assumption was rarely tested. It may be that the dissonance conditions actually produced very little dissonance. Both of these problems will tend to reduce any selective-exposure effects. To insure that a fair test of the hypotheses is being made, some measurement of the dissonance is necessary, and comparisons must be made with appropriate control groups.

Impact of the Information Choice

One common problem with many laboratory studies of selective exposure to information was that the choices of information typically had little impact. For example, in Feather's (1962, 1963) studies of selective exposure among smokers, the experimenter asked the subjects to "rank these articles in their order of interest to you" (1963, p. 158). The experimenter was asking the subjects to indicate their interest, not actually to choose information. There was no indication that the subjects would be faced with the articles or be required to read them. Thus, it is not surprising to find that few differences in information preference occurred in these studies.

Brock (1965) explicitly manipulated the impact of this choice and found that when subjects think they will actually be reading the information, selective exposure occurs. In order for selective exposure to be adequately tested in a laboratory situation, it must be real to the subjects. Simply indicating interest about different types of information is not enough. Subjects must believe they may be reading and facing the information they choose or avoid.

Demands for Honesty and Impartiality

Another situational factor affecting selective exposure is the norm of honesty or impartiality. Selective exposure can be considered a type of intellectual dishonesty. In a situation emphasizing norms for honesty, selective exposure would presumably be reduced. Sears' (1965) courtroom task would seem to emphasize this norm. If a person's life or freedom is at stake, a judge (the subject) is bound to be as conscientious, impartial, and honest as possible. Selectively avoiding discrepant information appears to be "cheating" in this context.

Because the subjects must indicate to the experimenter their choice of information, the experimenter can judge how well the subject performs. If honesty is part of performance, selective exposure will be reduced. This can then lead to subjects indicating information preferences which may be impartial, but contrary to their actual desires.

Usefulness or Utility of Information

A further factor that might sway people's choices of information is the utility of the information. People will obviously be more likely to select information that is more useful. In a study reviewed earlier, Freedman (1965b) had subjects make an evaluation of an interviewee and then choose some additional information (another evaluation) about the person they had rated. Freedman found that subjects desired information disagreeing with their evaluation.

This choice is not surprising if one argues that the subjects (being in a psychology experiment) believed they might have to justify their response. If they were to be assessed on their evaluation, the subjects would desire highly useful information to defend their choice. An evaluation disagreeing with them would be more useful than an evaluation that agreed. This effect for utility was also found by Cannon (1964).

Attractiveness of the Information

Yet another factor that probably moderates selective exposure to information is the attractiveness of the different types of information. All things being equal, a person will select information that is more attractive or more interesting.

Presumably, car owners will be more familiar with ads for their own car than with ads concerning other cars, as these ads helped guide them in their choice. Because of their greater familiarity, these ads will also be less interesting for the car owner than other, less familiar ads. Therefore, curiosity might predict the car owner would seek ads about other cars, ads with discrepant information. Familiarity and curiosity might motivate people to choose differently than dissonance theory would predict. This greater familiarity has generally not been controlled for in selective-exposure research.

Aside from simple curiosity, some information may be more attractive than other information simply through its contents or its form. A personal interview with the president of the United States would probably be more attractive than reading a newspaper editorial, regardless of whether the president's information was supportive or discrepant.

Whether this factor might augment or reduce selective exposure depends on the information involved. Mills (1965a) indicated that the desirability of a product will affect the interest in reading about the product. In his study, it was necessary to control for this statistically. However, other research on selective exposure has not attended to this factor, so one cannot be sure if attractiveness is of significance or not.

De Facto Selective Exposure

The final moderating factor is one that would always serve to increase the probability of finding selective-exposure effects. One can hypothesize that subjects may not always be actively seeking and avoiding information, but rather that their situation somehow moderates the information they are exposed to. For example, it may be that smokers see more prosmoking ads and also smoke because of some third variable, such as social class or culture. In this case, there is no motivation for selective exposure; it is simply due to other factors.

The problem of de facto selective exposure is critical in field studies. One advantage of the dissonance research on selective exposure is that the exposure is controlled so that information is offered equally to all subjects. Although Freedman and Sears (1965) may not be correct in concluding that de facto selective exposure is responsible for the effects in most studies, it is certainly a potential problem with much of the field research. Studies such as Ehrlich et al. (1957) are open to alternative explanations. Because of this, laboratory data (assuming no other problems) may be more effective evidence than field research for the occurrence of selective exposure to information.

Summary

There is now sufficient reason to suspect that many tests of selective exposure may have been ineffective. However, the general perception of selective exposure within social psychology was that of a weak, unreliable phenomenon. Although research continued, it progressed at a somewhat slower pace. This research, combined with the realization of the problems that have been discussed, may give us greater confidence in the existence of selective exposure.

LATER RESEARCH (1967–1983)

The later research, although not as frequent or as well-known as the earlier work, has tended to produce more favorable results for selective exposure. It has also tended to be more carefully controlled.

Lowin (1967) investigated how ease of message refutation moderates selective exposure in two studies. In the first experiment, he mailed offers of political brochures to Goldwater and Johnson supporters during the 1964 presidential campaign. The information (brochures) being offered was represented by a series of arguments that were easy or difficult to refute (as predetermined by judges). The information was also tested to insure that different information was equally interesting. The results indicated that hard to refute, supportive information and easily refuted, nonsupportive information were preferred to easily refuted, supportive information and hard to refute, nonsupportive information. In short, the selective-exposure predictions, as moderated by ease of refutation, were supported.

In a very similar second experiment, Lowin again sent offers of information to political partisans. In the second study, however, all subjects were offered all of the forms of information, making it a within-subjects design. The findings from this study did not replicate the earlier study. Whereas Republican subjects demonstrated the expected interaction between information supportiveness and ease of refutation, Democratic subjects showed no information preferences. Lowin explained the differing results as possibly due to the fact that the information in the second experiment involved a nonpartisan rather than a partisan source (as in the first study). By being nonpartisan, the easily refuted messages may have appeared stronger and/or the norm of impartiality may have been operating.

In another study of selective exposure to political information, Rhine (1967a) investigated the impact of several different levels of dissonance. Johnson and Goldwater partisans were confronted with different levels of contradictory information about their candidates. Then, subjects indicated their preference for informational pamphlets that favored either Johnson or Goldwater. The findings supported Festinger's (1957) predictions. Subjects with moderate levels of dissonance demonstrated strong selective-exposure effects, whereas subjects with low or very high levels of dissonance showed little effect.

Lowin (1969) manipulated both ease of message refutation and subject confidence. Employing Cannon's (1964) case study procedure, Lowin manipulated subjects' confidence through success or failure on the task, and ease of refutation through source expertise. (Difficult to refute information was credited to a prestigious panel of business experts, whereas easily refuted messages were ascribed to high school sophomores.) Although ease of refutation produced significant effects, subjects' confidence had no effect.

Thayer (1969) manipulated subjects' confidence, and then had them judge the attractiveness of a book jacket. After their evaluation, the subjects were offered information agreeing or disagreeing with their evaluation. The information was placed in front of the subjects, and which information the subject read (or read first) was recorded. No selective-exposure effects were found. However, it is uncertain whether or not dissonance was produced. In another attempt to test the effect of confidence on selective exposure, Schultz (1974) also found no effects for this variable.

Lowe and Steiner (1968) manipulated the reversibility of a decision, the consequences of the decision, and then offered their subjects information concerning the decision. They hypothesized that selective exposure would occur when the decision was irrevocable and had few consequences. Their logic was that if the decision was reversible, all types of information would still be sought. Additionally, if the decision had consequences, nonsupportive information would have greater utility. The subjects (undergraduate females) chose between two men for a blind date. In the nonreversible conditions, the choice was binding; in the reversible conditions, it was not. In the high-consequences conditions, the blind date was to occur; in the low-consequences conditions, the choice was hypothetical. The prediction was confirmed, as only subjects in the irreversible condition with no consequences demonstrated selective exposure.

In a study described at the beginning of this chapter, Brock and Balloun (1967) demonstrated selective exposure among smokers and nonsmokers to information concerning smoking and lung cancer. In contrast to most of the studies, subjects did not choose information, but had to respond by pushing a button in order to continue receiving information without static interference. In four experiments, Brock and Balloun found that smokers would push the button more than nonsmokers to eliminate static during a message disputing the smoking-cancer link. However, smokers pushed the button fewer times than nonsmokers during a message supporting the link. Similar effects were also found between religious and weakly religious subjects with regard to messages concerning Christianity.

In a very carefully designed experiment, Frey and Wicklund (1978) tested selective exposure after controlling for curiosity, utility, attractiveness, confidence, and norms for impartiality. Subjects (German high school students) experienced an onerous task (writing lists of random numbers) and then had a choice or no choice to continue the experiment. This is a classic dissonance manipulation because the subjects in the choice condition believe they have complete freedom of choice, yet most or all of them continue with the task. This free choice, coupled with their dislike of the task, produces dissonance in the high-choice subjects.

After the choice manipulation, the subjects were offered information supportive of continuing the task (its scientific value and positive effects on subjects) or nonsupportive information. Because the task is totally artificial, the attractiveness, utility, and curiosity value of the information are equal. In addition, because the task is novel and unusual, all subjects are equal in terms of confidence, and norms for impartiality should be nil. Finally, varying the level of dissonance through choice rather than through behavior (e.g., smokers vs. nonsmokers) also helps to eliminate alternative explanations for information preferences. The results supported the dissonance predictions. Frey and Wicklund manipulated the conditions of information seeking (subjects could choose 3 of 6, 3 of 10, or 10 of 10 pamphlets) and found similar selective-exposure effects under all conditions.

Cotton and Hieser (1980) also manipulated dissonance through choice by having subjects opposed to nuclear power plants write essays favoring such plants near populated areas. Subjects wrote the essay under high or low choice, this manipulation producing high or low dissonance. After writing the essay, subjects answered several questions concerning their information preferences and their attitudes toward nuclear power plants. The attitude questionnaire was to insure that dissonance had been produced. The order of the questionnaire was counterbalanced; half the subjects gave their information preferences first, and half gave their attitudes first. The information questions asked subjects how much they would like informational pamphlets and how much they would like to join discussion groups concerned with four issues, one of them being nuclear energy. The instructions were phrased to emphasize to the subjects that they would indeed be receiving pamphlets or joining a discussion group. Subjects who desired pamphlets on nuclear energy received them at the end of the experiment.

The results confirmed the selective-exposure hypothesis. High-choice (high-dissonance) subjects desired consistent information more and dissonant information less than did low-choice subjects. In addition, subjects who answered the attitude questionnaire before indicating their information preferences showed weaker selective-exposure effects than subjects who indicated information preferences first. This interaction indicated that some of the dissonance was already reduced through the attitude shift demonstrated on the attitude survey.

Otis (1979) found that individuals waiting to see a science fiction film (*Close Encounters of the Third Kind*) were more inclined to believe in flying saucers than patrons waiting to see two other films. Unfortunately, it is impossible to determine whether the belief motivated seeing the movie (i.e., selective exposure) or if expectations about the move affected the subjects' beliefs (or primed their responses).

Using a consumer choice manipulation similar to Mills, Frey (1981) manipulated the level of dissonance and the reversibility of the decision. He controlled the first by giving subjects a choice between two alternatives with varying degrees of attractiveness. Reversibility was manipulated by making the choice binding or not. Frey found greater selective-exposure effects after irreversible versus reversible decisions. With irrevocable decisions, there was greater selective exposure when the alternatives were more similar in attractiveness (i.e., high dissonance).

Summary

The later research on selective exposure, generally more carefully controlled, has produced more positive results. Almost every study found significant selective-exposure effects. These effects were moderated by refutability of the information (Lowin, 1967), the revocability of the decision (Frey, 1981; Lowe & Steiner, 1978), and other opportunities for dissonance reduction (Cotton & Hieser, 1980). In contrast to the conclusions of Freedman and Sears (1965), Sears (1968), and McGuire (1968), there does appear to be evidence for selective exposure to information, and several moderating factors have been identified.

UNANSWERED QUESTIONS
IN SELECTIVE EXPOSURE TO INFORMATION

Thus far, the major focus of this review has been on determining whether or not selective exposure to information can be induced via cognitive dissonance. A secondary aim has been to identify several factors that may moderate selective exposure. Such variables as the level of dissonance, the utility, attractiveness, and refutability of the information, as well as the impact of the decision, confidence of the person, and so forth have all been discussed and/or researched.

In this section, I would like to outline several questions that have not been given a great deal of attention. These issues have not been critical to demonstrating that selective exposure exists. However, they are important for a clearer understanding of the phenomenon and its practical importance.

Approach Versus Avoidance

Festinger (1957) hypothesized that people should seek consistent information *and* avoid dissonant information. However, the research on selective exposure has been far more successful in demonstrating the former than the latter. Most studies of selective exposure simply have not differentiated between seeking and avoidance. Some have combined both behaviors into an overall measure of selective exposure (i.e., Frey & Wicklund, 1978); others have examined only the seeking aspect (i.e., Frey, 1981).

In studies where both processes were sought and tested, the results have tended to support the seeking of consonant information, but not the avoidance of dissonant information. Studies by Mills et al. (1959), Mills (1965b), Jecker (1964), and others have not demonstrated avoidance. This failure to find avoidance of dissonant information was identified early by Brehm and Cohen (1962). Brock (1965) went so far as to argue that dissonance theory should be modified to reflect the fact that only seeking occurs. In contrast to these authors, however, Mills (1965a), Rhine (1967b), and Cotton and Hieser (1980) have demonstrated clear evidence for the avoidance of inconsistent information. Empirically, the question remains unanswered.

It seems reasonable that social norms should favor the seeking of consonant information more than the avoidance of dissonant information. In general, seeking information is valued; if that information is supportive, so much the better. Avoidance, however, smacks of irrational behavior and is not generally admired.

Selective exposure has been demonstrated, but its precise form is not clear. Although the seeking of consistent information appears certain, at present it can only be said that there is doubt whether or not active avoidance occurs. Further research on this aspect of selective exposure is needed.

Individual Differences

Part of the stock and trade of psychology is individual differences, that is, assessing how different people react to the same situation. Although personality factors have been investigated within cognitive dissonance (Wicklund & Brehm, 1976), this research for the most part has focused on individual differences in the perception of dissonance or tolerance for dissonance. Within the area of selective exposure, personality or other individual differences have only rarely been studied.

In one of the few studies, Olson and Zanna (1979) investigated the impact of one personality dimension on selective exposure. They pretested subjects on Byrne's (1964) repression-sensitization scale. Repressors are generally "avoid-ers,'' that is, people who emphasize positive or supportive information when faced with an anxiety-provoking situation. Sensitizers, however, are "approachers," people who employ intellectualization and confrontation as strategies for reducing anxiety.

Olson and Zanna predicted that repressors would tend to exhibit selective exposure to a greater extent than sensitizers. These authors had their subjects choose a painting, and then observed their eye gaze for 75 seconds after the choice. Control subjects viewed the paintings for the same period of time without making a choice. Olson and Zanna found that repressors looked at the painting they had chosen and avoided the painting they had rejected more than their controls. No differences were found between sensitizer subjects and their controls.

In one of his studies of smokers, Feather (1963) also included the personality variables of neuroticism and extroversion. No clear-cut results were found for these variables, except that smokers tended to be higher than nonsmokers on the extroversion scale.

In the only other personality study, Schultz (1974) investigated the impact of dogmatism and confidence as moderators of selective exposure. Schultz hypothesized that in his procedure, dogmatism should operate in the opposite direction as confidence, with subjects high in dogmatism showing more selective exposure under high confidence than low confidence. Schultz's results confirmed the hypothesis. His findings led him to suggest that the elusive relationship between confidence and selective exposure may be moderated by personality variables such as dogmatism.

In addition to personality, there is the question of whether demographic variables such as sex, age, economic status, and others affect selective exposure. Variables such as these might have some impact, but it is not known whether they significantly and consistently have an effect on selective exposure to information.

In short, the influence of individual differences on selective exposure has barely been addressed. Such variables as dogmatism, repression-sensitization, and self-esteem (possibly related to confidence?) require testing. Only additional research can determine whether these variables will prove to be important.

Temporal Factors

A third question that has been relatively unanswered concerns the timing of selective exposure to information. In a reformulation of his original theory, Festinger (1964) suggested that prior to dissonance reduction a person may focus on dissonant cognitions, thereby increasing the dissonance. This state, which Festinger labeled "regret," is necessary to provide the motivation that eventually leads to the dissonance reduction. One can then assume that dissonance reduction does not occur immediately following a contradiction of cognitions, but rather, after a short interval of regret. Selective exposure should also demonstrate this pattern.

Miller (1977) investigated the effects of timing on selective exposure. Following a procedure used earlier by Walster (1964), Miller produced dissonance in subjects (via a difficult choice), and then presented information immediately, 4 minutes later, or 12 minutes later. In the immediate condition, subjects tended to select relatively neutral information; at 4 minutes, they selected negative information about their choice; and at 12 minutes, they chose positive information. None of the subjects chose information about the unchosen alternative. Miller hypothesized that at 4 minutes, subjects were in a regret phase, where they were focusing on the dissonant information so as to justify their decision. At the 12-minute interval, dissonance reduction via selective exposure occurred. Additional research addressing these temporal issues has not been conducted.

In addition to short-term temporal questions, there are also long-term issues. How long will selective exposure continue? Dissonance has been shown to linger for up to 2 months (Freedman, 1965b); will selective exposure last as long? This has not been tested. Another interesting possibility is that as the motivation disappears, it may be replaced with situational or de facto selective exposure. It may be, for example, that selective-exposure effects last for a long time, first motivated by dissonance reduction and later simply as a result of altered habits or situational constraints. It would be interesting as well as useful to conduct research on temporal questions such as these.

Selective Exposure in the Real World

The final question yet to be addressed in theory or research is how common dissonance-motivated selective exposure is in the real world. This question involves two different issues.

First, how common is selective exposure as a means of reducing dissonance? Laboratory demonstrations of selective exposure are typically artificial situations in which dissonance is created and selective exposure offered as a convenient method to reduce the dissonance. It cannot be determined from this research, however, whether selective exposure typically occurs when the person has a variety of dissonance-reduction methods to choose from. Dissonance studies are well known for their careful preparations aimed at producing effects. For example, attitude change is only produced in these studies by blocking off other methods of dissonance reduction. Changing one's attitudes becomes the only alternative. Is this also true of selective exposure?

There is no direct evidence, but logically, selective exposure does not appear to be an artifact of the situation. One reason is that selective exposure is seldom the only method of dissonance reduction available; hence, it can easily be combined with other methods. In addition, studies investigating selective exposure have used a variety of procedures with different types of information exposure.

These have seldom been controlled as well as the typical attitude-change study, yet selective exposure has been demonstrated.

From the discussion of factors that may influence selective-exposure effects, it also appears that the laboratory situation may inhibit these effects. Demands for impartiality are probably stronger within the laboratory than outside, whereas the impact of the information choice is probably weaker. Therefore, it would appear that laboratory tests of selective exposure may understate the occurrence of this phenomenon.

A second issue of practical importance to selective exposure is the problem of differentiating dissonance-motivated from de facto selective exposure. Are people actively choosing consistent information and avoiding discrepant information, or is this simply an accident of the situation?

Unfortunately, much of the research outside the laboratory confounds the two types of selective exposure. For example, political partisans may be motivated to seek information favoring their candidate, but by being partisans, such information is also more easily available. Careful methodology is needed to determine whether selective-exposure effects outside the lab are due to motivation or to aspects of the situation.

In sum, more research such as Ehrlich et al.'s (1957) study of new car owners would be welcome. The political studies of Lowin (1967) and Rhine (1967a) are useful, but they are still *offering* information to subjects and seeing if it is taken. More research focusing on how people actively seek and avoid information *on their own* is needed. This research will allow us to assess the actual impact of selective exposure, and not its impact within the artificial cognitive dissonance study.

CONCLUDING REMARKS

A number of conclusions can be drawn from this review. First, dissonance-motivated selective exposure does appear to exist. Although the phenomenon has often been elusive and its support questioned, the research overall suggests that something is there.

Second, dissonance-motivated selective exposure is undoubtedly moderated by many variables. These factors include: (a) the level of dissonance; (b) the impact of the information choice, whether or not the choice is real; (c) demands for honesty and impartiality; (d) usefulness or utility of the information; (e) attractiveness of the information; (f) refutability of the information; and (g) de facto selective exposure.

Although several variables have been hypothesized as moderators of selective exposure, the research has not been very supportive of at least one. Confidence, which is expected to influence selective exposure, has seldom proven to be a factor. In five studies, only one found significant effects for confidence.

Part of the difficulty in clearly identifying the important moderating variables of dissonance-motivated selective exposure is the logical elasticity of dissonance theory. The theory predicts that people experiencing dissonance will seek out supportive information and avoid discrepant information (Festinger, 1957), but it can also predict that people will seek out discrepant information (Festinger, 1964). With this kind of maneuverability, it is not suprising that moderating variables are difficult to pin down.

Several interesting questions concerning dissonance-motivated selective exposure to information have yet to be fully investigated. Most measures of selective exposure lump together the seeking of consistent information with the avoidance of nonsupportive information. When these two processes are differentiated, it is not clear that both occur. Is selective exposure primarily just seeking consistent information, or does the active avoidance of inconsistent information also occur?

A second question is the extent to which individual differences modify selective exposure. Do individuals consistently differ in the degree to which they selectively expose themselves to information? Are some people more likely than others to seek out or avoid information?

A third unanswered question concerns the timing of the information. On the basis of Miller's (1977) experiment, it appears that information preferences change over time. Are these changes consistent across different situations? What about long-term changes in selective exposure?

The final question is probably the most important. Accepting that dissonance-motivated selective exposure does exist, how widespread is it? Are the laboratory experiments simply occurrences of isolated and unlikely behaviors, or are they examples of a general process? Although the laboratory research is useful for controlling extraneous factors and independently assessing variables, more field research is required to determine the final place of selective exposure.

Rather than simply repeating the obligatory call for more theory and research, I would like to make a somewhat different point. Writing about cognitive dissonance theory, Aronson (1978) stated: ''Although facts (ugly or otherwise) may slay theories in the natural sciences, in the social sciences, theories are almost never bumped off that easily or clearly. In the social sciences, what generally kills a theory is benign neglect—by its critics as well as by its advocates'' (p. 215).

The end of selective exposure by dissonance will probably not come from empirical disproof, but from neglect and inattention. Its dismissal by some theorists in the mid-1960s was only sufficient to reduce attention, not to eliminate the subject. However, if theory and research on selective exposure and cognitive dissonance are to continue, they must have new and interesting questions. Without this motivation, decline and eventual abandonment will undoubtedly occur. As long as intriguing questions remain, so will the phenomenon.

REFERENCES

Abelson, R. P., Aronson, E., McGuire, W. J., Newcomb, T. M., Rosenberg, M. J., & Tannen-baum, P. H. (Eds.). (1968). *Theories of cognitive consistency: A sourcebook.* Chicago: Rand McNally.

Adams, J. S. (1961). Reduction of cognitive dissonance by seeking consonant information. *Journal of Abnormal and Social Psychology, 62,* 74–78.

Aronson, E. (1978). The theory of cognitive dissonance: A current perspective. In L. Berkowitz (Ed.), *Cognitive theories in social psychology* (pp. 215–220). New York: Academic Press.

Berelson, B. R., Lazarsfeld, P. F., & McPhee, W. N. (1954). *Voting.* Chicago: University of Chicago Press.

Brehm, J. W., & Cohen, A. R. (1962). *Explorations in cognitive dissonance.* New York: Wiley.

Brock, T. C. (1965). Commitment to exposure as a determinant of information receptivity. *Journal of Personality and Social Psychology, 2,* 10–19.

Brock, T. C., & Balloun, J. L. (1967) Behavioral receptivity to dissonant information. *Journal of Personality and Social Psychology, 6,* 413–428.

Byrne, D. (1964). Repression-sensitization as a dimension of personality. In B. A. Maher (Ed.), *Progress in experimental personality research* (Vol. *1,* pp. 169–219). New York: Academic Press.

Cannon, L. K. (1964). Self-confidence and selective exposure to information. In L. Festinger (Ed.), *Conflict, decision, and dissonance* (pp. 83–95). Stanford, CA: Stanford University Press.

Cohen, A. R., Brehm, J. W., & Latane, B. (1959). Choice of strategy and voluntary exposure to information under public and private conditions. *Journal of Personality, 27,* 63–73.

Cotton, J. L., & Hieser, R. A. (1980). Selective exposure to information and cognitive dissonance. *Journal of Research in Personality, 14,* 518–527.

Davis, K. E., & Jones, E. E. (1960). Changes in interpersonal perception as a means of reducing cognitive dissonance. *Journal of Abnormal and Social Psychology, 61,* 402–410.

Ehrlich, D., Guttman, I., Schonbach, P., & Mills, J. (1957). Postdecision exposure to relevant information. *Journal of Abnormal and Social Psychology, 54,* 98–102.

Feather, N. T. (1962). Cigarette smoking and lung cancer: A study of cognitive dissonance. *Australian Journal of Psychology, 14,* 55–64.

Feather, N. T. (1963). Cognitive dissonance, sensitivity, and evaluation. *Journal of Abnormal and Social Psychology, 66,* 157–163.

Festinger, L. (1957). *A theory of cognitive dissonance.* Evanston, IL: Row, Peterson.

Festinger, L. (Ed.) (1964). *Conflict, decision, and dissonance.* Stanford, CA: Stanford University Press.

Festinger, L., & Carlsmith, J. M. (1959). Cognitive consequences of forced compliance. *Journal of Abnormal and Social Psychology, 58,* 203–210.

Freedman, J. L. (1965a). Confidence, utility, and selective exposure: A partial replication. *Journal of Personality and Social Psychology, 2,* 778–780.

Freedman, J. L. (1965b). Long-term behavioral effects of cognitive dissonance. *Journal of Experimental Social Psychology, 1,* 145–155.

Freedman, J. L. (1965c). Preference for dissonant information. *Journal of Personality and Social Psychology, 2,* 287–289.

Freedman, J. L., & Sears, D. O. (1965). Selective exposure. In L. Berkowitz (Ed.), *Advances in experimental social psychology* (Vol. 2, pp. 58–98). New York: Academic Press.

Frey, D. (1981). Reversible and irreversible decisions: Preference for consonant information as a function of attractiveness of decision alternatives. *Personality and Social Psychology Bulletin, 7,* 621–626.

Frey, D., & Wicklund, R. A. (1978). A clarification of selective exposure: The impact of choice. *Journal of Experimental Social Psychology, 14,* 132–139.

Hyman, H., & Sheatsley, P. B. (1947). Some reasons why information campaigns fail. *Public Opinion Quarterly, 11,* 412–423.

Jecker, J. D. (1964). Selective exposure to new information. In L. Festinger, (Ed.) *Conflict, decision, and dissonance* (pp. 65–81). Stanford, CA: Stanford University Press.

Katz, E. (1968). On reopening the question of selectivity in exposure to mass communications. In R. P. Abelson, E. Aronson, W. J. McGuire, T. M. Newcomb, M. J. Rosenberg, & P. H. Tannenbaum (Eds.), *Theories of cognitive consistency: A sourcebook* (pp. 788–796). Chicago: Rand McNally.

Lazarsfeld, P. (1942). Effects of radio on public opinion. In D. Waples (Ed.), *Print, radio, and film in a democracy* (pp. 114–158). Chicago: University of Chicago Press.

Lowe, R. H., & Steiner, I. D. (1968). Some effects of the reversibility and consequences of decisions on postdecision information preferences. *Journal of Personality and Social Psychology, 8,* 172–179.

Lowin, A. (1967). Approach and avoidance as alternative modes of selective exposure to information. *Journal of Personality and Social Psychology, 6,* 1–9.

Lowin, A. (1969). Further evidence for an approach–avoidance interpretation of selective exposure. *Journal of Experimental Social Psychology, 5,* 265–271.

McGuire, W. J. (1968). Selective exposure: A summing up. In R. P. Abelson, E. Aronson, W. J. McGuire, T. M. Newcomb, M. J. Rosenberg, & P. H. Tannenbaum (Eds.), *Theories of cognitive consistency: A sourcebook* (pp. 797–800). Chicago: Rand McNally.

Miller, R. L. (1977). The effects of postdecisional regret on selective exposure. *European Journal of Social Psychology, 7,* 121–127.

Mills, J. (1965a). Avoidance of dissonant information. *Journal of Personality and Social Psychology, 2,* 589–593.

Mills, J. (1965b). Effect of certainty about a decision upon postdecision exposure to consonant and dissonant information. *Journal of Personality and Social Psychology, 2,* 749–752.

Mills, J. (1968). Interest in supporting and discrepant information. In R. P. Abelson, E. Aronson, W. J. McGuire, T. M. Newcomb, M. J. Rosenberg, & P. H. Tannenbaum (Eds.), *Theories of cognitive consistency: A sourcebook* (pp. 771–776). Chicago: Rand McNally.

Mills, J., Aronson, E., & Robinson, H. (1959). Selectivity in exposure to information. *Journal of Abnormal and Social Psychology, 59,* 250–253.

Olson, J. M., & Zanna, M. P. (1979). A new look at selective exposure. *Journal of Experimental Social Psychology, 15,* 1–15.

Otis, L. (1979). Selective exposure to the film Close Encounters. *Journal of Psychology, 101,* 293–295.

Parker, E. C., Barry, D. W., & Smythe, D. W. (1955). *The television-radio audience and religion.* New York: Harper and Row.

Rabbie, J. M., Brehm, J. W., & Cohen, A. R. (1959). Verbalization and reactions to cognitive dissonance. *Journal of Personality, 27,* 407–417.

Rhine, R. J. (1967a). The 1964 presidential election and curves of information seeking and avoiding. *Journal of Personality and Social Psychology, 5,* 416–423.

Rhine, R. J. (1967b). Some problems in dissonance theory research on information selectivity. *Psychological Bulletin, 68,* 21–28.

Rosen, S. (1961). Postdecision affinity for incompatible information. *Journal of Abnormal and Social Psychology, 63,* 188–190.

Schultz, C. B. (1974). The effect of confidence on selective exposure: An unresolved dilemma. *Journal of Social Psychology, 94,* 65–69.

Sears, D. O. (1965). Biased indoctrination and selectivity of exposure to new information. *Sociometry, 28,* 363–376.

Sears, D. O. (1968). The paradox of de facto selective exposure without preferences for supportive information. In R. P. Abelson, E. Aronson, W. J. McGuire, T. M. Newcomb, M. J. Rosenberg,

& P. H. Tannenbaum (Eds.), *Theories of cognitive consistency: A sourcebook* (pp. 777–787). Chicago: Rand McNally.

Thayer, S. (1969). Confidence and postjudgment exposure to consonant and dissonant information in a free-choice situation. *Journal of Social Psychology, 77,* 113–120.

Walster, E. (1964). The temporal sequence of postdecision processes. In L. Festinger (Ed.), *Conflict, decision, and dissonance* (pp. 112–128). Stanford, CA: Stanford University Press.

Wicklund, R. A., & Brehm, J. W. (1976). *Perspectives on cognitive dissonance.* Hillsdale, NJ: Lawrence Erlbaum Associates.

3 Measuring Exposure to Television

James G. Webster
University of Maryland

Jacob Wakshlag
Indiana University

Exposure to television may well be the most extensively studied of all communication behaviors. For over 3 decades, rating services have regularly measured television audiences to satisfy the demands of those seeking to exploit the medium's commercial potential. Beyond such pragmatic and far-reaching efforts to document the extent of television viewership, scholars from a variety of disciplines have devoted considerable attention to assessing the uses and effects of exposure.

Given this wealth of research, one might imagine that the procedures for measuring exposure to television were well understood and universally applied in industry and academe alike. But this is not, in fact, the case. Exposure has been conceptualized in a number of ways, resulting in a wide range of operational definitions and an even wider array of measurement techniques. On the one hand, such diversity is an entirely appropriate reflection of the different theoretical assumptions and rationales of various research efforts. On the other hand, applying so many different approaches to measurement has made comparisons across studies difficult and has produced a rather confusing collection of results on the nature of exposure to television.

It is the purpose of this chapter to summarize and critique the methods that have been used, are being used, and can be used to measure exposure. Obviously, no single method of measurement will be appropriate to the objectives and resources of all researchers. We hope, however, that such a review will draw into sharper focus the strengths and weaknesses of different techniques and, so, encourage researchers to be more discerning in their application of these measures.

WHAT IS EXPOSURE TO TELEVISION?

An assessment of the methods used for measuring exposure to television must begin by considering exactly what is being measured. Although this might seem a relatively simple matter, even a casual review of the research on this topic reveals that the concept of exposure to television has assumed a variety of meanings. Logically enough, definitions have varied in response to two questions: (a) what is television? and (b) what is exposure?

What is Television?

Television as a Medium.   A considerable body of research has treated television as a single, undifferentiated medium. Such conceptualizations are evident in several early studies, which measured exposure by the presence or absence of a set in the home. Many contemporary research efforts have also focused on the medium of television, rather than its more discrete programming elements. For example, exposure to television has been measured as use of the medium during specific times of the day (e.g., Bower, 1973; Frank & Greenberg, 1980; Robinson, 1972), the amount of time individuals view on a daily basis (e.g., Allen, 1981; LoSciuto, 1972; Roper, 1969), and time spent viewing over some period of days (e.g., Bechtel, Achelpohl, & Akers, 1972).

Whether television is appropriately conceptualized as a monolithic entity can be, and often is, debated (e.g., Anderson & Meyer, 1975; Katz, Blumler, & Gurevitch, 1974). The utility of treating it as such ultimately depends on the purposes and theoretical underpinnings of the research. Aside from relatively straightforward descriptions of the amount of viewing done by various segments of the population (e.g., A. C. Nielsen Co., 1982; Bower, 1973) or analyses of the extent to which television lays claim to leisure time (e.g., Peterson, 1981; Sahin & Robinson, 1981), defining television as an undifferentiated medium seems justified under one of two rationales. First, if it can be assumed that at least some uses (e.g., Katz et al., 1974; Lull, 1980) or effects (e.g., Chaffee, 1980) of television are independent of its content, then employing a gross measure of exposure to television may be sufficient. Alternatively, measures of time spent viewing could be employed if one assumes that television's content is so homogeneous or interrelated that further content distinctions are inappropriate (e.g., Gerbner & Gross, 1976).

Television as Content.   Television is perhaps most commonly defined by specific program content. Although a great many typologies can be used to organize television's content, the basic element or building block of these is typically the television program.

Ratings research as practiced in the broadcasting industry ascertains the viewership of individual television programs. In fact, the measurement techniques used by the major ratings services (i.e., A. C. Nielsen and Arbitron) collect reports of viewership at intervals shorter than standard program lengths. In principle, then, such data can be used to identify exposure to a specific segment within a program.

Defining television as program content is also common in much academic research. By employing a variety of measurement techniques, scholars have assessed viewing of specific programs on the previous day (e.g., Greenberg, Dervin, & Dominick, 1968), over the course of a week (e.g., Goodhardt, Ehrenberg, & Collins, 1975; Palmgreen, Wenner, & Rayburn, 1981; Webster & Wakshlag, 1982), or across several weeks (e.g., Frank & Greenberg, 1980; Gensch & Ranganathan, 1974).

Measuring exposure to television at the level of specific television programs offers an important advantage to the researcher. Such information can be easily reduced into more manageable or theoretically relevant content categories. For example, data on the viewing of individual programs have been collapsed to index exposure to violence (Israel & Robinson, 1972), to assess program-type loyalty (Webster & Wakshlag, 1982) and channel loyalty (Goodhardt et al., 1975), and to derive program types defined by viewer preference (Kirsch & Banks, 1962). Indeed, Greenberg et al. (1968) have argued that such data can be reduced to provide a more serviceable measure of total time spent viewing than self-reports of overall television usage.

What is Exposure?

Exposure as Choice.   Just as researchers have defined television in different ways, so too has the concept of exposure assumed different meanings. Frequently, exposure is defined as an act of choice in which an individual selects from a range of possible activities or messages. This definition of exposure could be applied to media use if television viewing is conceptualized as one of a number of possible leisure activities (e.g., Robinson, 1969; Sahin & Robinson, 1981) or conceived of as a general "social-situational factor" (Allen, 1981; Salomon & Cohen, 1978). More typically, however, exposure as choice pertains to the selection of specific television content across the range of available programming (e.g., Salomon & Cohen, 1978; Webster & Wakshlag, 1983).

Defining exposure in this way has certain limitations. Such measures reveal little about the quality of a viewing experience, the level of attention paid to program selections, or the extent to which messages are perceived. Nevertheless, this concept of exposure underlies the vast data-gathering activities of the ratings services and is the operational definition of exposure in a considerable amount of academic research that has assessed, among other things, the impact of new technologies (e.g., Agostino, 1980; Webster, 1983b), patterns of viewing (e.g., Gensch & Shaman, 1980; Goodhardt et al., 1975), and theoretical constructs such as selective exposure (e.g., Atkin, Greenberg, Korzenny, & McDermott,

1979; Bryant & Zillmann, 1984; Freedman & Sears, 1965; Zillmann, Hezel, & Medoff, 1980). Choice also comes closest to the traditional measure of selective exposure as a function of attitudes (see chap. 2 by Cotton for a comprehensive review of this literature).

Exposure as Attention.   There is ample evidence that people engage in a variety of activities while the television set is in use (e.g., Bechtel et al., 1972; Lull, 1980; Robinson, 1969). As a result, many researchers have voiced concern that defining exposure as choice fails to measure more useful or theoretically relevant concepts of exposure (e.g., Clarke & Kline, 1974; Miller & Cannell, 1977). Alternative definitions of exposure might incorporate the level of attention paid to the screen (e.g., Bechtel et al., 1972; Israel & Robinson, 1972), the degree to which a viewer is psychologically involved with what is being presented (e.g., Levy & Windahl, 1984), the extent to which viewers discriminate televised messages (Clarke & Kline, 1974), or the degree to which viewers extract knowledge from the encoded "language" of television (e.g., Salomon & Cohen, 1978). Although these and many other potentially useful definitions of exposure reflect diverse perspectives, they are considered here under the general heading of exposure as attention.

If televised content is to have an effect on behaviors, interests, attitudes, inclinations, or cognitions, it must be perceived by the viewer (Salomon & Cohen, 1978). Because an individual's perception of content is not directly observable, this construct has been measured either by some test of message recall (e.g., Clarke & Kline, 1974) or, more frequently, by assessing the extent to which the viewer attends to what is on the screen. Measurement of the latter has variously included direct observation of viewing (e.g., Allen 1965; Anderson, Alwitt, Lorch, & Levin, 1979; Bechtel et al., 1972), direct questions on how much attention is paid to specific programs (e.g., Frank & Greenberg, 1980; Israel & Robinson, 1972), and indirect assessments made by asking respondents the extent to which they engaged in nonviewing activities while the set was on (Levy & Windahl, 1984).

Although important, defining the precise distinctions and relationships among choice, attention, and perception is too extensive a task to be dealt with in the present chapter. For our purposes, it is sufficient to note that these are interrelated phenomena that might, under various rationales, be defended as the appropriate meaning of exposure.

Exposure as Preference.   Though few would argue that preference for a program inevitably leads to viewership, measures of preference have, nevertheless, been widely used to assess exposure to program content. The underlying rationale for such an approach is imbedded in the theoretical assumption that an individual's exposure to specific program content is primarily, if not exclusively, a function of preference for program-content characteristics (e.g.,

Bowman & Farley, 1972). If such a one-to-one correspondence between a viewer's attitudes and behaviors does indeed exist, then program preferences would seem a reasonable indicant of exposure.

As Comstock, Chaffee, Katzman, McCombs, and Roberts (1978) have noted, survey research on aggressiveness in adolescents has commonly measured exposure to violent programs by gathering self-reports of "favorite programs." Similarly, experimental research designs have measured choice by ascertaining a subject's preference for or desire to view various program materials (e.g., Boyanowski, 1977; Fenigstein, 1979).

The validity of using preference as a measure of exposure or, for that matter, exposure as a measure of preference (e.g., Comstock et al., 1978; Gensch & Ranganathan, 1974) depends on the strength of the association between these factors. Although program preferences are undoubtedly one determinant of viewing behavior, a substantial body of research suggests that the strength of the relationship, at least outside the laboratory, is frequently overstated (e.g., Aske Research Ltd., 1975; Bower, 1973; Comstock et al., 1978). Patterns of exposure in natural environments are known to be affected by viewer availability (Barwise, Ehrenberg, & Goodhardt, 1982; Gensch & Shaman, 1980), group viewing configurations (Webster & Wakshlag, 1982), and the scheduling characteristics of programs (Anast, 1983; Ehrenberg, 1968; Goodhardt et al., 1975; Headen, Klompmaker, & Rust, 1979). All of these factors serve to diminish or at least complicate the relationship between preference and viewing behavior (see Webster & Wakshlag, 1983). As a result, using program preferences to measure actual exposure in the field is highly questionable.

Exposure to television, then, has been conceptualized in a variety of ways. Clearly, no one definition is inherently superior to all others. Under certain assumptions, gross measures of media use may be appropriate to the researcher's purposes. At other times, exposure might be more meaningfully defined as the choice of or attention paid to specific television content. As Salomon and Cohen (1978) have noted, however, all too often exposure has been measured without any explicit discussion of the construct it represents. This has inevitably led to a good deal of confusion and inconsistency in the literature on viewing behavior. At the very least, researchers must make clear their definition of exposure before adopting a particular measurement technique.

MEASURES OF EXPOSURE TO TELEVISION

We now turn to a review and critique of various methods used to measure exposure to television. Our discussion of these techniques draws a distinction between measurement in the field and in the laboratory. Some forms of measurement might be appropriate in either setting, but others clearly are not. For example, experimental designs make it possible to control the factors which, outside the laboratory, mediate the relationship between preference and choice (Webster & Wakshlag, 1983). Under such circumstances, it is reasonable to define a desire to view certain materials as a dependent measure of exposure. Employing the same measure of exposure in survey research, however, is problematic at best.

Measuring Exposure in the Field

The vast majority of research on exposure to television occurs in the field, where the viewing environment is beyond the immediate control of the investigator. Here, our discussion of measurement eschews viewer preferences and emphasizes those techniques that define exposure as the choice of specific program content. We have taken this approach for a number of reasons. First, considering the research activities of television ratings services, this is far-and-away the most common operationalization of exposure. Second, as we have noted, such measures offer the researcher a good deal of flexibility in assessing levels of exposure to content types or the medium itself (Greenberg et al., 1968). Finally, as we point out later, the devices used to measure exposure as program choice can often be adapted to provide some measure of attention.

Diaries.   If one were to rank the various measures of exposure by the sheer number of cases involved, television diaries would undoubtedly top the list. Arbitron, A. C. Nielsen, and a number of other research firms in the United States and abroad use the diary to generate estimates of audience size and composition. In one survey month, or "sweep," Arbitron alone collects and edits the viewing information contained in over 100,000 diaries (Arbitron, 1983). Although diaries might be conceptualized as just another kind of questionnaire, their widespread use, and the availability of methodological research specific to diaries, leads us to treat them as a distinct method of measurement.

In its simplest form, the diary is a small booklet in which a respondent is instructed to make some ongoing record of his or her viewing behavior. The format of diaries employed by major U.S. ratings services divides each day of the week into discrete 15-minute intervals beginning at 6:00 a.m. and extending through midnight to 2:00 a.m. the following morning. When the television set is on, respondents are instructed to write in the call letters and channel number of the station being viewed as well as the title of the program they are watching. Additionally, they are asked to report the presence of other family members or visitors, whose ages and sex have been recorded elsewhere in the diary. It is standard practice for a household to keep one diary for each television set over a period of 1 week.

Assuming for the moment that such diaries are completed with great care and accuracy, this measure of exposure to television provides researchers with a wealth of information. It contains a quarter hour by quarter hour record of when each set in the home was in use, as well as a list of exactly what programs were viewed. Unlike some other methods used to produce program ratings, it also identifies who in the household watched a particular program and with whom the program was viewed.

Obviously, making an accurate record of 1 week's television viewing can be a burdensome task. Indeed, only 50–60% of those households that agree to accept a diary return usable information to the rating services (Statistical Research Inc., 1975). Respondents who are either unwilling or unable to complete a diary might be systematically different from other subjects on a number of attributes including levels of education, occupation, literacy, ethnicity, and most important, media use. Additionally, diary keepers might fail to report certain instances of viewing or deliberately misrepresent their program choices. These potential problems can be broadly categorized as issues of nonresponse and response error, respectively.

Methodological research on nonresponse error associated with the diary technique suggests that although diary keepers do differ from the population with respect to certain demographic characteristics, such differences are generally minor. The most notable exception to this is race: Black households have response rates that are nearly half those of nonblack households (Statistical Research Inc., 1975). In practice, major ratings services employ special placement and retrieval procedures to improve rates of return among minority respondents (A. C. Nielsen, 1983b; Arbitron, 1982; Rubens, 1984). Significantly, though, diary keepers have been found to watch the same amount of television (Steeves & Bostain, 1982) or only slightly more (Statistical Research Inc., 1975) than the total population.

Although the nonresponse error associated with diaries could produce modestly inflated levels of viewing, response error appears to operate in the opposite direction (Statistical Research Inc., 1975). That is, diary keepers are inclined to be somewhat heavier viewers of television, but the diaries they keep do not report all instances of viewing. LoSciuto (1972) has noted that some respondents lost interest in keeping diaries after a few days and suggested that "the one week time period may have been overlong and tedious" (p. 42). In fact, response error and nonresponse error balance each other out such that, for most populations, the estimates of total television usage are reasonably accurate (Statistical Research Inc., 1975).

There is less evidence on the extent to which evaluation apprehension or social desirability factors might produce response error systematically related to program content. Unlike Steiner (1963), LoSciuto (1972) found that very few people expressed any guilt about the amount of time they spent watching television. That fact, in combination with the apparent failure of many critically acclaimed programs to attract large audiences as measured by diary data, suggests that response error is largely random with respect to program content. This does not mean, however, that response error will be uniform across all program types. It appears to be a function of when certain kinds of programs are scheduled rather than a function of their content per se. Specifically, the audience for programs broadcast late at night or at times when an adult diary keeper is unavailable may be underrepresented (Poltrack, 1983).

In spite of some limitations, the diary's popularity as a technique for measuring exposure to television is likely to remain. Diaries are relatively inexpensive when compared with other methods able to assess viewing at such regular intervals. Academic researchers have used conventional diary data either by distributing their own diaries (Wakshlag, Agostino, Terry, Driscoll, & Ramsey, 1983) or by exploiting data already collected for commercial purposes (e.g., Agostino, 1980; Goodhardt et al., 1975; Webster, 1983b; Webster & Wakshlag, 1982). Further, diary formats can be adapted to serve a variety of purposes by pairing diary reports with a number of program-specific questions. For example, how much attention was paid to the program (Israel & Robinson, 1972; Television Audience Assessment, Inc., 1983)? Who chose the program, and what activities occurred while the program was on (Murray, 1972)? How entertaining, different, useful, or informative was the program (Myrick & Keegan, 1981)? Diaries have also been the method most commonly employed to identify the program-specific uses of home video recorders (e.g., Agostino & Zenaty, 1980; Levy, 1983; Levy & Fink, 1984).

Meters.   Electronic metering devices are the second major method used by rating services to measure exposure to television. The best known metering device is A. C. Nielsen's "Storage Instantaneous Audimeter," which is used to monitor viewing behavior in a nationwide panel of 1,700 U.S. households. In addition to forming the basis of national network program-audience estimates, both Nielsen and Arbitron employ meter data in major U.S. cities to produce "overnight" projections of local market audiences.

Though the metering devices used by various firms have somewhat different capabilities, we can offer a general description of the meters in common use. Meters electronically monitor the on–off condition of all television sets in a household. When a set is in use, the meter produces a continuous record of the channel to which the set is tuned. Set usage data are typically stored in a separate unit, placed in an unobtrusive location. At least once a day, a central computer calls the storage unit on dedicated telephone lines and retrieves the information it contains. It is standard practice for metering devices to remain in sample households for a period of 5 years. In this way, 20% of the meter panel can be replaced each year while leaving the sample size constant (Arbitron, 1982).

Measuring exposure to television through metering devices has a number of advantages. Because no effort is required on the part of the viewer, response error associated with the rigors of keeping a diary is eliminated. In fact, the long-term records of household viewing behavior produced by meters have made possible longitudinal studies that would have been quite difficult to accomplish with diary collection methods (e.g., Besen & Mitchell, 1976; Gensch & Shaman, 1980). The nonresponse error associated with this method also appears to be limited. Virtually identical results are obtained when meter-based audience estimates are compared with those derived by the use of telephone coincidentals (Hoban, 1983; Statistical Research Inc., 1975). Perhaps because so much is invested tracking even one household, ratings services engage in elaborate sampling procedures to establish the viewing panel and offer sizable incentives to increase cooperation rates (e.g., Arbitron, 1982; Rubens, 1984). Finally, metered data can be collected and analyzed very quickly, an advantage which is of obvious importance to industry researchers.

As with any other measurement technique, however, meters have certain shortcomings. The hardware necessary to operate a metering system is expensive to buy and maintain. And despite the unobtrusive design of modern metering devices, sample households clearly know that they are the object of study. As a result, research firms typically assume "novelty" effects, and they will wait several weeks before making use of data from newly metered homes (Rubens, 1978). Further, there is anecdotal evidence that metered households occasionally attempt to misrepresent viewing. The most serious limitation of conventional metering, however, is that it provides the researcher with no information on who, if anyone, is watching the television set when it is in use. Indeed, ratings services must supplement meter data on set usage with diary data in order to make estimates of the demographic composition of program audiences (Arbitron, 1982; Rubens, 1978).

A new generation of meters currently under development may solve the problem of viewer-specific information. At this writing, A. C. Nielsen, Audits of Great Britain, and Arbitron are in various stages of field testing so-called "people meters" (Rubens, 1984; Webster, 1984). These systems combine the features of conventional meters with special push buttons assigned to each member of the household. When watching television, a person touches the appropriate button, and his or her presence is identified to a central computer which contains the viewer's demographic characteristics. In principle, then, this technology provides the person-specific information contained in diaries, but with the speed, accuracy, and long-term tracking characteristics of meters. Despite such an appealing prospect, it remains to be seen whether these relatively obtrusive devices can leave viewing behavior unaffected while still securing the kind of long-term respondent cooperation needed to make them a reliable and cost effective means of audience measurement.

Finally, meters, like diaries, have been modified to serve more specialized purposes. For example, the "VoX BoX" used by the Seattle based Percy company not only records set behavior, but also offers viewers a number of buttons to express their opinions about what it is they're watching. Responses range from "excellent" to "boring" to "zap" (Corporation for Public Broadcasting, 1980). These responses are, in turn, matched with video tapes of the programs that were aired at the time responses were made (Beville, 1984).

Questionnaires. Despite some novel adaptations in their design and application, the consequences of using either diaries or meters to measure exposure to television are fairly well understood. In a great many research efforts, however, media exposure is measured through some form of questioning. Unfortunately, less can be said about the error associated with questionnaire items, due in large part to the tremendous diversity in their wording and administration.

The designs of questionnaires seeking self-reports of television use are almost as varied as the imaginations of their authors. Total amounts of viewing have been measured by asking respondents to report an "average" or "previous" day's usage (e.g., Allen, 1981; LoSciuto, 1972) or to estimate the time they spent viewing over some period of days (Bechtel et al., 1972). Exposure to specific television programs has been measured by asking respondents what they are currently watching (Statistical Research Inc., 1975), what they watched one half-hour ago (Television Audience Assessment, Inc., 1983), what they watched the day before (e.g., Bechtel et al., 1972; Greenberg et al., 1968), what they have seen over some period of days or weeks (e.g., Frank & Greenberg, 1980; Murray, 1972; Palmgreen et al., 1981; Rao, 1975), or what they have regularly or "never" viewed over some unspecified period of time (e.g., Atkin et al., 1979).

Although the design of questionnaire items should always reflect the purposes and data-collection techniques of the researcher, two general factors appear to affect the validity of self-reports as measures of exposure: (a) the length of time over which a respondent is expected to recall his or her program choices, and (b) whether that recall is aided or unaided.

Telephone coincidental research, in which a respondent is asked what, if any, television programs are being watched by household members at the time of the call, clearly places the fewest demands on the respondent's memory. It is perhaps for this reason that carefully executed telephone coincidentals are frequently used as the standard against which other methods of measurement are evaluated (Hoban, 1983; Statistical Research Inc., 1975). Telephone coincidental or "near-coincidental" research (Television Audience Assessment, Inc., 1983) is limited, however, by time of day at which calls can be made and the expense of conducting enough calls to achieve adequate sample sizes.

More typically, questionnaires have required respondents to recall viewing over some period of time, placing increased demands on memory as the time interval is increased. Sudman and Bradburn (1982) have noted that the extent of "memory error" (p. 21) is in part a function of the salience of the topic. If, as much research and theory indicate (Csikszentmihalyi & Kubey, 1981; Gans, 1980; Goodhardt et al., 1975; Levy & Windahl, 1984; LoSciuto, 1972), watching television is a "low-involvement" activity, the common practice of asking respondents to report how many episodes of a particular series they have seen in the last 4 weeks (e.g., Frank & Greenberg, 1980; Gensch & Ranganathan, 1974; Rao, 1975) probably entails considerable error. Indeed, cluster analyses of claimed program viewing more closely resemble patterns found in studies of program preference than patterns in studies of actual viewing that use television diaries (cf. Aske Research Ltd., 1977). It would appear that as the demands on a respondent's memory increase, recollections of actual viewing are likely to be supplanted or at least colored by program preferences.

Aiding recall is one way in which memory error can be reduced. As a general rule, aided recall is appropriate where low-salience behaviors tend to be under-reported and an exhaustive list of those behaviors can be offered to prompt the respondent (Sudman & Bradburn, 1982). Questions on the extent to which specific television programs have been viewed would seem well qualified for this treatment. In practice, researchers have presented respondents with television program schedules (Bechtel et al., 1972; Greenberg et al., 1968) or otherwise listed specific programs (e.g., Frank & Greenberg, 1980) to aid in the reporting process. It does not appear that such aids induce overreporting or socially desirable responses (Greenberg et al., 1968).

Clearly, questionnaires offer researchers a very flexible tool for assessing exposure to television. Survey instruments can be designed to ascertain not only reports of program viewing, but also who decided to watch the program, whether its selection was planned, how much attention was paid to the program, and what activities occurred during viewing (e.g., Bechtel et al., 1972; Frank & Greenberg, 1980). Researchers should recognize, though, that even with aided recall, a respondent's memory of when or how some program was viewed is often very limited.

Observation.   Though relatively uncommon, exposure to television has been measured by direct observation in the field. One of two general approaches is typically employed. Photographic records of a family's viewing behaviors have been made by placing either a time lapse still camera (Allen, 1965) or video cameras (Bechtel et al., 1972) in the home. The activities and program selections recorded by these devices are later coded into a more useful form. Alternatively, viewing has been studied by placing participant observers in the home environment. These researchers may record activities by using a structured log and/or by less structured note taking (e.g., Lull, 1980).

The great virtue of direct observation is that it provides the researcher with a rich, sometimes overwhelming, store of data and impressions gathered in situ. Such studies have documented a range of behaviors and interactions associated with television watching. Further, they have illustrated that other measures of viewing tend to overstate the time that people actually spend attending to the screen. For example, Bechtel et al. (1972) found that for every 4 hours of reported viewing as measured in diaries, only 3 were actually spent watching the set. This result is generally consistent with other comparisons of attention levels and diary-based reports of viewing (e.g., Israel & Robinson, 1972).

The problems of direct observation, however, are numerous. Many people are understandably reluctant to allow the intrusion of either a camera or a stranger into their home for a period of days. After all, what types of people allow a total stranger to enter their home to observe how they live? Low acceptance rates suggest the possibility of considerable nonresponse bias. The time and expense involved place a practical limit on sample sizes and increase the likelihood of sampling error. Finally, there is the familiar problem of reactivity. Though many subjects report no change in their activities during observational periods, they clearly know that they are the object of study and may, consciously or not, alter their behavior accordingly.

Some academic researchers have attempted to overcome this problem by having students observe viewing in their own homes (e.g., Steiner, 1966). Although such a strategy may minimize reactivity, it introduces other difficulties regarding the objectivity of observers, biases due to nonprobability sampling, as well as ethical considerations.

Given these limitations, the methods we have already discussed seem to offer researchers more reliable and cost effective techniques for measuring set use and program choice in the home. If, on the other hand, the quality and gratifications of the viewing experience are to studied, direct observation constitutes a valuable alternative.

Scanning.   Television set usage has also been measured by various electronic devices that we describe here under the somewhat Orwellian title of "scanning." There are two basic ways in which scanning occurs. One technology employs radar-like devices that scan the airwaves and produce a reading on the number of sets within a certain area that are tuned to a particular frequency (Webster, 1983a). The second approach exploits the capabilities of modern two-way cable systems to scan subscribers and identify the channels to which sets are tuned. Of these two technologies, the latter appears to present scholars with more opportunities for studying patterns of choice, including tuning behaviors and exposure to programs over time (see chap. 10 by Heeter & Greenberg for a comprehensive discussion of this method of measurement).

In many respects, these techniques have the same advantages and disadvantages of more conventional meters. They require no effort on the part of the respondent, produce data quickly, are capable of monitoring set usage on a nearly continuous basis, and are unobtrusive. Scanning over a cable system also allows the researcher to match set-usage data with various household characteristics. But like meters, scanning cannot determine who in the household is watching.

Measuring Exposure in the Laboratory

Research on exposure in laboratory environments has been at a relative lull since dissonance theory ceased to be a major focus of study in psychology. Although some research on dissonance-based exposure has continued (see chap. 2 by Cotton in this volume for a review of this research), such experimentation has not been widespread. Rather, experimental work has tended to manipulate exposure as a treatment condition in a wide-ranging examination of media "effects." As a result, the measurement of exposure as a dependent variable in experiments has not been a matter of concern, until recently.

Research on media use has proceeded in the field via studies of "uses and gratifications" (Blumler & Katz, 1974), but it is only recently that experimentation on media use and exposure has begun to emerge. Such studies have focused on the extent to which subjects use media to satisfy needs produced by enduring traits or experimentally induced mood states. With this renewed emphasis on media as effect rather than cause, a range of experimental techniques has been developed to measure exposure. Usually, measurement of exposure in the field is undertaken for descriptive purposes. In the laboratory, explanation and prediction are typically of greater concern. Thus, a somewhat broader review of the theoretical and procedural landscape surrounding laboratory measurement is called for.

A major advantage of the experiment is the ease with which the researcher manipulates or controls the content of the televised messages available to the viewer. A number of researchers have been able to produce programs that control content features to judge their effects on selective exposure. Recent experimental work on selective exposure has looked at the effects of features such as humor (Wakshlag, Day, & Zillmann, 1981) and background music (Wakshlag, Reitz, & Zillmann, 1982) on measures of television exposure (see chap. 9 for more detail). By manipulating the affective states of subjects and allowing them to select from among programs, researchers (Boyanowski, 1977; Bryant & Zillmann, 1984; Christ & Medoff, 1984; Zillmann et al., 1980) have made initial strides toward understanding the relationship between mood-related affective states and selective-exposure behavior.

Mechanical recorders. Perhaps the most frequently employed device is some form of event recorder to monitor channel selection and/or duration of exposure. In many of these studies (cf. Bryant & Zillmann, 1984; Wakshlag et al., 1981; Zillmann et al., 1980), programs are fed to a special monitor from separate cassette recorders, with each program on a different channel. Subjects are told to watch some television while they are waiting for another experiment to begin. After flipping through the channels to familiarize the subject with the available content and operation of the tuner, the experimenter leaves the set on a vacant channel, once again invites the subject to watch television, and leaves the room. Subjects may, of course, choose to watch nothing and leave the set on the vacant channel or turn it off. These options are rarely taken, however. As in the home, when there is little to do, television is an attractive alternative. A recording device (usually an event recorder) located in an adjacent room is connected to the tuner. It produces an unobtrusively observed, permanent record of the subjects' tuning activity.

Although behavioral measures of tuning behavior have long been a part of commercial rating services, they have only recently emerged in experimental work. Such behavioral measures are particularly suited to assess initial program selection and duration of exposure. Through analyses of such data, we know that people generally settle down to their program of choice quickly and that, once settled, they generally view that program for an extended period of time (Bryant & Zillmann, 1984; Wakshlag et al., 1981, 1982). Goodhardt et al. (1975) corroborate this finding for field surveys by indicating that 95% of those watching the first quarter-hour of a half-hour program remain to watch the second quarter-hour. This "exposure inertia" has an interesting and probably related parallel in what Anderson et al. (1979) have labeled "attentional inertia": The longer persons pay attention to the screen, the more likely they are to continue to pay attention. Analyses of exposure behavior obtained via the scanning of homes with cable television (see chapt. 10 by Heeter & Greenberg in this volume) indicate that switching takes place at predictable places (at station breaks and commercials). Similar analyses in the commercial sector (A. C. Nielsen, 1983a) suggest that concerns with "zapping" (switching the channel so as to avoid commercials) expressed by commercial advertisers have been overemphasized. Thus, the use of mechanically recorded behavioral measures of exposure have yielded substantial knowledge of exposure behavior in the field and, more recently, in the laboratory.

Behavioral measures commonly used in the laboratory studies to date are associated with one potential difficulty, however. Most of these studies of exposure have used duration of exposure to a program as the dependent variable. Analyses of the distributions of scores indicate that this variable does not distribute normally, in general.

After a brief searching process, subjects generally settle on one show and stay with it (exposure inertia). The result, for the most part, is that subjects either view an entire show or almost none of it. Thus, means computed on the duration of exposure to any one program are subject to considerable error variance, as most subjects' scores are substantially above or below the mean, producing a U-shaped distribution of scores. This has not been too much of a problem for most experimental studies to date. The effects that have been assessed have been quite powerful and able to overcome the error variance problem. Nevertheless, it is a potential problem for assessing less potent effects.

Statistically speaking, the nonnormal distribution of scores does violate an assumption of the analytic procedure most often used in experiments to assess effects on exposure (viz., the analysis of variance). One possible solution is to transform the data. By taking the square root of each individual's deviation from the grand mean (but retaining the sign of the deviation) and using these values in the analysis, the U shape would be less pronounced. These transformed data would be preferable to raw data when initial analyses suggest that substantial error variance produces problems in assessing the effects of a variable on exposure. An alternative, of course, is to use nonparametric procedures. The major difficulty with them, however, is that they make the analyses of interactions difficult and do not lend themselves well to analyzing a mixture of independent and repeated measures. If exposure to a show does not vary substantially over time or if interactions between an independent factor and the repeated measures factor are inconsequential or irrelevant, mixed-measures analyses may not be required. Under these circumstances, nonparametric analyses should yield satisfactory results.

Observation.   A hidden camera was used by Christ and Medoff (1984) to record their subjects' tuning behaviors. Actually, having a visual record of what transpires on the set as subjects view and change channels could be very useful. A prototype known as the CARMA (Cable Audience Research Monitoring Acolyte) device has been developed and tested at Michigan State University and provides such visual records. The device video tapes the content as it is selected by the viewer while a microcomputer controls the taping and keeps a record. The record enables the researcher to relate content attributes to channel changing or to the decision to turn off the television altogether. Parallel research on attention (Anderson et al., 1979; Anderson & Lorch, 1983; Watt & Welch, 1983) has examined factors that are positively related to visual attention. Some of these studies have also identified elements that appear to turn viewers' attention away from the screen. As has been pointed out elsewhere (Anderson & Bryant, 1983), virtually nothing is known about why or when changes in program choice occur or why viewing stops. Continuous records of the content seen by a subject, collected along with attentional data, could contribute substantially to knowledge of the correlates and determinants of exposure.

Although the preponderance of experimental research on exposure behavior has given subjects the opportunity to select from among several alternatives, Masters, Ford, and Arend (1983) used a more basic procedure. After an experimental manipulation of affect, subjects were given the opportunity to control the duration of exposure to either nurturant or neutral television content. Only one type of content was available to each subject. In this case, observed differences in duration of exposure could be attributed to differences in the appeal of the program induced by the manipulation of affect.

This procedure appears to be acceptable, but there are reasons for preferring one that allows subjects to select from between at least two programs. Although the program to be viewed might be more attractive to subjects in one experimental group than to subjects in another, those in both groups might find their program far more attractive than viewing nothing. Under such conditions, the procedure used by Masters et al. (1983) might fail to yield reliable differences and would, at the very least, underestimate effects. Given the choice between two programs, however, between-group differences would emerge so long as the two shows were roughly equivalent in appeal. The critical variable, then, is the relative appeal of the alternative activity. If nonviewing is as attractive as viewing the program, the basic procedure used by Masters et al. (1983) is satisfactory. Otherwise, some alternate activity or option, roughly equivalent in appeal to the program, would be preferable. An alternative program is an acceptable alternate option.

A related reason for preferring a procedure that allows the subject to choose between program options is a practical one. As already noted, after a brief scanning of programs, viewers generally settle on one program and remain with it for some time. Because viewers choose among programs rather quickly (within 2 minutes or so) and because these choices are generally stable, data collection proceeds more rapidly when subjects are given a choice among programs than if one had to wait until each subject chose to stop viewing or until the program concluded. This may be even more of a problem when dealing with exposure to programs where an interesting or exciting ending is promised. In such cases, there is good reason for the subject to view until the program ends.

Collecting Exposure Data From Groups.   For researchers who must collect data from sizable samples in a short period of time, all the measures of exposure discussed so far present a particular difficulty. Data can be collected from only one subject (or family, if that is the unit of concern) at a time. A device that allows for group administration of a behavioral measure of selection has been described by Mielke (1983). Three monitors display three programs simultaneously, fed by three video-cassette players. The audio is fed through individual earphones to audience members. Using push buttons, they select the audio channel, and their audio selection patterns are recorded as an index of selective exposure.

On the surface, this procedure appears to be a good compromise between the rigors of other behavioral measures of exposure and the efficiency of running several subjects simultaneously. As long as subjects don't see each other's responses, individual choices are independent. A potential difficulty emerges when considering external validity, however. Viewers in the real world rarely have the opportunity to see all program options simultaneously. Rather, they scan both the video *and* audio tracks only as long as they tune in to a particular channel. Thus, under normal circumstances, an individual who is watching (and listening to) a particular program is unaware of particular events occurring on other channels.

In essence, when one chooses to watch a program, one also chooses not to watch others. Thus, deciding to watch a program at any given moment is really a choice between discrete events. Allowing viewers access to the video portion of competing fare provides them with information they would not normally have. One can readily imagine how a subject watching a drama while a boxing match is on another channel would respond as soon as he or she noticed one of the fighters about to be knocked out. Similarly, would viewers of the fight watch as long as they knew that they would not miss any knockouts? The extent to which subjects' behavior under these circumstances does, in fact, deviate from what would be the case under normal circumstances has yet to be assessed. Unfortunately, Mielke (1983) indicated that developmental work on this device has stopped.

Measures of Preference.   The behavioral methods outlined earlier assessed both initial program choice and duration of exposure. Other methods consider only initial program preference or choice. As noted earlier, preferences may be an acceptable substitute for actual exposure data obtained in the laboratory where viewer availability, viewing conditions, and program schedules are under the researcher's control. After manipulating degree of threat, Boyanowski (1977) had subjects rate their preference for each of six films on the basis of synopses provided. Subjects were told that they would be given the opportunity to view the three films they rated highest. Although the film descriptions were distinctive, there is no way to tell exactly how, and along what dimensions, they differed. Thus, the reasoning behind the choice of any film was not directly determinable. A modified procedure, which provides subjects the opportunity to select from among film descriptions that have been pretested and assigned scores along critical dimensions, has been used with success (Fenigstein, 1979; Wakshlag, Vial, & Tamborini, 1983).

Fenigstein (1979) had film descriptions rated (in a pretest) on three factors: aggression, interest, and action. Subjects in the main experiment were told to select 10 film clips from a list of 26. The total aggression, interest, and action scores of the 10 films chosen were the major dependent variables. As the principal concern of this study was the effect of aggressiveness on preferences for violent (aggressive) content, the interest and action scores were used as covariates in a second analysis, with the aggression score of the 10 selected films as the criterion variable. In this way, preferences for violent content were assessed independently of, and statistically controlling for, preferences for action or interest. Thus, even if a manipulation of film descriptions fails to yield independent manipulations, the covariance procedure can be used to remove covariation among measured factors statistically.

Various procedures can be used to generate scores on each dimension for each respondent. Most commonly, the scores of the selected films are summed for each measured dimension. Alternatively, one might weigh the selections, with scores associated with the first film selected weighted more heavily than the second, and so on. Although such weights might be arbitrary, assigning each film an equal weight (which is what happens when scores are summed) is also arbitrary. Alternatively, one could determine empirical weights by having the subjects who do the selecting assign each film a score on the basis of their desire to watch it. Such procedures seem overly complicated at this stage in the research, however. After all, the concern is with *choice* among a discrete set of viewing options rather than with measuring degrees of preference.

The general procedure, then, is to create film descriptions that differ along prespecified dimensions, to obtain scores on these dimensions via pretest, to provide subjects in the experiment with the opportunity to select from among these films, to sum the scores on each of the dimensions for the films chosen, and to use these summed scores either as dependent variables or as covariates while retaining one of them as the criterion variable. This procedure appears to hold substantial promise for both experimental as well as survey research. In the latter case, the main group of respondents engage in the program selection, and a parallel group rates the shows along specific dimensions or criteria. By relating these to program choice, one can evaluate the relative importance of each of several criteria in program selection.

Procedures such as these go a step beyond research in which subjects evaluate their own reasons for watching particular shows, types of shows, or television in general (for a review of these evaluative procedures, see chap. 4 by Atkin in this volume). This research, though a valuable initial step in understanding viewer motivations, draws concern regarding evaluation apprehension, demand characteristics, and so forth, which may encourage certain responses and bias others. Such problems have been acknowledged for reports of viewer behavior (Chaffee, 1972; Greenberg, Ericson, & Vlahos, 1972; Statistical Research Inc., 1975; Stipp, 1975). For example, mothers underestimate the amount of television— particularly the amount of violent television—their children view, and in general, people underestimate their viewing when asked (Cabletelevision Advertising Bureau, 1983; Statistical Research Inc., 1975). It is appropriate to consider the importance of these problems in the assessment of motivations for viewing. It appears naive to believe, without substantiation, that subjects know, remember, and are always willing to reveal their reasons for viewing. Such problems are likely to be particularly acute when the content of television or the reasons for viewing it might be socially objectionable.

Recently, Bryant and Zillmann (1984) presented some evidence concerning the degree to which people, on their own, can report on the processes that govern viewing decisions. Only 14% of their subjects (college undergraduates) ''were able to articulate a notion which might be considered an informal, personal theory'' (p. 19). Although these results were not obtained from a sample of the general population, they are most informative. In fact, one would expect a sample of the general population to be—if anything—even less proficient at articulating a reasoned rationale than these college students. Thus, it would appear that we may be asking too much of subjects—we may be planting ideas in their heads or forcing them to look for some ideas—when we ask them to rationalize an activity that is widely characterized as one which requires little effort, involvement, or reflection. The issue here, of course, is not whether viewer motivations influence viewing choices. Rather, the issue is whether respondents can and do know all their television viewing motives and, should they have an inkling, whether they are willing and able to divulge their true motives to the researcher.

Representativeness of Content.   A researcher concerned with generalizing results from an investigation to a particular population of individuals selects the sample of subjects that represents that population. A similar statement can be made regarding the representativeness of the content used in selective-exposure experiments. If the experimenter wants to generalize beyond the particular material used in the experiment—as he or she usually does—the content should be selected so as to be representative of a body of programming. Thus, if one wants to assess preferences for comedy or drama as a function of some experimental manipulation, using just one comedy or drama show is not unlike using only one subject in an experiment. It would appear to be desirable, then, to use a representative sample of programs rather than one or an arbitrary set of programs. If the sample of subjects and programs is large enough, programs can be selected randomly using combinations and/or permutations. If one does not have this luxury, a smaller number of combinations can be created by random choice or by procedures that match programs on relevant criteria. For example, in their study on selective exposure and affective state, Zillmann et al. (1980) gave each subject a set of program options (comedy, drama, and game shows) which were matched in terms of general appeal to each subject based on a pretest. Once we know more about the conditions that affect exposure and how they interact, such procedures may not be required. Until that time, however, these procedures are worthy of consideration, even though they may be arduous and time-consuming.

Forced Versus Selective Exposure and Effects Research

In studies where the effect of selective exposure to particular content is to be assessed, the Masters et al. (1983) procedure described earlier has a distinct advantage. The procedure insures that subjects are exposed to only the appropriate stimulus and to no other. Under conditions where subjects might not stay with a chosen program for very long and when control over the content is crucial, this would be an important advantage. Although most research supports the idea of exposure inertia, at least one has found systematic changes in exposure over time

(Zillmann et al., 1980). Thus, the researcher who must be certain that the subject is not exposed to alternative televised content would prefer the Masters et al. (1983) procedure over one that permits subjects to select from among a number of available programs. When making this choice, however, the researcher must consider problems with ecological validity. Persons generally select from among a number of programs. Restricting them to only one may be problematic.

Taking advantage of exposure inertia, Bryant and Zillmann (1984) conducted a study on the use (and effectiveness) of televised messages to alleviate boredom and stress. After inducing boredom or stress, they allowed subjects to select from among six television programs that varied in terms of how exciting or relaxing they were. Physiological measures of excitement were obtained before and after exposure, allowing calculation of excitatory changes. Subjects were assigned (in actuality, they assigned themselves) to an exposure condition on the basis of whether they spent most of their time with exciting or relaxing content. Results yielded effects for television exposure on excitatory changes as well as on a number of other factors, including enjoyment.

By manipulating the subjects' mood state, observing their subsequent choices from a controlled set of alternatives, and assessing the effects of these choices, Bryant and Zillmann (1984) have combined several important advantages of experimentation. This combination is a substantial methodological advance in the study of media-exposure effects. If the traditional mode of experimentation had been pursued, with subjects within each mood condition (stress vs. boredom) randomly assigned to view exciting or relaxing fare, any observed effects would have to be qualified by the contention that viewers in the real world *choose* the programs they watch. Although there might be substantial differences in the effects of relaxing media on bored versus stressed subjects, if bored subjects would not have chosen to watch relaxing fare on their own, the effect observed would have little external validity. Thus, although potential effects might be demonstrated, studies that use forced exposure do little to enhance knowledge about whether such effects happen under normal circumstances which allow selective exposure.

Experiments that randomly assign subjects to an exposure condition assess the impact of *forced* exposure. Research on the effects of *selective* exposure, exemplified by Masters et al. (1983) and Bryant and Zillmann (1984), goes a step further. The subject chooses content from among a controlled set of alternatives. As such, this type of experimental research provides an assessment of exposure effects in addition to a behavioral assessment of exposure itself.

As with all laboratory research, external validity is a matter of concern for studies of viewing behavior. These concerns are not particularly troublesome, as far as results are concerned, to the degree that: (a) the subject is unaware that his or her viewing is being monitored, (b) the laboratory viewing environment is natural and realistic, and (c) the programs used in the study are representative. The degree to which past laboratory studies on exposure may suffer regarding

external validity probably says more about the limits of laboratory experiment-
ers, and their limited resources, than about laboratory experiments per se. Laboratory studies are a valuable way to understand viewer motivations and their
causal role in program selection. They are an indispensable complement to field
research, given the likelihood that respondents may not be willing or able to
articulate their true motives for viewing television programs. Both laboratory and
field research provide complementary data and answers. They are correctly
viewed as complementary sources of information on television audiences.

CONCLUDING REMARKS

Exposure to television is the central variable in an enormous amount of communication research. It has long been studied as the cause of various cognitive,
attitudinal, and behavioral effects. Alternatively, it has been examined as a
function of numerous individual, familial, and societal factors. It has been the
object of research in industry and academic disciplines as diverse as economics,
education, political science, and social psychology. Yet the techniques for measuring exposure to television often seem arbitrary and ill-conceived, raising
important questions about the validity, reliability, and comparability of different
measurement procedures.

The validity of any measure of exposure to television must, in the first
instance, hinge on a clear definition of the construct. As we have noted, exposure
might be conceptualized in a variety of ways to suit the theoretical or applied
purposes of different research efforts. If, for example, ascertaining the perception of certain televised messages is the intent of the researcher, then measures of
program choice, however accurate, may have little construct validity. By the
same token, a measure of message discrimination or attention would be inappropriate as a dependent variable if one is studying the determinants of program
choice. Thus, it is difficult to make absolute statements about the validity of each
method for measuring exposure to television.

But if we confine ourselves to the techniques of measuring choice behavior,
which we reviewed earlier, certain generalizations seem warranted. Overall, the
procedures that yield the best results are those that place the fewest demands on
the subject or respondent. The validity of different techniques seems to be a
function of the extent to which the respondent must rely on memory, the time and
effort the respondent must devote to reporting his or her behavior, and the
obtrusiveness of the measuring procedure or device itself.

The ideal measurement, then, would be one that is completely unobtrusive,
records behavior as it occurs, and requires no particular effort on the part of the
respondent. Although conventional meters and scanning devices closely approxi-
mate these characteristics, they are not person-specific. If data on individual
viewers are necessary, then diaries, telephone coincidentals, and potentially,

TABLE 3.1
Procedures for Measuring Exposure to Television

	Brief Description	Relative Advantages and Disadvantages
In the Field		
1. Diaries	Booklet in which the respondent maintains an ongoing record of viewing	*Advantages:* records behavior as it occurs; records behavior of individuals; relatively inexpensive. *Disadvantages:* obtrusive; requires effort on the part of the viewer; long delay before data analyzed and reported.
2. Household meters	Device connected to the set, which records tuning activity	*Advantages:* unobtrusive; records behavior as it occurs; requires no effort on the part of the viewer; data analyzed and report available quickly. *Disadvantages:* does not record behavior of individuals; expensive.
3. People meters	Device connected to the set, which also allows viewers to record their viewing	*Advantages:* records behavior as it occurs; records behavior of individuals; requires little effort on the part of the viewer. *Disadvantages:* obtrusive; expensive.
4. Survey questionnaires	Self-reports of viewing collected at one time rather than as an ongoing record	*Advantages:* records behavior of individuals; inexpensive to administer. *Disadvantages:* obtrusive; requires substantial effort for respondent to give accurate information; does not record behavior as it occurs and thus is subject to memory failure.
5. Telephone coincidental	Self-reported viewing at the time the call is received	*Advantages:* records behavior as it occurs; records behavior of individuals; requires little effort on the part of the viewer; accuracy of data. *Disadvantages:* obtrusive; expensive; times for calling restricted.
6. Direct observation	Placement of camera or observer in the home	*Advantages:* richness of data; records behavior as it occurs; records behavior of individuals; requires little effort on the part of the viewer.

TABLE 3.1 (*Continued*)

	Brief Description	*Relative Advantages and Disadvantages*
7. Scanning	Measurement of tuning behavior via monitoring of tuner leakage or via interactive cable	*Disadvantages:* Highly obtrusive; expensive. *Advantages:* unobtrusive; records behavior as it occurs; requires no effort by the viewer; records the behavior of all in the area or all cable subscribers. *Disadvantages;* does not record behavior of individuals; expensive; invasion of privacy (ethical) issues.

In the Laboratory

1. Mechanical recorders	Recording devices attached to tuner; content under control of the experimenter	*Advantages;* unobtrusive; records behavior as it occurs; researcher knows composition of viewing group (e.g., individual, family, etc.) and who is viewing. *Disadvantages:* relatively high error variance; data collection is time consuming.
2. Observation	Visual recording of content or content and subject	*Advantages:* visual record of content as selective exposure is monitored; may be unobtrusive; records behavior as it occurs; composition of viewing group known. *Disadvantages:* high error variance; data collection is time consuming; expensive.
3. Simultaneous exposure choices from subjects in groups	Different content shown on each of several monitors; subjects (wearing earphones) select audio track corresponding with preferred content	*Advantages:* efficient data collection. *Disadvantages:* each subject sees all programs simultaneously and is thus acutely aware of competitive content each second; high error variance; obtrusive.
4. Measures of preference	Subjects given a set of program synopses, which have been pretested on critical dimensions; scores derived by summing the scores for programs chosen	*Advantages:* less response bias than questionnaires asking subjects for reasons for exposure; efficient data collection; appropriate stand-in for exposure when other factors are controlled. *Disadvantage:* obtrusive.

people meters would seem to offer the best alternatives. Unfortunately, gathering survey data using any one of these techniques is expensive. If a secondary analysis of commercially collected data is not feasible, then researchers may have to opt for less desirable measures. Alternatively, if the research question is appropriate, experimentation might be employed. In either case, researchers should at least consider the principles that we have outlined. A brief summary of the measurement techniques reviewed along with their strengths and weaknesses is presented in Table 3.1.

Our assessment of different methods for measuring exposure is premised on the assumption that the environment in which choice behavior occurs will remain relatively constant. In the long term, of course, this is unlikely. Over the last decade, we have witnessed the growth of many new technologies that promise viewers a far wider range of programming alternatives than is currently available. It seems reasonable to expect that viewing behaviors will become more varied and heterogeneous in the coming years (Rubens, 1984).

The measurement implications of such changes are only beginning to emerge. The reliability of diary-based measures, for example, suffers as an increasing number of options confront viewers (Cabletelevision Advertising Bureau, 1983; Webster, 1984). Keeping an accurate diary when there are only 3 or 4 channels to choose from is one thing. The same task is much more burdensome, and prone to error, if viewers are switching among, say, 50 or 60 channels.

As technological changes enable more and more viewers to schedule their own programs, select a news or music video channel to which they may selectively attend, or a video text service with which they may interact, gross measures of time spent viewing could become less useful. Ultimately, these changes may force us to reconsider just what television is, whether it can be understood as a single medium, and if not, how the new media should be organized and studied. These emerging changes regarding television and expanding choice are likely to require further refinement in conceptualizing and measuring exposure.

REFERENCES

A. C. Nielsen Co. (1982). *Television audience.* Northbrook, IL: Author.

A. C. Nielsen Co. (1983a). *Channel switching in prime time.* Northbrook, IL: Author.

A. C. Nielsen Co. (1983b). *Reference supplement 1983–84: NSI methodology techniques and data interpretation.* Northbrook, IL: Author.

Agostino, D. (1980). Cable television's impact on the audience of public television. *Journal of Broadcasting, 24,* 347–365.

Agostino, D., & Zenaty, J. (1980). *Home VCR owner's use of television and public television: Viewing, recording & playback.* Washington, DC: Corporation for Public Broadcasting.

Allen, C. (1965). Photographing the TV audience. *Journal of Advertising Research, 5,* 2–8.

Allen, R. (1981). The reliability and stability of television exposure. *Communication Research, 8,* 233–256.

Anast, A. (1983). *The role of content and scheduling in patterns of program audience duplication.* Unpublished doctoral dissertation, Ohio University.

Anderson, D., Alwitt, L., Lorch, E. P., & Levin, S. (1979). Watching children watch television. In G. Hale & M. Lewis (Eds.), *Attention and cognitive development* (pp. 331–361). New York: Plenum.

Anderson, D., & Bryant, J. (1983). Research on children's television viewing: The state of the art. In J. Bryant & D. Anderson (Eds.), *Children's understanding of television: Research on attention and comprehension* (pp. 331–353). New York: Academic Press.

Anderson, D., & Lorch, E. P. (1983). Looking at television: Action or reaction? In J. Bryant & D. Anderson (Eds.), *Children's understanding of television: Research on attention and comprehension* (pp. 1–33). New York: Academic Press.

Anderson, J., & Meyer, T. (1975). Functionalism and the mass media. *Journal of Broadcasting, 19,* 11–22.

Arbitron. (1982). *Description of methodology.* New York: Author.

Arbitron. (1983). November television reports delivered in record time! *Beyond the Ratings, 6*(1), 1.

Aske Research Ltd. (1975). Some possible programme-type effects. *Studies in television viewing.* London: Independent Broadcasting Authority.

Aske Research Ltd. (1977). Programmes viewers like to watch. *Studies in television viewing.* London: Independent Broadcast Authority.

Atkin, C., Greenberg, B., Korzenny, F., & McDermott, S. (1979). Selective exposure to televised violence. *Journal of Broadcasting, 23,* 5–13.

Barwise, P., Ehrenberg, A., & Goodhardt, G. (1982). Glued to the box?: Patterns of TV repeat-viewing. *Journal of Communication, 32*(4), 22–29.

Bechtel, R., Achelpohl, C., & Akers, R. (1972). Correlates between observed behavior and questionnaire responses on television viewing. In E. A. Rubinstein, G. A. Comstock, & J. P. Murray (Eds.), *Television and social behavior: Vol. 4. Television in day-to-day life: Patterns of use* (pp. 274–344). Washington, DC: U.S. Government Printing Office.

Besen, S., & Mitchell, B. (1976). Watergate and television: An economic analysis. *Communication Research, 3,* 243–260.

Beville, H. (1984). *Audience measurement in transition.* New York: Television/Radio Age.

Blumler, J., & Katz, E. (Eds.). (1974). *The uses of mass communications: Current perspectives on gratifications research.* Beverly Hills, CA: Sage.

Bower, R. (1973). *Television and the public.* New York: Holt, Rinehart & Winston.

Bowman, G., & Farley, J. (1972). TV viewing: Application of a formal choice model. *Applied Economics, 4,* 245–259.

Boyanowski, E. O. (1977). Film preferences under conditions of threat: Whetting the appetite for violence, information, or excitement? *Communication Research, 4,* 133–145.

Bryant, J., & Zillmann, D. (1984). Using television to alleviate boredom and stress: Selective exposure as a function of induced excitational states. *Journal of Broadcasting, 28,* 1–20.

Cabletelevision Advertising Bureau. (1983). *Cable audience methodology study.* New York: Author.

Chaffee, S. (1972). Television and adolescent aggressiveness. In G. A. Comstock, & E. A. Rubinstein (Eds.), *Television and social behavior: Vol. 3. Television and adolescent aggressiveness.* Washington, DC: U.S. Government Printing Office.

Chaffee, S. (1980). Mass media effects: New research perspectives. In D. C. Wilhoit & H. DeBock (Eds.), *Mass communication review yearbook* (pp. 77–108). Beverly Hills, CA: Sage.

Christ, W., & Medoff, N. (1984). Affective state and selective exposure to and use of television. *Journal of Broadcasting, 28,* 51–63.

Clarke, P., & Kline, G. (1974). Media effects reconsidered: Some new strategies for communication research. *Communication Research, 1,* 224–240.

Comstock, G., Chaffee, S., Katzman, N., McCombs, M., & Roberts, D. (1978). *Television and human behavior*. New York: Columbia University Press.

Corporation for Public Broadcasting. (1980). *Proceedings of the 1980 technical conference on qualitative television ratings: Final report*. Washington, DC: Author.

Csikszentmihalyi, M., & Kubey, R. (1981). Television and the rest of life: A systematic comparison of subjective experience. *Public Opinion Quarterly, 45,* 317–328.

Ehrenberg, A. (1968). The factor analytic search for program types. *Journal of Advertising Research, 8,* 55–63.

Fenigstein, A. (1979). Does aggression cause a preference of viewing media violence. *Journal of Personality and Social Psychology, 37,* 2307–2317.

Frank, R., Becknell, J., & Clokey, J. (1971). Television program types. *Journal of Marketing Research, 8,* 204–211.

Frank, R., & Greenberg, M. (1980). *The public's use of television*. Beverly Hill, CA: Sage.

Freedman, J., & Sears, D. (1965). Selective exposure. In L. Berkowitz (Ed.), *Advances in experimental social psychology* (Vol. 2, pp. 58–98). New York: Academic Press.

Gans, H. (1980). The audience for television—and in television research. In S. B. Withey & R. P. Abeles (Eds.), *Television and social behavior: Beyond violence and children* (pp. 55–81). Hillsdale, NJ: Lawrence Erlbaum Associates.

Gensch, D., & Ranganathan, B. (1974). Evaluation of television program content for the purpose of promotional segmentation. *Journal of Marketing Research, 11,* 390–398.

Gensch, D., & Shaman, P. (1980). Models of competitive ratings. *Journal of Marketing Research, 17,* 307–315.

Gerbner, G., & Gross, L. (1976). Living with television: The violence profile. *Journal of Communication, 26,* 172–199.

Goodhardt, G., Ehrenberg, A., & Collins, M. (1975). *The television audience: Patterns of viewing*. Westmead, England: D. C. Heath.

Greenberg, B., Dervin, B., & Dominick, J. (1968). Do people watch 'television' or 'programs'?: A measurement problem. *Journal of Broadcasting, 12,* 367–376.

Greenberg, B., Ericson, P., & Vlahos, M. (1972). Children's television behavior as perceived by mother and child. In E. A. Rubinstein, G. A. Comstock, & J. P. Murray (Eds.), *Television and social behavior: Vol. 4. Television in day-to-day life: Patterns of use* (pp. 395–410). Washington, DC: U.S. Government Printing Office.

Headen, R., Klompmaker, J., & Rust, T. (1979). The duplication of viewing law and television media schedule evaluation. *Journal of Marketing Research, 16,* 333–340.

Hoban, B. (1983, April 15). CAMS: What was learned? *Cable Television Business*, pp. 70–72.

Israel, H., & Robinson, J. (1972). Demographic characteristics of viewers of television violence and news programs. In E. A. Rubinstein, G. A. Comstock, & J. P. Murray (Eds.), *Television and social behavior: Vol. 4. Television in day-to-day life: Patterns of use* (pp. 87–128). Washington, DC: U.S. Government Printing Office.

Katz, E., Blumler, J., & Gurevitch, M. (1974). Utilization of mass communication by the individual. In J. Blumler & E. Katz (Eds.), *The uses of mass communications: Current perspectives on gratifications research* (pp. 19–32). Beverly Hills, CA: Sage.

Kirsch, A., & Banks, S. (1962). Program types defined by factor analysis. *Journal of Advertising Research, 2,* 29–31.

Levy, M. (1983). The time-shifting use of home video recorders. *Journal of Broadcasting, 27,* 263–268.

Levy, M., & Fink, E. (1984). Home video recorders and the transience of television broadcasts. *Journal of Communication, 34*(2), 56–71.

Levy, M., & Windahl, S. (1984). Audience activity and gratifications: A conceptual clarification and exploration. *Communication Research, 11,* 51–78.

LoSciuto, L. (1972). A national inventory of television viewing behavior. In E. A. Rubinstein, G.

A. Comstock, & J. P. Murray (Eds.), *Television and Social Behavior: Vol. 4. Television in day-to-day life: Patterns of use* (pp. 33–86). Washington, DC: U.S. Government Printing Office.

Lull, J. (1980). The social uses of television. *Human Communication Research, 6,* 197–209.

Masters, J., Ford, M., & Arend, R. (1983). Children's strategies for controlling affective responses to aversive social experience. *Motivation and Emotion, 7,* 103–116.

Mielke, K. (1983). Formative research on appeal and comprehension in *3-2-1 Contact.* In J. Bryant & D. Anderson (Eds.), *Children's understanding of television: Research on attention and comprehension* (pp. 241–263). New York: Academic Press.

Miller, P., & Cannell, C. (1977). Communicating measurements objectives in the survey interview. In P. Hirsh, P. Miller, & F. G. Kline (Eds.), *Strategies for communication research* (pp. 127–151). Beverly Hills, CA: Sage.

Murray, J. (1972). Television in inner-city homes: Viewing behavior of young boys. In E. A. Rubinstein, G. A. Comstock, & J. P. Murray (Eds.), *Television and social behavior: Vol. 4. Television in day-to-day life: Patterns of use* (pp. 345–394). Washington, DC: U.S. Government Printing Office.

Myrick, H., & Keegan, C. (1981). *Boston (WGBH) field testing of a qualitative television rating system for public broadcasting.* Washington DC: Corporation for Public Broadcasting.

Palmgreen, P., Wenner, L., & Rayburn, J. (1981). Gratification discrepancies and news program choice. *Communication Research, 8,* 451–478.

Peterson, R. (1981). Measuring culture, leisure, and time use. *The Annals of the American Academy of Political and Social Science, 453,* 169–179.

Poltrack, D. (1983). *Television marketing: Network, local and cable.* New York: McGraw-Hill.

Rao, V. (1975). Taxonomy of television programs based on viewing behavior. *Journal of Marketing Research, 12,* 355–358.

Robinson, J. (1969). Television and leisure time: Yesterday, today and (maybe) tomorrow. *Public Opinion Quarterly, 33,* 210–222.

Robinson, J. (1972). Television's impact on everyday life: Some cross-national evidence. In E. A. Rubinstein, G. A. Comstock, & J. P. Murray (Eds.), *Television and social behavior: Vol. 4. Television in day-to-day life: Patterns of use* (pp. 410–431). Washington, DC: U.S. Government Printing Office.

Roper, B. (1969). *A ten-year view of public attitudes toward television and other mass media, 1959-1968.* New York: Television Information Office.

Rubens, W. (1978). A guide to TV ratings. *Journal of Advertising Research, 18,* 11–18.

Rubens, W. (1984). High-tech audience measurement for new-tech audiences. *Critical Studies in Mass Communication, 1,* 195–205.

Sahin, H., & Robinson, J. (1981). Beyond the realm of necessity: Television and the colonization of leisure. *Media, Culture and Society, 3,* 85–95.

Salomon, G., & Cohen, A. (1978). On the meaning and validity of television viewing. *Human Communication Research, 4,* 265–270.

Statistical Research Inc. (1975). *How good is the television diary technique?* Washington, DC: National Association of Broadcasters.

Steeves, H., & Bostain, L. (1982). A comparison of cooperation levels of diary and questionnaire respondents. *Journalism Quarterly, 4,* 610–616.

Steiner, G. (1963). *The people look at television.* New York: Alfred A. Knopf.

Steiner, G. (1966). The people look at commercials: A study of audience behavior. *Journal of Business, 39,* 272–304.

Stipp, H. (1975). *Validity in social research: Measuring children's television exposure.* Unpublished doctoral dissertation, Columbia University.

Sudman, S., & Bradburn, N. (1982). *Asking questions: A practical guide to questionnaire design.* San Francisco: Jossey-Bass.

Television Audience Assessment, Inc. (1983). *Technical appendix.* Cambridge, MA: Author.

Wakshlag, J., Agostino, D., Terry, H., Driscoll, P., & Ramsey, B. (1983). Television news viewing and network affiliation changes. *Journal of Broadcasting, 27,* 53–68.

Wakshlag, J., Day, K., & Zillmann, D. (1981). Selective exposure to educational television programs as a function of differently paced humorous inserts. *Journal of Educational Psychology, 73,* 27–32.

Wakshlag, J., Reitz, R., & Zillmann, D. (1982). Selective exposure to and acquisition of information from educational television programs as a function of appeal and tempo of background music. *Journal of Educational Psychology, 74,* 666–677.

Wakshlag, J., Vial, V., & Tamborini, R. (1983). Selecting crime drama and apprehension about crime. *Human Communication Research, 10,* 227–242.

Watt, J., & Welch, A. (1983). Effects of static and dynamic complexity on children's attention and recall of televised instruction. In J. Bryant & D. Anderson (Eds.), *Children's understanding of television: Research on attention and comprehension* (pp. 69–102). New York: Academic Press.

Webster, J. (1983a). *Audience research.* Washington, DC: National Association of Broadcasters.

Webster, J. (1983b). The impact of cable and pay cable television on local station audiences. *Journal of Broadcasting, 27,* 119–126.

Webster, J. (1984, April). People meters. In *Research & planning: Information for management.* Washington: National Association of Broadcasters.

Webster, J., & Wakshlag, J. (1982). The impact of group viewing on patterns of television program choice. *Journal of Broadcasting, 26,* 445–455.

Webster, J., & Wakshlag, J. (1983). A theory of television program choice. *Communication Research, 10,* 430–446.

Zillmann, D., Hezel, R., & Medoff, N. (1980). The effect of affective states on selective exposure to entertainment fare. *Journal of Applied Social Psychology, 10,* 323–339.

4 Informational Utility and Selective Exposure to Entertainment Media

Charles K. Atkin
Michigan State University

Although entertainment media exposure is primarily motivated by anticipation of intrinsic gratifications, audience choices are partially shaped by utilitarian considerations. This chapter examines the role of informational needs in stimulating purposive selection of television programming and other entertainment content which has instrumental utility for guidance and reinforcement.

The two terms paired in the "uses and gratifications" label actually represent distinct concepts. Gratifications are transitory mental or emotional responses providing momentary satisfaction at an intrinsic level. The pursuit of immediate gratification underlies most of the channel consumption and message-selection decisions of mass media audiences (Bower, 1973; Buddenbaum, 1981; Compesi, 1980; Gantz, 1981; Greenberg, 1974; Herzog, 1944; Katz, Blumler, & Gurevitch, 1973-1974; Lometti, Reeves, & Bybee, 1977; LoSciuto, 1972; Palmgreen & Rayburn, 1982; Rubin, 1977, 1979, 1981, 1983; Rubin & Rubin, 1982; Schramm, Lyle, & Parker, 1961). Although this is often inertial or indiscriminant, some exposure is "selective" in the sense that general tastes or interests and specific cognitive or affective states motivate choices among entertainment offerings.

By contrast, uses are characterized by anticipated postexposure application of the mediated experience to attaining pragmatic goals (this is sometimes termed "delayed" gratification). Exposure is a means to an end, as the individual seeks helpful informational inputs for extrinsic purposes such as learning new behaviors, solving problems, making decisions, coping with environmental forces, and strengthening predispositions; this is frequently based on uncertainty-reduction needs. Nonexposure may also be utilitarian as the individual avoids or ignores messages that may increase uncertainty, particularly content that challenges predispositions. Instrumental utility has conventionally been treated as a feature of nonentertainment media content, such as news, political campaigns, and advertising.

The seemingly simple act of mass media exposure can be traced to a complex set of determinants involving receiver needs and message attributes. Following an informal cost–benefit analysis, content is selected when the individual anticipates that the message reward value will exceed the expenditures and liabilities associated with acquiring and processing it. This decision is based on a combination of (a) the learned expectations concerning the likelihood that media offerings will provide certain outcomes, and (b) the subjective evaluation of these consequences.

On the benefit side of the equation, the dominant positive motivation is enjoyment-seeking, where entertainment content is chosen for emotional arousal and cognitive stimulation gratifications that enhance transitory satisfaction. Mediated entertainment may also be selected for compensatory reasons, as an individual experiencing a transitory deficiency seeks to alleviate the negative state; several gratifications commonly sought by audience members can be considered as deficit-motivated, including the benefits of relaxation, to relieve tension or fatigue; killing time, to avoid boredom; companionship, to compensate for loneliness; and escape, to evade social conflict or psychological problems (Compesi, 1980; Greenberg, 1974; Lull, 1980; Rubin, 1977; Rubin & Rubin, 1982; Smith, 1971–1972; Surlin & Dominick, 1970–1971; Wenner, 1976).

Assessment of these gratification-oriented benefits is beyond the scope of this chapter, however. The concepts and evidence described here focus on rewards of an instrumental nature that account for selective exposure to entertainment. Among utilitarian benefits, guidance-seeking prompts message selection for learning purposes, and reinforcement-seeking leads to selection of supportive content that is consistent with predispositions.

These rewarding uses and gratifications must be balanced against cost factors. Obtaining and decoding messages involves expenditures of resources in terms of money, time, physical exertion, and mental effort. Message content may pose certain psychological liabilities, such as guilt feelings, fear arousal from threatening portrayals, irritation due to offensive depictions, and dissonance from discrepant messages that undermine predispositions. Entertainment media may also have liabilities at the social level, as exposure to certain genres results in embarrassment.

This chapter has been prepared with several goals in mind. The first is to demonstrate that instrumental utilities, along with transitory gratifications, play a role in the selection of entertainment messages; this represents an extension in the application of these extrinsic motivations beyond the usual informational and persuasive categories of media content. A second goal is the identification of which utilitarian factors are significant in accounting for exposure to various types of content (e.g., selective exposure to soap operas for advice or to violent programs for reinforcing aggressive attitudes). Third, there is an attempt to assess the strength of each type of motivation, in terms of absolute degree of importance and comparative weighting relative to intrinsic reasons for exposure. To a limited extent, it is also possible to examine the conditions under which utilities affect message choices.

This is accomplished by reviewing a wide assortment of published research that has never been systematically organized from a selective-exposure perspective; some of these studies were not even designed for purposes of investigating the predictors of content selection. The presentation of relevant evidence from the mass communication literature is supplemented by new data from a pilot study conducted for this chapter.

The research findings on this subject are exclusively nonexperimental and suffer from some key deficiencies of survey methodology. Many investigators have relied on introspective self-reports of motivations, usually rated along a numerical scale. The validity of this approach is restricted by respondents' ability to accurately estimate underlying reasons for routine and multifaceted exposure decisions, which is complicated by vagueness in defining both the content referents and the nature of the motives; respondents may also be unwilling to disclose the extent to which less socially desirable needs prompt exposure.

Other studies use correlational survey methods, where the issue of spuriousness is especially problematic. Due to the multiplicity of uses and gratifications that might be derived from a specific message, there is substantial ambiguity regarding the functional contribution of a particular motivation that is indexed by respondent characteristics. For example, a positive association between aggressiveness and the viewing of violence may be due to needs for reinforcement (to justify antisocial behavior), for guidance (to learn criminal techniques), for relaxation (to reduce hostility), or for excitement (to satisfy tastes for fast-paced action). The application of standard multivariate controls might not be sufficient in such cases. There is also a problem in drawing inferences of causal direction, because an attitude or behavior may be a consequence of exposure to corresponding content portrayals (e.g., television violence has an impact on viewer aggression, which accounts for at least a portion of the correlation). Thus, time-order designs offer a valuable advantage in unraveling questions of causality.

The chapter is divided into two major segments. The first describes guidance-oriented selective exposure for purposes of learning information. The second describes reinforcement-oriented selectivity as a means of defending predispositions.

GUIDANCE-ORIENTED SELECTIVE EXPOSURE

Researchers have long recognized that mass media audiences utilize entertainment content for various forms of learning, such as advice, interpretation, surveillance, behavioral modeling, and the acquisition of conversational material. Despite the predominantly fictional nature of entertainment, such messages can provide useful inputs at the cognitive, affective, and behavioral levels, serving as helpful tools for daily living. This guidance function frequently operates without explicit intention on the part of the receiver, who absorbs the information incidentally while exposed for other purposes.

Nevertheless, the needs experienced by the individual occasionally produce uncertainty that motivates selection of entertainment for instrumental reasons. Entertaining stimuli are used as a source of learning when characterizations, plot lines, or settings are perceived as offering information that contributes to uncertainty reduction at three levels. The content may be useful in formulating cognitive orientations by providing awareness or understanding of environmental phenomena relevant to the individual's life (e.g., learning about people and society or self-identity). At the affective level, the individual may want to develop evaluative dispositions or reach decisions among options (e.g., forming attitudes toward social groups or obtaining problem-solving advice). Behaviorally, content portrayals may aid in the enactment of overt actions (e.g., performance of a social behavior sequence or participation in interpersonal conversations).

McGuire (1974) has discussed this form of motivation in the context of utilitarian theories (e.g., Lewin, Tolman), which treat the individual as a positive problem solver seeking to develop coping skills or acquire relevant information for cognitive growth. He notes that "even entertainment content conveys a great deal of information to viewers or readers about taste in clothes and furnishings, styles of life, and appropriate interpersonal relationships" and that the messages are "instructive regarding how to live, how to manage, what is happening, and what it means" (p. 182).

General Learning Motivations

A number of research investigations over the past 2 decades have explored the broad range of motivations for viewing television. These studies have typically measured self-reported motives along numerical rating scales. In considering this evidence, it should be recognized that researchers are measuring self-appraisals as perceived and reported by respondents; unfortunately, there has been little systematic measurement validation of the type performed by McLeod and Becker (1974) for political uses and gratifications. Moreover, it is often unclear which specific types of television programming respondents are using as a referent in making their ratings.

This review of evidence focuses on those motivations involving instrumental utilities, with comparisons to intrinsic gratification-seeking noted briefly. Without a coherent conceptualization of the various dimensions of learning-oriented motivations, a diverse set of measures has been employed. Only in the case of communicatory utility has a distinctive aspect of guidance-based selective exposure been isolated; this is considered in the next section. Researchers have almost exclusively examined the medium of television; the single investigation assessing all media is reported following the description of the findings for television only.

Viewing Television to Learn. Most studies that measure learning motivations for viewing have looked at television in general rather than at specific genres of programming. The most comprehensive research effort has been Rubin's series of investigations, which explores both guidance uses and transitory gratifications of general television viewing. In a large sample of children and adolescents, Rubin (1981) reported that an informational set of items (watch TV to learn new things, to learn about self and others, and to learn what could happen) averaged 2.3 in importance on a 1 to 5 scale. This rating is lower than the three-item averages for entertainment (3.3), relaxation (2.9), habit/pass time (2.6), but slightly higher than viewing television for escape (2.2), arousal (2.2), companionship (2.1), and social interaction (2.0).

Rubin (1983) then performed both factor analyses of viewing motivations and canonical correlations between motivations and viewing patterns in the adult subsample. He found that the nonselective motivation items representing habit and passing time loaded on a first factor that accounted for 50% of the common variance. The three information items, along with the communicatory utility item ("so I can talk with other people about what's on"), constituted the second factor accounting for 16% of the variance. The other three factors were entertainment, companionship, and escape. It should be noted that the information factor was positively related to each of the other four, with an average correlation of + .31, indicating the multiplicity of gratifications accompanying television viewed for learning purposes. This factor was moderately correlated with perceived reality of television, which Rubin (1979) also discovered in a survey of children and adolescents. In the canonical analysis, the information motivation, unlike the other four factors, correlated more strongly with the second root, which also includes viewing of talk-interview programs, newscasts, and game shows. Rubin concluded that the first type of viewer uses television out of habit, to pass time, and for entertainment, displaying indiscriminant consumption of the *medium* itself without obvious programming preferences. The second type of viewer uses television to learn (and not for escape), utilizing genres of informational *content* in the medium for instrumental purposes such as learning about people and events and extracting material for interpersonal communication.

Two other studies in this research program tested youthful and elderly groups. Among children and adolescents, three items measuring viewing for purposes of learning averaged 2.3 on the 1 to 5 scale (Rubin, 1977). Although this level is the same as for adults, it is relatively weaker than for ratings on the gratificatory dimensions. In a sample of older persons, Rubin and Rubin (1982) measured motivations with single-item descriptors. Viewing to provide topics for communication was rated 2.8 on a 5-step scale, and viewing to help know how to act with others or in new situations was rated 2.6. Both variables were positvely related to amount of social interaction, indicating the utilitarian nature of some television-exposure decisions.

A survey of British children's motivations for viewing television (Greenberg, 1974) measured two sets of learning reasons, along with items tapping habit, passing time, companionship, relaxation, arousal, and diversion. A factor analysis showed that the four items in the "learning about things" category loaded with the four from the "learning about myself" category, in a factor distinct from the other motivations. Children were asked if they watched to learn about things happening in the world, to learn how to do things they haven't done before, to get new ideas, to learn things they don't learn in school, to learn things about themselves, to see how they're supposed to act, to learn about what could happen to them, and to see how other people deal with the same problems they have. Averaging across the eight reasons, the mean score was 2.9 on a 1–4 scale, which was midway in the ranking of all factors.

In a survey of U.S. Hispanic youth, Greenberg and Heeter (1983) discovered moderate levels of utilitarian motives for media usage. One factor examined was Social Learning, operationalized as finding out about new places and people, learning how to do new things, and seeing how others deal with similar problems. Motivation scores averaged near the midpoint of the scale for both television viewing and newspaper reading. For television motivations, an Advice factor was also obtained from reasons such as watching to know how to act and to get advice on problems; scores were substantially lower, however.

In their pioneering exploration of the role of television in children's lives, Schramm et al., (1961) reported that television is viewed predominantly for the passive pleasure of being entertained. They did find evidence that utilitarian acquisition of information occurs; for example, children said they learn about fashion, manners, and athletic skills, which are clearly in the behavioral guidance domain. However, the investigators described this as primarily incidental learning rather than an active motivation accounting for program selection.

According to a survey of black and white youth in the fourth through eighth grades, more than two fifths of the viewers said they watch television to learn how different people behave, talk, dress, and look, and to learn what police, doctors, secretaries, and nurses are like (Greenberg & Atkin, 1982). For both types of learning motivation, young blacks were significantly more likely than whites to cite each reason.

A few surveys have focused more narrowly on certain types of television fare. Heavy viewers of soap operas were asked to describe the usefulness of the information in these serials for dealing with real-life problems in the health, marital, pregnancy, and legal domains; most rated soaps as moderately useful for these instrumental purposes (Greenberg, Neuendorf, Buerkel-Rothfuss, & Henderson, 1982).

In another study focusing on a single socially relevant soap opera, one set of motivational items that formed a separate factor included watching for advice and exploring reality, for solving one's own problems, and for understanding others; these reasons were rated somewhat lower than more immediate gratifications such as entertainment and relaxation (Compesi, 1980).

In a study of adults with specific maladies, most said they watched medical programs on television, and almost half reported that they got some useful health information (Wright, 1975).

Multimedia Motivations.   Lichtenstein and Rosenfeld (1983) asked college students to rate how much each of 10 reasons for exposure applied to their use of seven mass media channels. For all media but newspapers, the gratification "to be entertained" ranked first. The utilitarian motive "to obtain information about daily life" was second in importance overall, particularly for the four primary mass media (it ranked first for newspapers, second for television and magazines, and third for radio). Two other ostensibly instrumental purposes ranked high for the major media: "to keep up with the way the government is doing its job" and "to get to know the quality of our leaders." Two other reasons ranked lower: "to learn about myself" and "to feel I'm involved in important events." There were also four deficit-motivated gratifications that received varied rankings: "to kill time," "to release tension," "to get away from usual cares and problems," and "to overcome loneliness."

The most interesting findings involve comparisons across media. Newspapers and television were used quite differently, according to students' rankings. For newspapers, the reasons for exposure followed this order of importance: life information, monitoring government, knowing leaders, entertainment, feeling involved, time killing, learning about self, release, escape, and loneliness. For television, the ordering was: entertainment, life information, time killing, monitoring government, escape, release, loneliness, feeling involved, knowing leaders, and learning about self. Radio was similar to television, although release and loneliness ranked higher and escape lower. Magazine rankings were similar to newspaper rankings, except entertainment was higher and feeling involved was lower.

The profiles for three minor media (books, films, recorded music) were very similar to each other and distinct from the four major media. This was the average ordering: entertainment, escape, release, time killing, loneliness, and learning about self, life information, feeling involved, knowing leaders, and monitoring government.

Examining the four reasons most closely linked to informational utility (including learning about self, life information, monitoring government, and knowing leaders), the average ranking was highest for newspapers (3.3), followed by magazines (4.0), television (5.5), radio (6.5), books (7.0), films and recorded music (both 8.0). On the other hand, average rankings were reversed for the four deficit motivations for channel use: films and recorded music scored highest (both 3.5), followed by books (4.5), radio (5.0), television (5.8), magazines (7.3), and newspapers (8.3).

Thus, utility-based exposure varies considerably from channel to channel, although there is obviously considerable variance across content categories within each medium. Clearly, newspapers and magazines are most often sought for utilitarian material.

Communicatory Utility

Although most assessments of exposure motivations yield broad and indistinct indicants of generalized learning utilities, one relatively discrete aspect involves message selection for purposes of acquiring conversational material. For example, the studies by Rubin and Rubin (1982) and Rubin (1983) found that viewing television to provide topics for interpersonal communication was rated as somewhat important by respondents. Because a number of investigators have focused specifically on this motivation, it is treated separately here.

Assessing the heavy television viewing patterns of the elderly, Meyerson (1961) advanced the notion that a crucial function of television is to provide universal conversation pieces that can be used in social interaction with persons from younger generations who share few other common experiences.

In their early study of children's uses of television, Schramm et al. (1961) noted that communicatory utility plays a secondary but significant role in attracting viewers to television. They reported that the programs provide a fertile common ground of shared experience for the next morning's conversations at school; those who can't talk about the latest performers or plot lines are less able to participate in peer-group interaction. However, this seems more of an incidental function than an explicit motivation for viewing.

Smith (1971–1972) asked adolescents whether they used various media for conversation topics. Almost all cited television, whereas less than half used comic books or radio as sources of discussion material.

A survey by Gantz (1981) examining the motivations for viewing televised sports showed that many persons watch in order to have something to do with friends or to provide material for sports-related conversations. Compesi (1980) asked regular viewers of the soap opera *All My Children* to identify reasons for watching; the second-ranking motivation was social utility (operationalized as a tool for facilitating social interaction and talking with friends).

Using ethnographic observations in family settings, Lull (1980) examined how individuals used television to satisfy structural and relational needs. The key relational function was communicatory facilitation, as family members used stories, themes, and characters as illustrations and common referents and program content as an immediate agenda for talk.

A pair of studies show the extent to which people talk with others about the programming they have seen. Preadolescents ranked television programs second only to school events as the most likely peer conversation topics (Lyle & Hoffman, 1972). When Bernstein (1975) interviewed employees of beauty shops, barbershops, and pharmacies to determine the conversational material occurring in casual interactions with customers, a majority said they frequently talked about entertainment topics and half cited sports. Of course, the finding that people subsequently discuss certain television content does not demonstrate the existence of explicit motivations; acquiring discussion material may be an incidental byproduct rather than an intentional reason for viewing.

New Data on Guidance Motivations

To gather preliminary evidence on the degree to which instrumental motivations influence message selection, the author conducted a modest pilot survey with 70 college students. Although the sample is small and unrepresentative and the measurement relies on self-report estimates, the study provides some rudimentary indications of the reasons for choosing media and content for four purposes.

The motivations were defined in detail rather than merely labeled, and respondents were asked to rate the importance of each factor in their exposure to 22 types of media messages along a scale ranging from 0 (not at all important) to 10 (extremely important). These are the definitions presented:

Conversational material: Media content is selected because it provides subject matter for interpersonal communication with friends and acquaintances; you decide to be exposed in order to talk with others who may have seen it, or to relay the information to someone who is not exposed, or simply because it may come up as a discussion topic some time.

Advice: Media content is selected because it provides useful guidance for decision making or problem solving regarding some specific matter that you expect to deal with in your daily life; you choose the messages in order to help make up your mind about what to do, such as forming attitudes toward leaders, coping with health problems, choosing among products, or improving a romantic relationship.

Learning about life: Media content is selected because it provides information about people, places, and the way society operates; you decide to be exposed in order to better understand the way other persons think and feel, and to learn about different social groups, races, occupations, life styles, and events that are happening in the outside world.

Learning new behaviors: Media content is selected because it provides helpful suggestions and illustrations about how to do things that you haven't done before; you decide to be exposed in order to find out the appropriate way to act in certain situations, to follow current fads and fashions, to improve your techniques in playing games or deceiving people, to obtain a blueprint for losing weight or taking a trip or cooking a certain meal, and to learn how to take drugs or get ahead on the job, and so forth.

The first 9 media categories listed in Table 4.1 involve broad ranges of content in key channels of mass communication (because scores differed little between news magazine vs. male/female magazine reading, and between radio music vs. record/tape listening, these are combined in the analysis). The other 13 categories represent major genres of television programming, as listed in Table 4.2.

For general consumption of each medium, the mean levels of importance for the four purposes vary substantially from 1.5 to 7.0 on the 0 to 10 scale. Newspaper reading is most often motivated by utilitarian considerations, with an overall average of 5.7 across the four dimensions studied; learning information about people and places scores highest, according to these self-reports. Magazine reading ranks second, with a grand mean of 5.5; the information-learning motive is again most important. This is followed by nonfiction book reading at 5.0, general television viewing at 4.4, and film attendance at 4.0. The average rating for fiction book reading is 3.2, and listening to radio music and recordings ranks last at 2.5; in both cases, the advice motive is relatively low in degree of importance.

Comparing motives across media, conversational material and information learning are rated somewhat higher, with an average of 4.9. Learning new behaviors is the third reason overall, with a mean rating of 4.2. Consuming media for purposes of advice is least important; the score is substantially lower at 3.2.

Moving to the television programming data in Table 4.2, it is clear that utilization of content in conversations is the most important motive for entertainment viewing; over all 12 types of television shows, the mean rating is 5.0. This factor seems to be especially central relative to the other three reasons for soaps, action-adventure programs, sports, comedies, and musical shows; only game shows provide little raw material for interpersonal communication. News and

TABLE 4.1
Mean Level of Media Consumption for Four Instrumental Purposes

Medium	Conversation Material	Advice	Learning About Life	Learning New Behaviors
General newspaper reading	5.5	5.1	7.0	5.2
News and M/F magazine reading	5.0	4.7	6.5	5.7
Nonfiction book reading	4.7	4.3	5.8	5.3
General television viewing	5.0	2.9	5.0	4.6
Theater film viewing	5.9	1.8	4.7	3.6
Fiction book reading	4.4	2.1	3.2	3.1
Radio music and record/tape listening	3.7	1.5	2.6	2.0

Note. Figures are mean scores on a 0 to 10 scale representing self-reported ratings of importance of each motivation for each medium.

TABLE 4.2
Mean Level of Television Content Viewing
for Four Instrumental Purposes

Content Genre	Conversation Material	Advice	Learning About Life	Learning New Behaviors
Daytime soap operas	5.2	1.2	3.0	3.1
Prime time soap operas	5.4	1.2	2.9	2.8
Action-adventure shows	3.8	1.2	2.5	2.5
Game shows	2.2	0.8	1.5	2.0
Newscasts	6.1	5.5	7.4	5.0
Weather news	4.9	6.1	4.3	2.4
Sports news	5.7	2.8	3.6	2.6
Football/baseball games	5.8	1.7	2.9	2.5
Situation comedies	4.2	1.3	2.7	2.5
Talk/interview shows	5.4	4.7	6.4	5.1
Late-night comedy	5.4	1.3	3.0	2.8
MTV/rock music shows	4.9	0.9	2.2	2.1
Political broadcasts	6.1	5.0	5.7	3.6

Note. Figures are mean scores on a 0 to 10 scale representing self-reported ratings of importance of each motivation for each television genre.

political broadcasts are also sought for purposes of conversation, but other factors are important as well.

The second-ranking motive overall is learning about life, with an average score of 3.7. The informational genres of news and talk/interview shows are rated higher on life learning than on other motives, and political broadcasts are also rated high.

Watching television for purposes of learning new behaviors has an overall score averaging 3.0, and the average is 2.6 for the advice motive. There is much more variation in mean scores across genre categories for advice (from 0.8 for game shows to 6.1 for weather news) than for behavior learning (all falling between 2.0 and 5.1).

The type of programming viewed for the greatest degree of utilitarian motivation is newscasts, averaging 6.0 across the four dimensions. Three other information-oriented genres yield fairly high overall averages: talk/interview shows (5.2), political broadcasts (4.9), and weather news (4.4). Sportcasts and games are somewhat above average, along with late-night comedy. The daytime and evening soap dramas rank next. Situation comedies and action-adventure shows are less strongly sought for utility; ranking lower are musical content (2.5) and game shows (1.4). For these four low-rated categories, only conversational reasons are widely cited as determinants of viewing.

Examining the total set of findings, it is clear that the classic informational media content generates the highest levels of utility-based message selection.

Newspapers, magazines, and nonfiction books lead the way, along with television news, political broadcasts, and talk/interview programs. All of these are rated near the middle of the 0 to 10 scale of importance across the four motive dimensions studied. The entertainment-oriented content is rated mostly in the 2.0 to 4.0 range of the scale, with moderately high scores only for conversational material. This communicatory utility dimension appears to be most important overall, as many people select messages in order to talk about the subject matter with friends and acquaintances. Exposure for purposes of advice in problem solving or decision making is least important; the scores are surprisingly low for certain forms of content considered to be functional in this respect, such as magazines, nonfiction books, and soap operas. Cognitive and behavioral learning are both somewhat important reasons for exposure, particularly for serious print-media reading and the viewing of information-oriented television programming.

Although these data show that media consumption patterns are not predominantly guided by utilitarian considerations (none of the rating scores were above 7.0), learning-based motivations do seem to play a significant role for a broad range of content. This indicates that many exposure decisions are at least partially influenced by instrumental rather than purely gratificatory considerations.

Of course, there are a number of methodological limitations in this study. The sample is atypical; the general public may have distinctly different motivations than do college students. The particular definitions provided for each motivational dimension undoubtedly affected responses; alternate wording or examples may generate different levels of reported importance. The degree of specificity in categorizing media messages also shapes the responses; for instance, the ratings for television in general on the two learning motives are substantially higher than for the average of the 13 television-content genres measured, and there is considerable variation from one genre to the next. The global newspaper item yielded motivation ratings that are probably far different than if individual sections of the paper were measured. Finally, the basic deficiencies associated with the self-report survey approach apply to this investigation. In particular, evaluation apprehension may produce inaccurate reporting of certain message-selection patterns in the direction of social acceptability or psychological self-concept maintenance (e.g., overreporting learning motivations for newspaper use or underreporting advice seeking from broadcast media).

REINFORCEMENT-ORIENTED
SELECTIVE EXPOSURE

A venerable proposition in the literature of social psychology and mass communication is that people prefer messages that are supportive of, rather than discrepant with, predispositions (Atkin, 1973; Festinger, 1957; Katz, 1968; Klapper,

1960; Mills, 1968). This preference will lead to selection of content that is consistent with existing beliefs, attitudes, and practices as a means to reinforcement. A corollary predicts that contrary content will be avoided in an effort to preserve prior commitments. Thus, mass media audiences are expected to exhibit a defensive stance in message selection.

Although the broad array of needs underlying reinforcement-based motivations has not been adequately conceptualized, several basic reasons for selectivity can be advanced. The first is a form of deficit motivation, where content is sought as a means of addressing a perceived negative condition. The individual may be motivated by existing tension generated by dissonant relationships perceived among orientations; those experiencing this unpleasant psychological state will seek supportive material for purposes of rationalization and avoid contact with content that might increase the salience of the inconsistency. Social norms may also play a role in stimulating message selection for compensatory purposes. Individuals with beliefs, attitudes, or behaviors that are socially deviant may seek media content for purposes of legitimization to increase the feeling that such orientations are normal and proper; information that accentuates the unacceptable nature of the orientations may be evaded. For example, smokers, delinquents, racists, adulterers, and others practicing guilt-inducing, disapproved, or questionable behavior are likely to be defensive in choosing among mediated messages, giving preference to content that protects rather than threatens established dispositions.

A second form of reinforcement-oriented selectivity results from genuine uncertainty about the correctness of certain beliefs, attitudes, or practices. The individual who is committed to a particular orientation may want to be more certain that it is valid or appropriate. Where there is doubt or lack of confidence, selective exposure may occur for purposes of reassurance, confirmation, and fortification. For example, a heavy drinker may prefer messages indicating that alcohol is minimally harmful; such selectivity would not be based on felt discrepancies (e.g., the explicit need to reduce guilt or distort normative standards), but on the desire to bolster the cognitive underpinnings of the behavior. Voters who are unsure about the appropriateness of their attitudinal support for a candidate may shun information that challenges their viewpoint so as not to undermine the fragile orientation.

Beyond deficit motivation and uncertainty reduction, a third type of reinforcement-guided exposure occurs as an expression of securely held orientations. In this case, individuals find it comforting to observe mediated portrayals verifying their beliefs, celebrating their values, and affirming their behavior patterns; such messages contribute to a positive affective state during exposure and serve a modest instrumental function. Avoidance of contrary information is based more on minimizing irritation than on preserving cognitive consistency. As examples, persons who revere doctors or respect police officers seek enjoyment from favorable depictions of these occupational roles, whereas patriots tune out antimilitary themes that might offend their sensibilities.

Social scientists have engaged in a long-running controversy over the viability of the reinforcement-oriented selective-exposure proposition since Freedman and Sears (1965) severely questioned the existence of a general psychological preference for supportive versus discrepant information. Subsequent reviews of the evidence by Mills (1968), Katz (1968), and Atkin (1973) clearly demonstrate the existence of de facto selectivity in field settings and suggest reinforcement seeking as a motivation accounting for certain exposure preferences (see also chap. 2 by Cotton in this volume). However, this research has focused almost exclusively on news and persuasive messages in the public affairs domain; little is known about selective exposure to entertainment content. This section examines evidence of selectivity in television program viewing and other entertainment use based on antisocial, prosocial, political, moral, and social role predispositions of the audience. New data are presented concerning preferences for reinforcing versus discrepant television entertainment themes.

Selective Exposure to Television

Physical aggression is a prevalent feature of entertainment television programming. Characteristically aggressive individuals are more likely than nonaggressive people to prefer televised violence for several reasons. Some persons with aggressive attitudes and behavior patterns will watch violent portrayals to affirm or revitalize their antisocial predispositions; others may exalt in viewing content glorifying the acts that they commit, or they may feel satisfaction when characters express the sentiments that they value. Certain aggressive viewers may be attempting to rationalize their deviant inclinations; according to Heusmann (1982): "The justification hypothesis posits that people who are aggressive like to watch violent television because they can then justify their own behavior as being normal. A child's own aggressive behaviors normally should elicit guilt in the child, but this guilt could be relieved if the child believed that aggression was normal" (p. 134). On the other hand, nonaggressive individuals are likely to avoid or ignore violent programming because it is psychologically unsettling to observe actions at variance with their value system; others may simply find such content offensive.

The huge volume of research on television violence provides a basis for assessing selectivity in viewing patterns. Correlational surveys showing that aggressive youths tend to watch a greater amount of violence on television (e.g., McLeod, Atkin, & Chaffee, 1972) are only suggestive with regard to the operation of selective exposure. Because direction of causality is ambiguous, it is not clear whether aggressiveness produces violent viewers or viewing stimulates aggression. Chaffee (1972) suggested that selectivity could be more adequately inferred from studies that measure exposure to violent "favorite" programs rather than the amount of violence viewed across all programs in the television diet. He reasoned that those few shows that viewers identify as favorites are more appropriately considered as a dependent variable (resulting from predispositions) than as an independent variable (producing attitudes or behavior patterns), because the small number of preferred programs would not constitute a strong stimulus.

Studies of favorite program viewing have yielded modest evidence of selectivity. Robinson and Bachman (1972) discovered that delinquent aggressiveness in late adolescence was associated with level of violence in favorite programs. McIntyre and Teevan (1972) found that deviance and violence approval were both related to preference for violent programs among adolescents. In a survey by Friedman and Johnson (1972), aggressive students, both self-identified and as selected by school officials, had more violent programs as favorites.

A survey of Ohio prison inmates found no association between incarceration for violent versus nonviolent crimes and preference for watching violence-filled crime programs such as *Baretta, Starsky and Hutch, Cannon,* and *Kojak* (Balon, 1978). Indeed, those imprisoned for assault showed a tendency to select family dramas such as *The Waltons,* and *Little House on the Prairie.*

Lefkowitz, Eron, Walder, and Huesmann (1972) reported a positive relationship between aggressiveness and violent program preference in childhood, but this initial level of aggression was a negative predictor of viewing violence measured in the same sample 10 years later. However, this time lag was probably too long, because aggressive dispositions changed markedly between the childhood and early adulthood measuring points; aggressiveness as a predictor of program selection 10 years hence is of questionable validity.

More suitable causal evidence concerning the relationship between violence viewing and aggression is provided by a panel survey across a 1-year lag (Atkin, Greenberg, Korzenny, & McDermott, 1979). Inasmuch as this investigation constitutes the most definitive assessment of violence selectivity, the data can be examined in detail.

Questionnaires were administered to 227 children in the fourth through eighth grades in 1976 and again in 1977, and mothers of each child were also interviewed. The pertinent variables in this analysis are exposure to physically and verbally aggressive programming and reports of physical and verbal aggressiveness. In both years, the children marked how often they watched 29 prime time and Saturday morning shows popular with the age group; three shows from the 1976 list were replaced by new shows debuting in the following season. Content analyses provided data on the frequency of acts of physical and verbal aggression for each program; the rate of depicted aggression was multiplied by the frequency of viewing, and the products were summed for both forms of aggression.

Indices of physical and verbal aggressiveness were constructed each year to correspond to the two exposure indices. The disposition measures were hypothetical responses to a series of vignettes of various frustrating situations (e.g., "What if someone cut in front of you in a long line? What would you do?—

Would you push them out? . . . yell at them?''). The response alternatives for each possible reaction were "yes," "maybe," and "no." Mothers were also asked to indicate how their child would react to the situations.

Physical aggressiveness at Time 1 correlated +.24 with Time 2 exposure to televised physical aggression. In a regression analysis adding in Time 1 exposure, age, and sex as predictors, the beta weight between initial aggressiveness and subsequent exposure was +.14 (significant at the .05 level). An important supplemental finding was that the two new series featuring a high amount of violence both attracted aggressive children; initial physical aggression correlated +.31 with becoming a viewer of *Baa Baa Black Sheep* and +.25 with watching *Charlie's Angels* when these shows aired 1 year later.

Because parental control over viewing violent programming may limit the child's exercise of selective exposure, the degree of prohibition of programs was examined as a contingent condition. The sample was divided into those experiencing moderate versus minimal levels of parental constraints (few parents or children reported extensive control), and the relationship between aggressiveness and viewing was computed in each subgroup. The over-time correlation between the indices of physical agression and violence exposure was +.30 where few restrictions existed, and +.16 in the restricted subgroup. Turning to verbal aggression, Time 1 aggressiveness correlated +.17 with Time 2 viewing of verbally aggressive programming. The beta weight was +.13 after Time 1 viewing, age, and sex were entered in the regression.

This panel survey provides evidence that young people are selectively exposed to aggressive television entertainment programming that is compatible with their predispositions. Even with conservative regression analyses controlling for age, sex, and initial viewing patterns, a significant relationship remains between prior orientations and subsequent program choices. In particular, aggressiveness is a predictor of selection of new programming that becomes available.

A similar time-order design for testing the direction of causality was used in a study reported in Huesmann (1982) and Eron and Huesmann (1980). A sample of children was measured in a three-wave panel with 1-year lags. Aggressiveness in 1977 correlated +.18 with violence viewing in 1978, and 1978 aggressiveness correlated +.18 with 1979 violence viewing (in both cases, the reverse viewing-to-aggression lags were slightly stronger, indicating effects of exposure as well). For boys, there is a +.18 correlation between first-year aggression and second-year viewing of violence by male characters; the relationship between girls' initial aggression and subsequent viewing of violent female characters is +.15.

Of course, these correlational data do not yield unequivocable evidence regarding the aggression-reinforcement motive. Other aspects of the content of violent programming could be serving other needs of viewers. For example, learning motivations may produce exposure among aggressive subgroups who want to acquire new techniques of committing violence or evading punishment, or to become aware of plots and characterizations in order to discuss the portrayals with peers. There may also be competing reinforcement motives for viewing violence based on predispositions other than aggressiveness, such as chronic fear of victimization.

In reviewing the evidence on the relationship between television violence and both fearfulness (estimated risk of being victimized, avoidance of perceived risky behavior) and pessimism (estimated crime rate, mistrust of others, worsening quality of life), Comstock (1982) focuses primarily on the cultivation effect of viewing. Nevertheless, he suggests that selective exposure may be operative: "Still another alternative explanation is that fearful and pessimistic persons are motivated to view violent television because of the consistent theme that transgressors of the law are eventually punished, thereby deriving solace and comfort from viewing" (p. 122).

The cultivation analysis research by Gerbner and his associates, which contains numerous measures of fears, values, attitudes, and behaviors that might predict defensive selectivity, is unfortunately of little use for assessing utilitarian viewing motivations. The reason is Gerbner's focus on general television viewing time rather than specific content selection patterns. The only exception comes from a secondary analysis of national sample data presented in Gerbner, Gross, Jackson-Beeck, Jeffries-Fox, and Signorielli (1978). They reported that persons who are fearful of crime (taking precautionary measures, e.g., owning a watchdog, keeping a gun) tend to watch police-crime shows on television more frequently. This may be interpreted as a cultivation effect, but it may also indicate a preference for viewing programs that enhance emotional security by depicting law and order maintained by effective police.

Prosocial Program Viewing

Just as aggressive persons are expected to seek out violent programs, those who display positive social behavior may be motivated to view prosocial programming. In a survey of elementary school children, Sprafkin and Rubinstein (1979) examined the relationship between these two variables. Prosocial behavior was measured with peer ratings of helping, sharing, caring, cooperating, following rules, avoiding fights, and doing other nice things. Frequency of viewing 55 programs on a checklist was weighted according to the number of prosocial acts per episode as determined by a content analysis. There was a correlation of +.11 controlling for demographic variables.

There are several reasons why this prosocial association is weaker than the aggression relationship. First, there may be less need for reinforcement of socially acceptable behavior; because persons who behave positively receive interpersonal approval, there is a weaker motivation to seek content that supports such habits. Second, there is little impetus to watch behaviorally compatible portrayals for purposes of psychologically justifying prosocial behavior, because a person is likely to feel self-assured in this pattern of action. Third, prosocial content is relatively subtle and mild in intensity, and thus a less salient feature in attracting audience attention while choosing programs. Finally, there is less chance that the observed relationship is inflated by the reverse causal link from exposure to behavior, because mechanisms for impact are fewer and restricted.

Political and Moral Values as Predictors

A number of studies have examined how basic values in the sociopolitical and moral-religious spheres relate to the selection of relevant content themes in entertainment or quasi-entertainment programming.

For a period in the late 1960s and early 1970s, popular music available on radio and records presented several distinctive sociopolitical messages in addition to the standard romantic love themes (Mashkin & Volgy, 1975). Rock music featured lyrics expressing social alienation, traditional male chauvinism, and some political alienation. Folk music focused more centrally on political protest along with antiestablishment social views, but tended to take a more liberated stance regarding feminism. Both forms of music conveyed a "post-bourgeois" rejection of materialistic values. On the other hand, country music was characterized by minimal political and social alienation and by traditional sex-role orientations, reflecting a generally conservative perspective.

Mashkin and Volgy (1975) argued that preferences for these musical genres would be related to the corresponding sociopolitical attitudes of listeners. They created indices measuring degree of political alienation (distrust of government and estrangement from political processes), social alienation (rejection of conventional social norms), traditional sex-role orientations, and post-bourgeois ideology. In a sample of college social science students, the investigators found that greater political alienation was significantly associated with preference for folk and rock music rather than country music; this trend occurred to a lesser extent for social alienation. Those with the most traditional sex-role orientations favored country music; folk adherents tended to reject traditional sex roles, and rock fans fell in between. Finally, support for post-bourgeois ideology was highest for those preferring rock and lowest for country fans.

In a similar study, Fox and Williams (1974) obtained both contrasting and consistent results. Based on attitudinal dispositions toward political and social problems of the early 1970s, they divided a college student sample into conservative, moderate, and liberal subgroups. When asked to describe their preferences for nine musical styles, the conservatives scored significantly higher for popular hits and easy listening music; these two genres tend to be apolitical and socially conventional. Liberals were significantly more likely to prefer protest, blues, folk, and jazz music; for the politically relevant protest genre, preference was expressed by 52% of the liberals, 31% of the moderates, and 17% of the conservatives. Rock music, which was widely popular across the sample, correlated only slightly with liberal orientation. Surprisingly, country music, which was low in popularity, held a relatively stronger appeal for the liberal subgroup.

Finally, a survey of adolescents during this period by Robinson, Pilskaln, and Hirsch (1976) showed a strong association between antiestablishment attitudes and preference for "protest rock" music.

Political selectivity is most likely to occur when exposure requires a major time-cost investment and the content is both high in partisan valence and low in entertainment value. During the Vietnam war era, Paletz (1972) reported that the vast majority of persons attending an antiwar film (*Tell Me Lies*) expressed strong opposition to U.S. involvement in Vietnam and that more than half had taken part in protest demonstrations.

Sports programming can also be considered as providing attitudinally reinforcing inputs that may motivate viewing behavior. Prisuta (1979) argues that the leading sports in this country are inherently conservative in a sociopolitical sense, with strict regulation of activity, emphasis on competition, male domination, authoritarian structure and order, and nationalistic flavor (domestic sports, e.g., football, baseball, and basketball, are most popular, whereas foreign sports, e.g., soccer, have not attracted substantial audiences). He reported that teen-agers holding conservative values more frequently view sports programming. There is a moderately positive relationship with nationalism (loyalty to the country) and with authoritarianism (opposition to dissent, acceptance of legitimacy of those in power, intolerance for ambiguity). These correlations remain significant when controls are applied for potentially contaminating variables such as demographics, peer values, and general television viewing. Because the data are correlational, both selective exposure and effects inferences are tenable; it is likely that such fundamental values as nationalism and authoritarianism are at least partial predictors of sports viewing rather than consequences.

One other survey germane to the sociopolitical realm examined correlates of viewing *All in the Family* and a counterpart black program, *Sanford and Son* (Leckenby & Surlin, 1976). Because the lead character in each series was a working class individual buffeted by the social undercurrents and frustrated by an inability to control his situation, alienated whites and blacks were expected to watch these shows more often. Indeed, heavier viewers of each program tended to score higher on two dimensions of alienation: powerlessness and meaninglessness,

Another predisposing orientation that may affect content selection is moral-religious philosophy, particularly the strongly held views of fundamentalist Christians. In a study comparing members of a local Moral Majority chapter and a cross-section of local citizens, Roberts (1983) measured exposure to television entertainment programs, religious programs, and magazines. Moral Majority adherents were expected to avoid certain shows and periodicals portraying sex or violence and to seek out religious programming, due to their predominantly conservative prolife, protraditional family, promoral and proevangelical values.

There was a small, nonsignificant tendency for the Moral Majority sample to report less viewing of 14 prime time programs criticized by right-wing pressure groups as presenting too much sex or violence (e.g., *Vegas, Charlie's Angels, Dukes of Hazzard, Love Boat, Three's Company,* and *Hill Street Blues*). Apparently, the entertainment qualities of these popular series largely counteracted any motivation to avoid morally objectionable themes. On the other hand, members were much less likely than the general sample to report reading the sexually explicit magazines *Playboy* and *Penthouse.* They were also far more attentive to the set of 22 religious programs measured in the survey. This latter finding is consistent with research showing strong tendencies for persons with conservative Protestant affiliations to attend radio stations featuring gospel music (Johnstone, 1971–1972) and television programming presenting fundamentalist religious philosophy and entertainment (Buddenbaum, 1981). Thus, there is clear evidence for the selective seeking of reinforcing religious-oriented content, but only limited avoidance of value-discrepant entertainment.

A survey of the general public provides evidence of reinforcement-oriented use of pornography. According to Wilson and Abelson (1973), exposure to explicit sexual materials is much greater for sociopolitical activists, persons holding liberal political views, and those who are less religious.

In a survey of a diverse sample of jail inmates, college students, and members of religious organizations, Davis and Braucht (1976) measured the relationship between pornography exposure and both moral character and sexually deviant life styles. There was a mild positive correlation between the frequency of reading and viewing hard-core pornography and exploitative and psychopathic character structures reflecting hedonistic, instrumental conceptions of right and wrong. In an effort to determine whether pornography contributed to defective character development or whether those with low moral character sought out pornography, the authors examined the correlations separately for those initially exposed before versus after age 17. For those first exposed at a younger age, the coefficient was near zero; those initially experiencing pornography at an older age showed a moderately strong coefficient. The researchers concluded that this pattern of findings supports the pornography-seeking hypothesis, because older persons have a more fully developed morality, which is an antecedent to voluntary exposure at the age of maturity. Moreover, the lack of relationship for those starting pornography use in their formative years casts doubt on the causal effects hypothesis, because this subgroup would have had a greater cumulative amount of exposure during a period of vulnerability to media influence. There was also a moderately positive relationship between exposure frequency and various forms of sexual deviance, regardless of age of initial contact. This leaves the directionality issue unresolved, but the authors suggest that pornography use is likely to be a partial consequence of deviance.

Social-Role Attitudes and Selectivity

The attitudes of viewers toward certain categories of role-holders can shape the selection of programs portraying these subgroups. Race roles and occupational roles have attracted research interest, producing correlational data regarding preferences for reinforcing content.

Several studies have assessed the relationship between viewer race and exposure to television programming prominently featuring black characters. Greenberg (1972) found that 60% of the black children watched at least nine series with black stars, compared to just 20% of the whites sampled. A substantially higher frequency of viewing three black-oriented situation comedies was reported by black adolescents than by whites in a survey by Dates (1980). Reviewing five studies of viewership of the highly rated *Roots* docudrama miniseries, which treated the history of slavery in a manner sympathetic to the black perspective, Surlin (1978) concluded that blacks had a much higher rate of exposure than whites. Greenberg and Atkin (1982) cited Nielsen data showing that blacks are two to three times more likely than whites to be in the audience for television series with black casts.

These differential viewing patterns suggest reinforcement-oriented selective exposure based on preference for own-race portrayals, assuming that the stereotyping of blacks in these programs is generally positive. However, there are several other utilitarian and gratification-based interpretations that must be considered. Blacks may watch black programs for purposes of role-modeling guidance regarding appropriate behaviors, talk, and dress, or to obtain conversational material for subsequent discussion of episodes with the large number of fellow blacks who view the programs. Aside from these pragmatic motivations, blacks may exhibit higher viewing simply due to differences in entertainment taste for plots and characterizations in these black shows. Finally, part of the higher program viewership can be accounted for by the general tendency for blacks to watch a greater absolute amount of television rather than to be selective in program choice. Nevertheless, the findings are consistent with utilitarian selective exposure, and this set of defensive and guidance motivations probably explains a substantial proportion of the racial differences in viewing.

Studies of the *Roots* miniseries have specifically examined attitudinal correlates of viewing. In analyses of their white subsample, Hur and Robinson (1978) discovered that level of viewership was related to support for open-housing laws, to feelings that blacks are more intelligent and trustworthy, and to beliefs that black slavery produced severe hardships. The relationships are not strong, however, and may reflect impact of the programming as well as selective exposure.

Ball-Rokeach, Grube, and Rokeach (1981) focused on the follow-up installment of the saga (*Roots: The Next Generation*), which depicted the blacks' post-Civil War struggle for equality. Before the miniseries was aired, the investigators measured whites' valuation of egalitarianism (desirability of equality as an

American value, holding equality as a personal priority, expressing nonprejudicial racial attitudes, and perceiving social support for whites' joining a civil rights organization). There was a modest correlation between level of general egalitarianism and subsequent amount of viewing of the miniseries. The association held up under controls for usual television viewing, demographics, and religious orientation, indicating that de facto selective exposure can be eliminated as an explanation.

Exposure to another landmark television series, *All in the Family,* has been scrutinized by researchers because of the socially relevant content themes. This program sought to satirize bigotry with ostensibly unflattering portrayals of ethnocentric prejudice expressed by authoritarian lead character Archie Bunker. Investigators expected that prejudiced persons would be less likely to view the program due to selective avoidance. But an early study by Vidmar and Rokeach (1974) showed that persons scoring high in ethnocentrism regarding blacks, hippies, and homosexuals actually watched the program more frequently than did less prejudiced persons. Brigham and Giesbrecht (1976) found no relationship between racially prejudiced attitudes and viewing frequency. A survey of Dutch audiences also found no association between ethnocentrism and exposure to the program; both authoritarianism and intolerance for divergent life styles were inversely related to viewing as predicted (Wilhoit & de Bock, 1976).

Although some of these findings appear to contradict defensive selectivity in viewing, each study demonstrates a high degree of selective perception that has significant implications for drawing inferences about selective exposure. Ethnocentric viewers displayed a strong tendency to admire the bigoted character, to approve of his prejudicial actions, and to perceive that his views are valid. Thus, the content was widely misinterpreted by these viewers to be reinforcing of their prejudiced attitudes, such that the program may actually have been selected for purposes of defending predispositions.

Attitudes toward certain occupational groups may lead to the viewing of entertainment portrayals consistent with predispositions. For example, doctors are depicted in a uniformly favorable fashion in television dramas at both the professional and personal levels. Volgy and Schwarz (1980) discovered an exceptionally strong relationship between the amount of medical-series viewing and the degree of positive affect toward doctors (rating them as wise, helpful, intelligent, empathetic, and able); the raw gamma coefficient was $+.70$. This relationship is subject to several interpretations, including a causal sequence from viewing positive portrayals to holding positive stereotypes, or the coincidental seeking of such programming for guidance information or intrinsic interest. Nevertheless, it seems likely that a substantial portion of the variance is explained by supporters of the medical profession seeking reinforcing entertainment content, and possibly by detractors avoiding the flattering portrayals.

Nonsupportive findings were obtained by Dominick (1974), who measured several affective orientations toward police and the frequency of viewing each of

21 crime shows featuring law enforcement themes in a sample of preadolescents. Because content analysis indicated that police on television were competent in solving crimes and predominantly heroic rather than villainous, young people with favorable views of police officers might be expected to view the programs more frequently. However, there was no significant correlation between either attitude toward police or occupational prestige rankings of police/private detectives and crime show viewing. Perceived efficacy of the police was positively related to the viewing index, but this probably reflects content effects rather than selective exposure.

New Evidence of Reinforcement-Oriented Selectivity

Two portions of the pilot study conducted for this chapter focused on selective exposure to television programming based on attitudinal predispositions paralleling several of the substantive domains reviewed earlier. In one part of the questionnaire, respondents were asked directly to report the extent to which they selected or avoided content for reinforcement purposes. A second part of the survey measured the relationship between preferences for hypothetical new TV programs and relevant attitudes expressed by respondents.

Self-report Evidence.   The first test of defensive selectivity involves introspective reports of reinforcement seeking and avoidance of television content portraying police, blacks, physical aggression, alcohol, and sexuality. In each case, respondents were first asked to describe their attitude along a five-step scale (strongly positive, somewhat positive, mixed/neutral, somewhat negative, and strongly negative; in the case of sex, the terms liberal and conservative were substituted for positive and negative). Respondents also rated their level of confidence that they hold the correct attitude (very certain, fairly certain, not certain).

This was followed by a series of three items describing valenced television content and asking about degree of motivation for content selection along a 0 to 10 scale. The first item identified supportive TV portrayals and asked respondents to report the extent to which such content was selected for purposes of reinforcement. For example, the wording of the sexual question for those with a liberal attitude was as follows: "On television, there are many comedy shows, dramas, and soap operas that portray sex in a permissive manner. To what extent do you select these programs because they support your viewpoint?" For those holding a conservative attitude, the question stem stated: "There are some dramas, soap operas, and comedy shows that treat sexual matters conservatively by emphasizing traditional morals or portraying unfavorable consequences of permissive sexuality."

The second item identified discrepant portrayals and asked: "To what extent do you avoid watching these shows because the content is contrary to your values?'' To determine whether respondents sought to counterargue rather than evade certain discrepant content, a follow-up question asked about the extent to which the contrary depictions are viewed "because you want to challenge the themes presented."

The basic analyses simply describe the degree of self-reported exposure for each reason. Averaging the responses of persons with positive and negative attitudes across the five topics, the mean level of watching to support attitudinal dispositions is 4.7 on the 0 to 10 scale. The mean level of reported avoidance of contrary content is 3.3. The relatively lower level of avoidance may be partially due to the desire to challenge the discrepant portrayals; this phenomenon occurs to a limited degree with a mean of 2.8.

The overall level of defensive selective exposure (combining selection and avoidance) differs little from topic to topic, and those holding positive attitudes are generally no more selective than those with negative perspectives. However, there are some distinctive interactions between direction of attitude and topic. There is high selectivity for sexual conservatives (mean = 10.3, summing selection and avoidance ratings) but low selectivity for sexual liberals (mean = 6.0). Similarly, those with negative views of alcohol are high in selectivity (mean = 10.0), whereas those who regard alcohol positively show lower selectivity (mean = 6.0). The subgroup holding positive dispositions toward black people displays high level of selectivity (mean = 9.9); the small antipolice subgroup is low in selectivity (mean = 3.6).

Across the topics, there are no consistent differences in selectivity levels among respondents with strong versus mild attitudes. This may be due to contrasting tendencies for those with strongly held attitudes: They should be more selective because of greater ego-involvement and a more distinctive position, but they should be less selective because of higher self-assurance that the position is correct.

The prediction for level of certainty is clear-cut: Those with greater confidence that they are right have less need for reinforcement and should display lower selectivity than persons who are uncertain. However, the respondents who state they are "very certain" tend to report somewhat higher levels of program selection based on content supportiveness; averaging across the five topics, the difference is about 1 point on the scale, compared to those in the "fairly certain" and "not certain" categories. There is no difference in avoidance of contrary material. The less certain respondents are actually slightly more likely to report challenging discrepant material, scoring about ½ point higher than the very certain subgroup on the average. These findings are far from definitive because of the low numbers of respondents in the not certain categories on each attitude.

Correlational Evidence.   A second test of the defensive selectivity involves the relationship between attitude and preference for hypothetical new programs. For each of the five attitudinal domains, a 50-word description of the basic content concept was provided. For example, the potential television series *Shore*

Patrol was described as depicting a "special police unit working along the east coast of Florida to combat drug smuggling. Despite tempting bribes, these men are devoted to arresting smugglers and Mafia chieftains. Every week, they successfully solve a case using high technology techniques. The police are competent, honest, and efficient in carrying out their dangerous duties." In each case, the sketch describes a clearly valenced portrayal supportive of the positive attitudinal position (pro-alcohol, pro-violence, pro-police, pro-sexuality, and pro-black). Respondents were asked to rate their "degree of interest in watching along a scale ranging from +5 (definitely would watch) to 0 (might watch or might not) to −5 (definitely would avoid watching)." This directional measurement was used to help determine absolute levels of seeking or avoidance, along with relative preference across attitudinal subgroups.

In each case, those holding a positive attitude give a higher rating than the neutral or negative subgroups, and the difference is significant at the .05 level. For example, pro-police respondents give a mean interest rating of +1.3 for the *Shore Patrol* concept; the mean score is +0.01 for those with neutral or mixed feelings about police, and −1.4 for the antipolice subgroup. Averaging across the five attitudes, the positives give a rating of +0.6, the neutrals a rating of −0.5, and the negatives a rating of −1.9. (It should be noted that there were too few persons in the neutral sex-attitude category and the negative racial-attitude category for analysis.)

Thus, there is evidence that exposure preferences are shaped by attitudinal predispositions in a manner consistent with the reinforcement proposition. There are also indications that persons are affirmatively avoiding discrepant content as well as simply preferring it less than supportive content, because most scores are on the negative side. However, this may partly be due to the unattractive quality of the proposed programming, because the hypothetical story lines generated little enthusiasm among those neutral or favorable toward the thematic content.

The methodological caveats mentioned in the earlier description of this pilot study apply to these data, particularly the limitations of the atypical sample and the unwillingness of respondents to accurately report psychologically or socially unacceptable message-selection decisions.

SUMMARY

This chapter presents evidence showing that informational needs of the audience play a significant role in selective exposure to entertainment media. Although intrinsic gratification seeking is the primary determinant of exposure decisions, the research demonstrates that many choices are based on the instrumental utility of the content for purposes of guidance and reinforcement.

According to self-reported motivations for media use, entertainment messages are selected for various forms of learning, such as advice, interpretation, surveillance, behavioral modeling, and acquiring conversational material. These guidance motives are generally moderate in importance, ranking below enjoy-ment-oriented reasons. Among the utilities studied, message selection in order to learn subject matter for interpersonal communication is most central.

Individuals also choose entertainment content as a means of reinforcing or defending predispositions. Correlational data indicate that aggressive persons seek out violent television programming and that sociopolitical attitudes shape preferences for radio music and televised sports; moral-religious values are relat-ed to exposure patterns to content such as sexual depictions. The degree of association is moderately strong in most cases. To a limited extent, racial and occupational attitudes appear to influence choices of television programs portray-ing those social roles. Self-report data show that television viewers exhibit a moderate tendency to select depictions of social roles and behaviors for purposes of supporting predispositions, but selective avoidance of discrepant content is less widespread.

Although the evidence currently available is far from definitive and the degree of importance of utilitarian determinants is far from powerful, it can be tenta-tively concluded that guidance- and reinforcement-oriented selective exposure to entertainment media occurs to a modest extent. Future research is needed to assess the strength of various types of instrumental motivations and to specify the conditions under which anticipated utilities influence message choices in the entertainment domain.

REFERENCES

Atkin,C. (1973). Instrumental utilities and information seeking. In P. Clarke (Ed.), *New models for mass communication research* (pp. 205–242). Beverly Hills, CA: Sage.

Atkin, C., Greenberg, B., Korzenny, F., & McDermott, S. (1979). Selective exposure to televised violence. *Journal of Broadcasting, 23,* 5–14.

Ball-Rokeach, S., Grube, J., & Rokeach, M. (1981). "Roots: The Next Generation"—Who watched with what effect? *Public Opinion Quarterly, 45,* 58–68.

Balon, R. (1978), TV viewing preferences as correlates of adult dysfunctional behavior. *Journalism Quarterly, 55,* 288–294.

Bernstein, J. (1975). Conversations in public places. *Journal of Communication, 25,* 85–95.

Bower, R. (1973). *Television and the public.* New York: Holt, Rinehart & Winston.

Brigham, J., & Giesbrecht, L. (1976). "All in the Family": Racial attitudes. *Journal of Commu-nication, 26,* 69–74.

Buddenbaum, J. (1981). Characteristics and media-related needs of the audience for religious TV. *Journalism Quarterly, 58,* 266–272.

Chaffee, S. (1972). Television and adolescent aggressiveness. In G. Comstock & E. Rubinstein (Eds.), *Television and social behavior: Television and adolescent aggressiveness* (pp. 1–34). Washington, DC: U.S. Government Printing Office.

Compesi, R. (1980). Gratifications of daytime TV serial viewers. *Journalism Quarterly, 57,* 155–158.

Comstock, G. (1982). Violence in television content: An overview. In D. Pearl, L. Bouthilet, & J. Lazar (Eds.), *Television and behavior: Ten years of scientific progress and implications for the eighties* (pp. 108–125). Rockville, MD: Department of Health and Human Services.

Dates, J. (1980). Race, racial attitudes, and adolescent perceptions of black television characters. *Journal of Broadcasting, 24,* 549–560.

Davis, K., & Braucht, G. (1976). Exposure to pornography, character, and sexual deviance: A retrospective survey. *Journal of Social Issues, 29,* 183–196.

Dominick, J. (1974). Children's viewing of crime shows and attitudes on law enforcement. *Journalism Quarterly, 51,* 5–12.

Eron, L., & Huesmann, L. (1980). Adolescent aggression and television. *Annals of the New York Academy of Sciences, 347,* 319–331.

Festinger, L. (1957). *A theory of cognitive dissonance.* Evanston, IL: Row, Peterson.

Fox, W., & Williams, J. (1974). Political orientation and music preferences among college students. *Public Opinion Quarterly, 38,* 352–371.

Freedman, J., & Sears, D. (1965). Selective exposure. In L. Berkowitz (Ed.), *Advances in experimental social psychology* (pp. 57–97). New York: Academic Press.

Friedman, H., & Johnson, R. (1972). Mass media use and aggression: A pilot study. In G. Comstock & E. Rubinstein (Eds.), *Television and social behavior: Television and adolescent aggressiveness* (pp. 336–360). Washington, DC: U.S. Government Printing Office.

Gantz, W. (1981). An exploration of viewing motives and behaviors associated with televised sports. *Journal of Broadcasting, 25,* 263–275.

Gerbner, G., Gross, L., Jackson-Beeck, M., Jeffries-Fox, S., & Signorielli, N. (1978). Cultural indicators: Violence profile no. 9. *Journal of Communication, 28,* 176–207.

Greenberg, B. (1972). Children's reactions to TV blacks. *Journalism Quarterly, 49,* 5–14.

Greenberg, B. (1974). Gratifications of television viewing and their correlates for British children. In J. Blumler & E. Katz (Eds.), *The uses of mass communication* (pp. 71–92). Beverly Hills, CA: Sage.

Greenberg, B., & Atkin, C. (1982). Learning about minorities from television: A research agenda. In G. Berry & C. Mitchell-Kernan (Eds.), *Television and the socialization of the minority child* (pp. 215–243). New York: Academic Press.

Greenberg, B., & Heeter, C. (1983). Mass media orientations among Hispanic youth. *Hispanic Journal of Behavioral Sciences, 5,* 305–323.

Greenberg, B., Neuendorf, K., Buerkel-Rothfuss, N., & Henderson, L. (1982). The soaps: What's on and who cares? *Journal of Broadcasting, 26,* 519–536.

Herzog, H. (1944). What do we really know about daytime serial listeners? In P. Lazarsfeld & F. Stanton (Eds.), *Radio research 1942–1943* (pp. 3–33). New York: Duell, Sloan, & Pearce.

Huesmann, L. (1982). Television violence and aggressive behavior. In D. Pearl, L. Bouthilet, & J. Lazar (Eds.), *Television and behavior: Ten years of scientific progress and implications for the eighties* (pp. 126–137). Rockville, MD: Department of Health and Human Services.

Hur, K., & Robinson, J. (1978). The social impact of "Roots." *Journalism Quarterly, 55,* 19–24.

Johnstone, J. (1971-1972). Who listens to religious radio broadcasts anymore? *Journal of Broadcasting, 16,* 91–102.

Katz, E. (1968). On re-opening the question of selectivity in exposure to mass communications. In R. Abelson, E. Aronson, W. McGuire, T. Newcomb, M. Rosenberg, & P. Tannenbaum (Eds.), *Theories of cognitive consistency* (pp. 788–796). Chicago: Rand McNally.

Katz, E., Blumler, J., & Gurevitch, M. (1973-1974). Uses and gratifications research. *Public Opinion Quarterly, 37,* 509–523.

Klapper, J. (1960). *The effects of mass communication.* New York: Free Press.

Leckenby, J., & Surlin, S. (1976). Incidental social learning and viewer race. *Journal of Broadcasting, 20,* 481–494.

Lefkowitz, M., Eron, L., Walder, L., & Huesmann, L. (1972). Television violence and child aggression: A follow-up study. In G. Comstock & E. Rubinstein (Eds.), *Television and social behavior: Television and adolescent aggressiveness* (pp. 35–135). Washington, DC: U.S. Government Printing Office.

Lichtenstein, A., & Rosenfeld, L. (1983). Uses and misuses of gratifications research: An explication of media functions. *Communication Research, 10,* 97–109.

Lometti, G., Reeves, B., & Bybee, C. (1977). Investigating the assumptions of uses and gratifications research. *Communication Research, 4,* 321–338.

LoSciuto, L. (1972). A national inventory of television viewing behavior. In E. Rubinstein, G. Comstock, & J. Murray (Eds.), *Television and social behavior: Television in day-to-day life: Patterns of use* (pp. 33–86). Washington, DC: U.S. Government Printing Office.

Lull, J. (1980). The social uses of television. *Human Communication Research, 6,* 197–209.

Lyle, J., & Hoffman, H. (1972). Children's use of television and other media. In E. Rubinstein, G. Comstock, & J. Murray (Eds.), *Television and social behavior: Television in day to day life: Patterns of use* (pp. 129–256). Washington, DC: U.S. Government Printing Office.

Mashkin, K., & Volgy, T. (1975). Socio-political attitudes and musical preferences. *Social Science Quarterly, 21,* 450–459.

McGuire, W. (1974). Psychological motives and communication gratification. In J. Blumler & E. Katz (Eds.), *The uses of mass communication* (pp. 167–196). Beverly Hills, CA: Sage.

McIntyre, J., & Teevan, J. (1972). Television violence and deviant behavior. In G. Comstock & E. Rubinstein (Eds.), *Television and social behavior: Television and adolescent aggressiveness* (pp. 383–435). Washington, DC: U.S. Government Printing Office.

McLeod, J., Atkin, C., & Chaffee, S. (1972). Adolescents, parents, and television use. In G. Comstock & E. Rubinstein (Eds.), *Television and social behavior: Television and adolescent aggressiveness* (pp. 173–313). Washington, DC: U.S. Government Printing Office.

McLeod, J., & Becker, L. (1974). Testing the validity of gratification measures through political effects analysis. In J. Blumler & E. Katz (Eds.), *The uses of mass communication* (pp. 137–166). Beverly Hills, CA: Sage.

Meyerson, R. (1961). A critical examination of commercial entertainment. In R. Kleemeier (Ed.), *Aging and leisure* (pp. 275–292). New York: Oxford University Press.

Mills, J. (1968). Interest in supporting and discrepant information. In R. Abelson, E. Aronson, W. McGuire, T. Newcomb, M. Rosenberg, & P. Tannenbaum (Eds.), *Theories of cognitive consistency* (pp. 771–776). Chicago: Rand McNally.

Paletz, D. (1972). Selective exposure: The potential boomerang effect. *Journal of Communication, 22,* 48–53.

Palmgreen, P., & Rayburn, J. (1982). Gratifications sought and media exposure: An expectancy value model. *Communication Research, 9,* 561–580.

Prisuta, R. (1979). Televised sports and political values. *Journal of Communication, 29,* 94–102.

Roberts, C. (1983). Attitudes and media use of the moral majority. *Journal of Broadcasting, 27,* 403–410.

Robinson, J., & Bachman, J. (1972). Television viewing habits and aggression. In G. Comstock & E. Rubinstein (Eds.), *Television and social behavior: Television and adolescent aggressiveness* (pp. 372–382). Washington, DC: U.S. Government Printing Office.

Robinson, J., Pilskaln, R., & Hirsch, P. (1976). Protest rock and drugs. *Journal of Communication, 26,* 125–136.

Rubin, A. (1977). Television usage, attitudes, and viewing behaviors of children and adolescents. *Journal of Broadcasting, 21,* 355–369.

Rubin, A. (1979). Television use by children and adolescents. *Human Communication Research, 5,* 109–120.

Rubin, A. (1981). An examination of television viewing motivations. *Communication Research, 8,* 141–165.

Rubin, A. (1983). Television uses and gratifications: The interactions of viewing patterns and motivations. *Journal of Broadcasting, 27,* 37–51.

Rubin, A., & Rubin, R. (1982). Contextual age and television use. *Human Communication Research, 8,* 228–244.

Schramm, W., Lyle, J., & Parker, E. (1961). *Television in the lives of our children.* Stanford, CA: Stanford University Press.

Smith, D. (1971-1972). Some uses of mass media by 14 year olds. *Journal of Broadcasting, 16,* 37–50.

Sprafkin, J., & Rubinstein, E. (1979). Children's television viewing habits and prosocial behavior: A field correlational study. *Journal of Broadcasting, 23,* 265–276.

Surlin, S. (1978). "Roots" research: A summary of findings. *Journal of Broadcasting, 22,* 309–320.

Surlin, S., & Dominick, J. (1970-1971). Television's function as a "third parent" for black and white teenagers. *Journal of Broadcasting, 15,* 55–64.

Vidmar, N., & Rokeach, M. (1974). Archie Bunker's bigotry: A study in selective perception and exposure. *Journal of Communication, 24,* 26–47.

Volgy, T., & Schwarz, J. (1980). TV entertainment programming and sociopolitical attitudes. *Journalism Quarterly, 57,* 150–155.

Wenner, L. (1976). Functional analysis of TV viewing for older adults. *Journal of Broadcasting, 20,* 77–88.

Wilhoit, G., & de Bock, H. (1976). "All in the Family" in Holland. *Journal of Communication, 26,* 75–84.

Wilson, W., & Abelson, H. (1973). Experience with and attitudes toward explicit sexual materials. *Journal of Social Issues, 29,* 19–39.

Wright, W. (1975). Mass media as sources of medical information. *Journal of Communication, 25,* 171–173.

5 Determinants of Television Viewing Preferences

Barrie Gunter
Independent Broadcasting Authority

This chapter examines survey and experimental evidence for selective exposure to and preferences for television programming. This evidence is both behavioral and attitudinal, and it relates viewing behaviors and program preferences to a variety of psychological characteristics of viewers including personality factors, values, and beliefs. The chapter is divided into three main sections. The first section examines behavioral evidence for selectivity of viewing based on television diaries and meter measures of what people watch. This research has been conducted with large representative national and regional samples in the United Kingdom, and it ties in with recent American work on selective exposure to television, which has also used behavioral measures of viewing (Gensch & Raganathan, 1980; Headen, Klompmaker, & Rust, 1979; Wakshlag, Agostino, Terry, Driscoll, & Ramsey, 1983). The second section reports survey evidence from the United Kingdom in which respondents' beliefs and personality characteristics have been related to diary measures of television viewing. This work has attempted to uncover links between the psychological makeup of individuals and what they choose to watch on television. The third section reports findings collected from smaller groups of people in experimental settings in which they have provided evaluative judgments about different kinds of program materials shown to them during the study. Measures of personality, values, and beliefs were related to program evaluations and preferences to indicate relationships between program appreciation or nonappreciation and psychological traits of individuals.

EVIDENCE FOR SELECTIVE TELEVISION VIEWING

Although overshadowed for a long time by concern over the medium's effects on public attitudes, values, and behavior, the question of how people use television has been of interest to broadcasters and advertisers for many years. With the recent unprecedented expansion of television channels and the fragmentation of the mass audience consequent upon the rapid growth in quantity and variety of available programming, more emphasis has been placed on the need to understand the nature and antecedents of television viewing patterns and program preferences. A fundamental question concerning viewing patterns is whether people watch television selectively, and if so, which criteria are the major determinants of the way they watch.

Some researchers, concerned with identifying patterns of television viewing behavior, have reported strong support for the belief that television programs form clusters or patterns of viewership (Banks, 1967; Kirsch & Banks, 1967; Swanson, 1967; Wells, 1969). Typically, program categories have been generated empirically via factor analyses of viewers' evaluative ratings of programs. However, some writers have argued that these typologies may be neither universal (but unique to the sample from which program judgments were obtained) nor stable over time with the same population (Gandy, 1982). As viewers' interests and the content of network schedules change over time, so one could expect the factor structures of tastes and program types to vary as well.

Pioneering explorations of viewing behavior patterns by Goodhardt and Ehrenberg have indicated that program type is largely unrelated to the way audiences flow over television schedules (Goodhardt, Ehrenberg, & Collins, 1975). Based on observation of audience overlaps for each of thousands of pairs of programs, Goodhardt et al. (1975) proposed a "duplication of viewing law." According to this law, the major influence on the level of audience overlap between two programs is usually the rating level or audience size for each program. The law states: "The proportion of the audience of any TV programme who watch another programme on another day of the same week is directly proportional to the rating of the latter programme (i.e., equal to it times a certain constant)" (p. 11).

Although a program's type is undoubtedly related to the size of the audience it attracts, it does not have much influence on the degree to which its viewers watch any other program. Goodhardt, Ehrenberg, Collins (1975) claim that audience overlap for two or more programs can be effectively predicted by the duplication of viewing law and that such predictions are not dependent on information about the particular program or type of program an audience is watching.

More important determinants of viewing patterns than program type are "inheritance" and "channel loyalty." Consecutive or near consecutive programs on the same evening share their audience to an above average extent, but this audience inheritance does not extend to programs further apart. Furthermore, overlap scores for pairs of programs on the same channel tend to be somewhat larger than for those on different channels. However, there are no special duplication patterns for programs of any particular type, such as action-adventure, soap opera, comedy, sports, or news. According to the audience-flow analyses of Goodhardt and Ehrenberg, different programs of the same type do not appeal especially to the same viewers. One serious problem that this model of viewing behavior poses for broadcasters is that weekly episodes of a television series do not appear to attract a substantial core of loyal viewers who follow the series through.

The Goodhardt–Ehrenberg thesis has not gone unchallenged, however, and other researchers using both similar and alternative measures of viewing behavior have reported findings indicative of selective viewing by programs or program types. Headen et al. (1979), for example, found important differences in audience flow between the United States and the United Kingdom, including an apparent preference in the U.S. for specific program types. United States audiences showed considerable variation in duplication for programs of the same type across different program categories. Average duplication levels varied from 34% for comedy shows to 61% for serial dramas. Even more recently, the Goodhardt–Ehrenberg group has begun to modify its original position to interpret differential levels of duplication across different programs as weak evidence for program loyalty, following another study of viewing patterns among United States audiences. Although only about half the people viewing a program one day were found to view it again on another day, this was largely because they were not viewing television at all on the second occasion, rather than because they were watching a different program. Once a decision to watch had been reached, viewers were highly likely to view the same program they watched last time (Barwise, Ehrenberg, & Goodhardt, 1982).

Published evidence of selective TV viewing by program or program type has emerged mostly from the United States. But research has also emerged recently that indicates a certain degree of viewing loyalty to programs even among audiences in the United Kingdom. Wober (1981) assessed the uptake by United Kingdom viewers of different a priori program types relative to their availability across 1 year. He found that certain categories of programs, such as information and general interest programs (e.g., documentaries, magazine and feature shows), were underviewed compared with their availability, whereas films, action-adventure series, and situation comedies were overviewed. More recent analyses of viewing patterns among United Kingdom audiences have produced further evidence of loyalty to programs and program types.

Gunter (1984a) found evidence of program-type loyalty as well as of channel loyalty following an analysis of network television news viewing data among two regional samples in London and the Midlands regions of England. About 1,000 viewing diaries were distributed, by mail or by interviewer, in each region during 2 separate weeks in May 1983, of which over 700 were returned from the

London sample and over 600 returned from the Midlands. These diaries listed all programs broadcast by the four United Kingdom television networks during each week, and respondents indicated how much each program seen was enjoyed. Thus, completed diaries could be used to produce appreciation scores for programs and to indicate how many programs had been seen and of which types. The current analyses focused specifically on viewing patterns for the six main weekday network news broadcasts on BBC1 (at 12:30 p.m., 5:40 p.m., and 9:00 p.m.) and on ITV (at 1:00 p.m., 5:45 p.m., and 10:00 p.m.).

Table 5.1 shows correlations between viewing of one network newscast with viewing of another for each regional survey. Viewing patterns were largely replicated across regions, and the findings provided evidence for channel and program-type loyalty. Channel loyalty was demonstrated by significant correlations between watching midday and early evening news bulletins, and between early evening and late evening news bulletins on the same channel. There was no evidence of switching between channels across these pairs of bulletins, however. Channel loyalty was also indicated by the negative relationship between watching the early evening news on BBC1 or ITV. The latter news bulletins are transmitted at approximately the same time. This means that viewers can watch either one or the other on any evening, although they can switch around between these programs across evenings. However, there was no indication that any channel switching occurred over different evenings in either week. The tendency to watch two news bulletins on the same channel became weaker as the time

TABLE 5.1
Correlations between Viewing of Main Network News Broadcasts
on BBC1 and ITV

		BBC1 *12:30p.m.*	*ITV* *1:00p.m.*	*BBC1* *5:40p.m.*	*ITV* *5:45p.m.*	*BBC1* *9:00p.m.*	*ITV* *10:00p.m.*
BBC1	London	—	29*	23*	ns	10**	ns
12:30p.m.	Midlands	—	25*	27*	ns	15*	ns
ITV	London		—	ns	31*	ns	16*
1:00p.m.	Midlands		—	ns	31*	ns	ns
BBC1	London			—	−.14*	20*	ns
5:40p.m.	Midlands			—	−.10**	21*	ns
ITV	London				—	ns	26*
5:45p.m.	Midlands				—	ns	27*
BBC1	London					—	16*
9:00p.m.	Midlands					—	19*
ITV	London						—
10:00p.m.	Midlands						—

*$p < 0.001$.
**$p < 0.01$.

interval between them in the schedule increased. Thus, though there were significant correlations between the viewing of midday and late evening news bulletins on the same channel, these relationships were weaker than those between midday and early evening news broadcasts or between bulletins in early and late evening.

Of more importance in the context of this discussion is the fact that, in addition to channel loyalty, reliable evidence emerged of channel switching to watch the news. This pattern of viewing was indicated by significant correlations between the viewing of midday news bulletins on BBC1 and ITV, and between the viewing of both channels' late news broadcasts across both survey weeks. Thus, at certain times of the day, there seem to be deliberate tendencies for the audience to flow straight from one news broadcast to another, even though this requires changing the channel.

Another study by the author has indicated that audiences may also exhibit loyalty to major drama series and return to one episode after another more often than they would have normally watched a particular television channel at the same times prior to the series. Wober and Gunter (1984) conducted a special analysis of audience sizes and audience flows for *The Winds of War,* produced by the United States television network ABC and promoted as the most expensive TV series ever made. The series was televised by the ITV network in the United Kingdom as eight episodes transmitted over 4 weeks at 7:45 p.m. on Sundays and at 8:00 p.m. on Mondays in the autumn of 1983. Audience research on the series was designed to examine how many people watched it, and how many episodes on average viewers saw. Audience sizes and viewing frequencies analyses were computed on data obtained by the agency Audits of Great Britain (AGB), which carries out audience size measurement work for the Broadcasters Audience Research Board (BARB), a company jointly owned by the British Broadcasting Corporation and the Independent Television Companies Association. Data are obtained from a panel of over 3,000 homes nationwide, representative of the viewing public in the United Kingdom. Television sets in each of these households have meters attached, which record when the set is switched on and to which channel it is tuned. A viewing diary is also kept to record the times, in clock quarter-hours, when each member of the household watched any television.

In the analysis of audience sizes, data were obtained for the first quarter-hour segment of *The Winds of War,* for equivalent periods on BBC1, and for similar times on both ITV and BBC1 over the four pairs of Sunday and Monday evenings prior to the first episode of the series. The frequency-of-viewing analyses were performed on the four sets of 8 o'clock quarter-hour spots to indicate in each set the percentages of viewers who saw one, two, three, continuing up to eight spots out of eight.

Based on the continuous viewing records of 6,084 individuals across the United Kingdom, analysis indicated that audiences for *The Winds of War* were much higher than for BBC1 programming shown opposite to the series, and also were much higher than audiences for ITV at the same times over a 4-week period prior to the series. On the average, 23% of the viewers tuned into episodes of *The Winds of War*, compared with an average of 15% who watched ITV at the same times over a similar period before the series began. Audiences for BBC1 at these times exhibited no change, averaging 12% both before and during *The Winds of War*.

However, although the series attracted larger audiences than usual, this alone is not evidence of loyalty. To what extent did viewers of one episode of *The Winds of War* return to watch subsequent episodes? Did viewers return to ITV during the series more often than they normally did across several Sunday and Monday evenings prior to the series? Table 5.2 sheds light on these important questions concerning program loyalty. The table shows that out of eight episodes across four Sunday and Monday evenings, greater percentages of viewers watched any number of spots on ITV (i.e., *The Winds of War*) than on BBC1. However, a comparison of viewing frequencies for ITV and BBC1 over the 4 weeks before *The Winds of War* showed that this difference occurred anyway. Of more significance was the shift in viewing frequency for ITV during the network's transmission of the miniseries.

Although there was no substantial change in the percentage of viewers who saw one episode out of eight, during *The Winds of War* markedly higher percentages of viewers saw two, three, four, five, and six episodes. Although only 20% of all viewers saw as many as half the episodes of the series, this was twice as many as had previously shown this degree of loyalty to ITV on Sunday and Monday evenings at around 8:00 p.m. Thus, not only did *The Winds of War*

TABLE 5.2
Frequency of Viewing ITV and BBC1 at 7:45p.m. on Sundays
and 8:00p.m. on Mondays over 4 Weeks during
and 4 Weeks prior to *The Winds of War*

Number of Episodes Seen	Over 4 Weeks Prior to The Winds of War		Over 4 Weeks during The Winds of War	
	ITV (%)	*BBC1 (%)*	*ITV (%)[a]*	*BBC1 (%)*
1	60	54	58	46
2	37	26	43	25
3	21	11	31	13
4	10	4	22	6
5	5	1	15	2
6	2	0	10	1
7	1	0	5	0
8	0	0	2	0

Note. Data from BARB/AGB. Base = 6,084.
[a]*Winds of War* on this channel.

boost audiences for the ITV network, but also among those who were watching the channel, substantially larger percentages than usual were returning to it week after week.

To sum up, evidence from diary records of viewing behaviors among regional and national samples in the United Kingdom has indicated that viewers may exhibit selective viewing of a program type such as news and enhanced loyalties to television channels in the presence of certain major drama series. In the next section, research evidence is examined which shows that degrees of preferential viewing for certain programs or program types may vary according to the demographic and psychological characteristics of viewers.

VIEWER CHARACTERISTICS
AND SELECTIVE VIEWING

Not all viewers like the same programs or watch television to the same extent. With the increased availability of TV channels, many of which now specialize in particular categories of programming, the audience has become fragmented. Television channels that provide all-news, all-weather, all-music, or all-film services appeal differently to different viewers, and some sections of the general audience may flow more than other sections toward one or another of these specialist channels. Similarly, on the networks, some viewers may be inclined to watch more action-adventure series, whereas others may prefer news or documentary output. To what extent can regular viewers of one category of programming be distinguished by their personal (demographic or psychological) characteristics? Does a certain type of person tend to be especially likely to watch soap operas, or action-drama series, or news broadcasts? Several recent studies done by the author have examined relationships between patterns of TV viewing behavior for particular program types and television series, and the demographic and psychological characteristics of viewers.

Demographic Differences
in Television Viewing Patterns

In the study of United Kingdom audiences for *The Winds of War* discussed earlier, Wober and Gunter (1984) examined audience sizes and audience flow for the series not simply for the viewing population in general, but also for particular demographic segments of it. Table 5.3 shows the audience sizes for the eight episodes of *The Winds of War,* where each score represents the percentage of all viewers within a particular demographic group who watched the first quarter-hour of each episode. It can be seen that on the average, the series was watched by more women than men, by more middle-aged and older people than young

TABLE 5.3
Audience Sizes for *The Winds of War*
among Different Demographic Groups

Day	Date	Sex (%)		Age (%)			Class (%)	
		Men	*Women*	*16–34*	*35–54*	*55+*	*ABC1*	*C2DE*
Sun.	Sept. 11	23	26	23	26	25	20	25
Mon.	Sept. 12	25	30	25	28	30	22	28
Sun.	Sept. 18	21	25	22	25	24	18	24
Mon.	Sept. 19	24	29	23	26	31	19	27
Sun.	Sept. 25	20	23	19	23	23	18	22
Mon.	Sept. 26	22	28	23	25	29	20	26
Sun.	Oct. 2	22	26	21	26	25	18	25
Mon.	Oct. 3	24	30	23	27	31	23	26
Mean Audience		23%	27%	22%	26%	27%	20%	25%
Base		2,250	2,604	1,430	1,633	1,790	2,174	3,909

Note. Data from BARB/AGB.

adults, and by more working-class people (C2DEs) than middle-class people (ABC1s).

The demographic pattern observed for audience sizes for *The Winds of War* was reflected in viewing frequencies for the series. Table 5.4 shows the percentages of viewers in each demographic category who saw one, two, or three, up to all eight episodes. This table indicates that markedly larger percentages of women than men, of older adults than younger adults, and of working-class than middle-class people saw between two and six out of eight episodes. Although an average of only about one-quarter of the United Kingdom viewers were likely to have seen at least half the episodes, variations in viewing frequencies across demographic groups were indicative of differential loyalty to the series among different segments of the audience.

Further evidence of varying loyalties to a television series across demographic groups emerged from a special study on United Kingdom audiences for another imported American program—*The A-Team* (Gunter, 1984b). The first series was televised in the United Kingdom by the ITV network between mid-July and mid-November, 1983. Following the first feature-length episode to open the series, the next seven hour-long episodes were scheduled at 9:00 p.m. on Friday evenings. Beginning with the next episode, however, the series was brought forward to 7:30 p.m., as the network wished to take advantage of the program's strong appeal to younger members of the audience.

The author carried out special analyses of viewing frequencies for the series when it was televised at 9:00 p.m. and then again among its 7:30 p.m. audiences. These analyses were computed on behavioral viewing data obtained from the BARB/AGB national panel in the United Kingdom. Viewing frequencies were examined for different sex, age, and social class groups among adults and among children.

Table 5.5 presents the viewing frequencies for different demographic groups within the United Kingdom television audience over the first six 9:00 p.m. and the first six 7:30 p.m. episodes of *The A-Team*. For control purposes, viewing frequencies were also computed for six 9:00 p.m. and six 7:30 p.m. Friday slots on ITV before the series began to run at these times. The data indicate that both the series and the time at which it was broadcast made a difference to viewing frequencies for the ITV channel. Among adults at 9:00 p.m., there was little change in viewing frequencies between the 6-week pre-*A-Team* period and over the first 6 weeks of the series. But as the table shows, when *The A-Team* was switched to 7:30 p.m., a substantial increase occurred in the percentages of viewers who watched ITV on one or three Fridays out of six at this time. Although viewing frequencies increased across all demographic groups, women, young people, and middle-class people established the greatest increases in their regularity of viewing on Friday evenings after *The A-Team* had been moved forward in the schedule.

Table 5.5 also presents the viewing frequencies for *The A-Team* among children (aged up to 15 years) in the United Kingdom. When the series was broadcast at 9:00 p.m., it made only a small difference to viewing frequencies among children for ITV on Friday evenings. It is generally true that fewer children watch after 9:00 p.m. than earlier in the evening, so any increase at all in the regularity of viewing, as did occur to some extent here, was a sign of the strong appeal the series had for young viewers.

Following the rescheduling of *The A-Team*, there was a substantial increase in viewing frequencies for ITV on Friday evenings at 7:30 p.m. compared with a similar period immediately prior to the series being shown at this earlier time.

TABLE 5.4
Viewing Frequencies for *The Winds of War*
among Different Demographic Groups

Number of	Sex (%)		Age (%)			Class (%)	
Episodes Seen	Men	Women	16–34	35–54	55+	ABC1	C2DE
1	58	63	56	64	61	52	62
2	42	49	41	47	48	37	46
3	30	37	30	34	36	27	34
4	22	29	22	24	28	18	24
5	15	19	14	17	20	12	17
6	9	13	9	11	13	7	11
7	5	8	5	6	8	4	6
8	2	3	2	2	3	1	1

Note. Data from BARB/AGB. Base sizes are as for Table 5.3.

TABLE 5.5

Viewing Frequencies for *The A-Team* among Different Demographic Sections of the Television Audience in the United Kingdom

Number of Episodes Seen	All Adults	Sex (%) Men	Sex (%) Women	Age (%) 16–34	Age (%) 35–54	Age (%) 55+	Class (%) ABC1	Class (%) C2DE	All Children (%)	Sex (%) Boys	Sex (%) Girls	Age (%) 4–9	Age (%) 10–15	Class (%) ABC1	Class (%) C2DE
9:00 p.m. pre-A-Team															
1	46	42	49	41	46	49	41	48	35	38	33	29	43	34	36
3	14	11	16	21	14	15	9	16	7	8	6	6	8	4	8
6	1	1	1	0	1	1	0	1	0	0	0	1	0	0	1
A-Team															
1	44	42	47	46	48	41	40	46	39	41	38	40	39	37	41
3	15	14	17	15	14	17	11	17	12	11	13	13	12	13	12
6	1	1	1	1	0	2	1	1	1	0	1	1	1	0	1
7:30 p.m. pre-A-Team															
1	46	42	48	40	42	53	34	51	42	44	41	46	38	40	44
3	17	14	19	11	14	24	9	21	11	17	7	10	12	9	11
6	2	2	2	1	1	4	1	3	0	0	1	1	0	1	0
A-Team															
1	54	51	56	54	53	55	46	58	53	61	47	58	49	50	55
3	25	23	26	21	24	28	19	28	25	30	21	30	20	25	25
6	3	2	3	2	2	4	2	3	3	4	3	4	3	4	3

The A-Team was particularly popular among boys, and the percentages who watched ITV at 7:30 p.m. on Fridays for 3 weeks out of 6 doubled compared with before the series. Among 4–9-year-olds, the same percentages more than doubled to indicate the series' especially strong appeal to the youngest viewers.

Psychological Characteristics and Television Viewing Patterns

The Independent Broadcasting Authority's Audience Research Department runs a weekly survey designed to measure audience appreciation of programs. Each week a diary is placed with or mailed to representative samples of over 1,000 respondents in one of twelve ITV regions around the United Kingdom. Diaries list all the programs broadcast by the four television channels during one week and provide an indication not only of appreciation levels, but also how many and which kinds of programs have been seen. This facility is often used to carry out special public opinion surveys in which questionnaires are sent out with the diaries. At the analysis stage, questionnaire data can be treated as separate entities, or they may be related to the viewing information contained in completed diaries. Several studies of this kind have been employed to investigate relationships between television viewing patterns and measures of respondents' attitudes, beliefs, and personality characteristics.

In a series of papers published during the 1970s, Gerbner and his associates reported that heavy viewers of television in the United States tended to endorse different beliefs about the world in which they lived than did lighter viewers (Gerbner & Gross, 1976; Gerbner, Gross, Jackson-Beeck, Jeffries-Fox, & Signorielli, 1978: Gerbner, Gross, Signorielli, Morgan, & Jackson-Beeck, 1979). In particular, it was reported that heavy viewers who watched for more than 4 hours every day tended to indicate a greater fear of being victims of crime and violence, greater mistrust of authority, and less hope for the future than did lighter viewers who saw less than 2 hours of daily television on the average. Gerbner et al. argue that these findings indicated a cultivation effect of viewing, whereby television conditions a distorted view of the world among those who are heavy consumers of its content. Heavy viewing may cause misconceptions not only about levels of crime and violence, but also with regard to other aspects of the social environment, such as the appropriate roles for women (Morgan, 1982) and the characteristics of old people (Gerbner, Gross, Signorielli, & Morgan, 1980).

Early attempts to replicate Gerbner's findings concerning TV viewing and perceptions of social danger in the United Kingdom failed to produce the same results (Piepe, Crouch, & Emerson, 1977; Wober 1978). Several reasons have been discussed to account for the discrepancies in the two sets of findings. It could be that there are significant cross-national differences in viewing habits and levels of exposure to television violence. Another important factor may be the differences in the way television viewing has been measured. Gerbner, for example, relied on gross personal estimations of viewing in hours per day, whereas Wober's sample filled in a viewing diary listing all programs broadcast over 1 week. Another possible explanation of the relationships reported by Gerbner and his colleagues between amount of television watched and social anxiety is a "third variable" hypothesis, which posits that both social beliefs and TV viewing may be effects of some additional factor not previously taken into account. Doob and MacDonald (1979) reported, for example, that fear of environmental crime among residents of Toronto, Canada, was related more closely to actual levels of such crime than to TV viewing. But in addition to making people more fearful, it could be argued that high local crime rates might encourage people to stay indoors and watch more television.

Developing this argument further, one might explain the relationship between viewing television and social fearfulness in terms of a reverse hypothesis, whereby those individuals who are more anxious to begin with also watch more television. It has been shown that mood states can affect the tendency not only to watch television per se, but can also influence the type of content a person prefers to watch. Boyanowsky, Newtson, and Walster (1974) found that threatened individuals showed a distinct preference for viewing potentially fear-inducing events under safe conditions. Girls who had shared a dormitory with a murder victim showed greater preference subsequent to the murder for a movie depicting a cold-blooded murder than for a nonviolent romantic film, whereas girls from another dormitory, who were presumably less directly affected by the murder, showed no such preference. In a subsequent contrived experiment, Boyanowsky (1977) was able to add further support to his initial findings. If transient mood states can influence short-term preferences for films, to what extent may longer term television viewing behaviors and program preferences be related to more lasting dispositions of individuals?

Wober and Gunter (1982) noted that many of the social beliefs measured by Gerbner and his colleagues exhibited a striking resemblance, at least on the surface, to those included by Rotter (1965, 1967) in an instrument developed to measure a personality characteristic known as locus of control. This dimension, which indicated the extent to which people believed events in their lives to be determined by fate or self-control, was conceptualized as a fundamental characteristic of the individual conditioned by a whole array of social and developmental factors and therefore, as something more than simply a reaction to television viewing. Wober and Gunter were interested in finding out whether locus of control was in any way related either to viewing television or to responses on the social anxiety and interpersonal mistrust items used by Gerbner.

Diary data on television viewing habits and completed questionnaires concerning personal fearfulness, mistrust, and locus of control were collected from over 300 individuals in the London ITV region during 1 week of routine audience-appreciation measurement. Results showed that although fear of being a victim of crime correlated significantly with TV viewing initially, this relationship disappeared when the influence of locus of control was partialed out. Locus of control, however, was related to amount of TV viewing even in the presence of statistical controls for other social beliefs and demographic factors. This evidence suggested that whatever is measured by the Gerbner questions is less robustly related to viewing behavior than the dimension measured by locus of control items (at least for viewers in the United Kingdom). Furthermore, it could be that the relationships observed here do not demonstrate a conditional reaction to regular TV viewing, but indicate a psychological antecedent of volume of viewing.

A subsequent survey suggested even more clearly a link between psychological characteristics of viewers and how much television and what kinds of programs they choose to watch. Although Gerbner and his associates have emphasized the cultivation, via heavy TV viewing, of exaggerated fears about personal safety and of increased mistrust of others, some writers have suggested that another message may be transmitted by television drama which ought to condition a completely different kind of social perception.

VIEWER CHARACTERISTICS
AND PROGRAM EVALUATION

The research discussed in the previous two sections indicated that degrees of loyalty to programs or program types can be identified via behavioral measures as prominent features of television viewing. Furthermore, selective viewing of programs is related to certain demographic and psychological characteristics of viewers. This behavioral evidence for program preferences has been corroborated by attitudinal research that has demonstrated relationships between the psychological characteristics of individuals and their appreciation of different kinds of programming. Although what people say about programs may not reflect how often those programs are actually viewed, attitudinal data can usefully supplement behavioral data on selectivity in viewing and give some idea of what viewers think or feel about programs.

Research discussed in the previous section indicated that relationships exist between certain psychological characteristics of viewers and the kinds of programs they watch. To a great extent, the latter research has utilized a priori or factor analytically defined program types. Some writers have expressed the concern, however, that these typologies, which offer relatively wholistic classifications of programs, may well miss out on other important program attributes that mediate the decision to watch (Gandy, 1982). Thus, Comisky and Bryant (1982) examined factors that were most important in generating feelings of suspense in the audience. Suspense is a stylistic attribute, which may mediate attraction to and appreciation of a program. It is not restricted to any particular genre of programming, and according to Comisky and Bryant, suspense depends on two major components: uncertainty of story outcome and degree of liking for the protagonist.

One attribute of program content, long considered by network executives as an essential ingredient guaranteed to attract large audiences, is violence. Research evidence on the efficacy of violence in enhancing the entertainment value of television programs, however, has been equivocal (Gunter, 1979). Recent studies have shown no relationship between audience sizes for prime time programs on major TV networks in the United States and the amount of violence such programs contain (Diener & De Four, 1978; Sprafkin, Rubinstein, & Stone, 1977).

Although dramatic story lines in fictional television programming often feature violent conflict between criminal elements and the forces of law and order, thus giving the impression of a "violent world," by the end of nearly all such programs, this conflict is typically resolved with the triumph of good over evil and the eventual bringing to justice of lawbreakers. Therefore, if television teaches anything about the world at all, it is equally or more likely to be that the world is a just and secure place than that it is a dangerous one (Zillmann, 1980).

To test this, Gunter and Wober (1983) carried out a survey in which program-appreciation diaries with attached opinion questionnaires were sent to the IBA's London region panel from whom nearly 500 usable replies were returned. The questionnaire contained items on personal fearfulness, interpersonal mistrust, anomie, and beliefs in a just world. The latter scale was developed by Rubin and Peplau (1975) to measure the extent to which people believe the world is a just place. This dimension is regarded, much as locus of control has been, as an enduring characteristic that can reliably discriminate between individuals.

Respondents received scores on each of the foregoing social-belief dimensions, and viewing behavior was classified not simply in terms of general amount of TV viewing, but also by the viewing of different program categories such as action-adventure, soap operas, news and current affairs, and United States TV series. Results showed that in the presence of multiple statistical controls for sex, age, and social class, just two significant relationships survived between viewing behavior and social beliefs.

Respondents who had strong beliefs in a just world tended to be heavy viewers of action-adventure programs and United States TV series (which consisted mainly of action-adventure). These relationships suggest a cultivation effect of television, which opposes that proposed by Gerbner and his colleagues. The message assimilated by viewers from action-drama programs relates to the triumph of justice over the wrongdoer rather than to the harm that criminals are frequently shown to inflict on innocent others in these programs. However, it could also be said that these results do not reflect a cultivation effect of television at all, but instead indicate that people who believe that the world is a just place turn selectively to dramatic story lines to obtain reinforcement and clarification of their beliefs.

In one recent investigation, Diener and Woody (1981) found that violent television programs were actually enjoyed somewhat less than nonviolent programs among 62 families who viewed these shows at home. Among a sample of British viewers, Himmelweit, Swift, and Biberian (1980) found no relationship between judgments of how violent programs were perceived to be and how much they were enjoyed.

Although findings of a number of survey and experimental studies have offered little support for the belief that violence makes programs more attractive to viewers in general, there is research evidence to show that viewers may vary widely in their personal preferences for televised violence and that selection and appreciation of violent programs may be mediated by transient mood states and by more enduring personality dispositions.

Mood States and Enjoyment of Television Violence

Preferences for media violence have been shown to relate to transient mood states of individuals. People who have been put into an angry mood or aggressive frame of mind have been found to exhibit stronger preferences for violent over nonviolent media content when compared with nonangered people. Some researchers have found that aggressive fantasizing can induce preferences for violent films over nonviolent films, especially among men (Fenigstein, 1979; Goldstein, 1972). Actually, the insulting and angering of individuals, and the encouragement to display overt physically aggressive acts, may also influence preferences for violent film material (Fenigstein, 1979; Freedman & Newtson, 1975). Further effects of mood states on program preferences are discussed by Zillmann and Bryant in chapter 8 of this volume.

Personality and Enjoyment of Television

Much of the massive literature concerning television violence has focused on the impact of violent TV material on viewers' attitudes and behaviors. Much less attention has been paid to whether or not violent programs are viewed selectively, in particular by individuals whose personalities are already characterized by strong aggressive dispositions, and if so, whether and to what extent this may account for the relationships so frequently observed in correlational surveys between the viewing of violent programming and personal aggressiveness. For example, many correlational studies have used favorite program choices as a measure of exposure to TV violence.

Thus, Robinson and Bachman (1972) found that delinquent aggressiveness in late adolescence was associated with the amount of violence in favorite programs. Elsewhere, adolescent deviance and attitudes approving of violence were found to be related to preferences for violent programs (McIntyre & Teevan, 1972). However, although these studies have been cited as evidence for the *effects* of viewing televised violence, an alternative interpretation equally consistent with their findings is that they indicate selectivity in viewing violence by aggressive individuals.

In comparing the television viewing preferences of aggressive and nonaggressive boys, Friedman and Johnson (1972) found that aggressive boys named more violent programs among their favorites than did nonaggressives. In addition, the former were only half as likely as the latter to name a violent program as one they would most like to take off the air. Although these correlational analyses cannot provide conclusive indicators of causality, Chaffee (1972) has argued that it may be more meaningful to think of programs identified as favorites as a dependent variable, which is influenced by personal dispositions of viewers, than as an independent variable, which produces those dispositions, because the small number of best liked programs would not provide a strong stimulus. However, this argument needs to be empirically verified because the most preferred programs may also be the most salient or vivid for the viewer, and therefore constitute a very potent stimulus indeed.

Evidence supporting the thesis that aggressive predisposition may underlie the enjoyment of violent television content has emerged from several recent studies in which viewing behavior and content preferences were clearly identified as dependent variables. Atkin, Greenberg, Korzenny, and McDermott (1979) used a time-order design to draw causal influences from correlational data. A two-wave panel study of young people across a 1-year lag was used to explore relationships between aggressive attitudes and television viewing behavior over time. Measures of attitudinal dispositions were used one year to predict viewing patterns a year later. Although general patterns of viewing changed little over the year, some evidence did emerge that individuals who exhibited aggressive attitudes at the beginning of the study expressed particularly strong preferences for violent programming after 1 year, even when other important variables such as sex, age, and initial viewing patterns had been statistically controlled. The reverse correlation between viewing television violence initially and the development of aggressive attitudes over time was much smaller.

Finally, further evidence indicating differences in preferences for different forms of televised violence among different personality types has emerged from work completed during the early 1980s by the author. A series of experiments was conducted in which a panel of viewers, from diverse age groups and social backgrounds, judged the content of sets of brief TV sequences that depicted different kinds of violent incidents. In these experiments, judgments included ratings of how violent, realistic, disturbing, and exciting viewers thought the scenes to be. These ratings were related to a range of personality measures obtained from panel members, including personal aggressiveness on four subscales of the Buss–Durkee (1957) Hostility Inventory, and Extraversion, Neuroticism, and Psychoticism on the Eysenck Personality Questionnaire (Eysenck & Eysenck, 1975), and self-perceived masculinity and femininity on the Bem (1974) Sex Role Inventory.

In one study, which was designed principally to examine differences in viewers' reactions to television violence perpetrated by law enforcers or by criminals, viewers who exhibited strong self-reported tendencies toward physical and verbal aggressiveness rated TV series depicting law enforcers as perpetrators of violence more exciting than did viewers with only weak aggressive tendencies (Gunter, 1985). In another study, which looked at the effects of program context or setting on viewers' perceptions of television violence, self-proclaimed physically aggressive people were found to judge shootings and fist-fights from British produced crime-detective shows (though not from shows produced in America of the same genre) as more exciting than did less aggressive individuals (Gunter & Furnham, 1984).

Personal aggressiveness was not the only personality dimension found to be a potential mediator of viewers' preferences for different kinds of violence. Again, comparing perceptions of violent portrayals from different categories of programming, it was found that high scorers on Eysenck's neuroticism dimension perceived TV violence generally, but especially that from contemporary British drama, in more serious and less favorable terms than did less anxious individuals (Gunter & Furnham, 1983). Meanwhile the psychoticism dimension, an indicator of tough-mindedness and emotional coolness, was found to be related to differential preferences for harmful violence. Scenes that depicted physical injury and harm to a victim were perceived as more violent and disturbing by lower than by higher psychoticism scorers (Gunter, 1983). Reactions to TV violence also varied according to sex of the attacker and victim, but this particular feature of violent portrayals interacted with program type and viewers' self-perceived masculinity or femininity to mediate judgments. Results showed that male violence on a female victim (whether a shooting or a fight) was rated as more serious than female violence on a male in contemporary British crime-drama settings. However, in American crime or futuristic science fiction settings, the reverse was true. More important in the context of the current discussion though, was the finding that viewers (male or female) who perceived themselves strongly in masculine terms and weakly in feminine terms on the Bem (1974) Sex Role Inventory perceived male attacks on female victims as relatively more serious, compared with viewers who exhibited the opposite masculinity–femininity tendencies (Gunter, 1985). These findings imply a complex interrelationship between certain personality dispositions of individuals and their preferences for different types of violent content.

SUMMARY

From the evidence reviewed in this chapter, it is clear that differential loyalty to programs or program types is a prominent feature of television viewing behavior. It is also evident that selective patterns of viewing or preferential attitudinal dispositions toward certain kinds of programming are not constant across all viewers. How people think or feel about programs or the extent to which the audience flows toward or across certain programs or program types varies between demographic divisions of the population. More significantly, however, are those findings that indicate differences in viewing patterns or attitudinal preferences for programs associated with enduring psychological characteristics of viewers. Although much more work still needs to be done to clarify and test the reliability of these findings, early indications are that this line of research is well worth pursuing. It could prove to be work of no small practical worth to broadcast institutions, who in the face of the ever more fragmenting audiences, need to understand better why audiences behave in the ways they do. Then, from both an academic and social policy standpoint, understanding why audiences flow toward programs in different ways could contribute significantly to a better understanding of the effects of television, research on which in the past has all too often ignored how people watch television. Unless we can be clear on this last point, we can never hope to demonstrate properly the extent to which television influences the way people think, feel, and behave.

REFERENCES

Atkin, C., Greenberg, B., Korzenny, F., & McDermott, S. (1979). Selective exposure to televised violence. *Journal of Broadcasting, 23,* 5–13.

Banks, S. (1967). Patterns of daytime viewing behaviour; Marketing for tomorrow . . . today. *Proceedings* June 1967 Conference, Chicago: American Marketing Association, 1967, pp. 139–142.

Barwise, T. P., Ehrenberg, A.S.C., & Goodhardt, G. J. (1982). Glued to the box? Patterns of TV repeat-viewing. *Journal of Communication, 32,* 22–29.

Bem, S. C. (1974). The measurement of psychological androgyny. *Journal of Consulting and Clinical Psychology, 52,* 155–162.

Boyanowsky, E. O. (1977). Film preferences under condition of threat: Wetting the appetite for violence, information or excitement? *Communication Research, 4,* 133–144.

Boyanowsky, E. O., Newtson, D., & Walster, E. (1974). Film preferences following a murder. *Communication Research, 1,* 32–43.

Buss, A. H., & Durkee, A. (1957). An inventory for assessing different kinds of hostility. *Journal of Consulting Psychology, 21,* 343–349.

Chaffee, S. (1972). Television and adolescent aggressiveness. In G. Comstock & E. A. Rubinstein (Eds.), *Television and social behavior: Vol. 3. Television and adolescent aggressiveness* (pp. 1–34). Washington, D.C.: U.S. Government Printing Office.

Comisky, P., & Bryant, J. (1982). Factors involved in generating suspense. *Human Communication and Research, 9,* 49–58.

Diener, E., & De Four, D. (1978). Does television violence enhance programme popularity? *Journal of Personality and Social Psychology, 36,* 333–341.

Diener, E., & Woody, L. W. (1981). TV violence and viewing liking. *Communication Research, 8,* 281–306.

Doob, A. N., & MacDonald, C. E. (1979). Television viewing and fear of victimization: Is the relationship causal? *Journal of Personality and Social Psychology, 37,* 170–179.

Eysenck, H. J., & Eysenck, S. B. G. (1975). *Manual for the Eysenck Personality Questionnaire.* London: Hodder & Stoughton.

Fenigstein, A. (1979). Does aggression cause a preference for viewing media violence? *Journal of Personality and Social Psychology, 37,* 2307–2317.

Freedman, J., & Newtson, R. (1975). *The effect of anger on preference for filmed violence.* Paper presented at the annual conference of the American Psychological Association, Chicago.

Friedman, H., & Johnson, R. L. (1972). Mass media use and aggression: A pilot study. In G. A. Comstock & E. A. Rubinstein (Eds.), *Television and social behavior:* Vol. 3. Television and adolescent aggressiveness (pp. 336–360). Washington, D.C.: U.S. Government Printing Office.

Gandy, O. H. (1982). Television audience size and composition. In B. Dervin & M. Voight (Eds.), *Progress in communication studies* (Vol. 5). Norwood, NJ: Ablex.

Gensch, D., & Ranganathan, B. (1980). Evaluation of television programme content for the purpose of promotional segmentation. *Journal of Marketing Research, 17,* 307–315.

Gerbner, G., & Gross, L. (1976). Living with television: The violence profile. *Journal of Communication, 26,* 173–199.

Gerbner, G., Gross, L., Jackson-Beeck, M., Jeffries-Fox, S., & Signorielli, N. (1978). Cultural indicators: Violence profile no. 9. *Journal of Communication, 28,* 176–207.

Gerbner, G., Gross, L., Signorielli, N., Morgan, M., & Jackson-Beeck, M. (1979). The demonstration of power: Violence profile no. 10. *Journal of Communication, 29,* 177–196.

Gerbner, G., Gross, L., Signorielli, N., & Morgan, M. (1980). Ageing with television: Images on television drama and conceptions of social reality. *Journal of Communication, 30,* 34–47.

Goldstein, J. H. (1972). *Preferences for aggressive movie content. The effects of cognitive silence.* Unpublished manuscript, Temple University, Philadelphia.

Goodhardt, G. J., Ehrenberg, A. S. C., & Collins, M. A. (1975). *The television audience: Patterns of viewing.* Lexington, MA: D.C. Heath.

Gunter, B. (1979). Television violence and entertainment value. *Bulletin of the British Psychological Society, 32,* 100–102.

Gunter, B. (1983). Personality and perceptions of harmful and harmless TV violence. *Personality and Individual Differences, 4,* 665–670.

Gunter, B. (1984a). *Patterns of network news viewing in Britain.* Research Paper, Independent Broadcasting Authority, London, England.

Gunter, B. (1984b). *UK viewing of The A-Team: A demonstration of audience loyalty to a TV series?* Unpublished manuscript.

Gunter, B. (1985). *Dimensions of television violence.* Aldershot, England: Gower.

Gunter, B., & Furnham A. (1983). Personality and the perception of TV violence. *Personality and Individual Differences, 4,* 315–321.

Gunter, B., & Furnham, A. (1984). Perceptions of television violence: Effects of programme genre and type of violence on viewers' judgements of violent portrayals. *British Journal of Social Psychology, 23,* 155–164.

Gunter, B., & Wober, M. (1983). Television viewing and public trust. *British Journal of Social Psychology, 22,* 174–176.

Headen, R. S., Klompmaker, J. E., & Rust, R. T. (1979). The duplication of viewing law and television media schedule evaluation. *Journal of Marketing Research, 16,* 333–340.

Himmelweit, H. T., Swift, B., & Biberian, M. J. (1980). The audience as critic: A conceptual analysis of television entertainment. In P. Tannenbaum (Ed.), *The entertainment functions of television* (pp. 67–106). Hillsdale, NJ: Lawrence Erlbaum Associates.

Kirsch, A. D., & Banks, S. (1967). Programmes types defined by factor analysis. *Journal of Advertising Research, 2,* 29–32.

McIntyre, J., & Teevan, J. (1972). Television violence and deviant behavior. In G. A. Comstock & E. A. Rubenstein (Eds.), *Television and social Behavior: Vol. 3, Television and adolescent aggressiveness* (pp. 383–435). Washington, D.C.: U.S. Government Printing Office.

Morgan, M. (1982). Television and adolescents' sex-role stereotypes: A longitudinal study. *Journal of Personality and Social Psychology, 43,* 947–955.

Piepe, A., Crouch, J., & Emerson, M. (1977). Violence and television. *New Society, 41,* 536–538.

Robinson, J., & Bachman, J. (1972). Television viewing habits and aggression. In G. A. Comstock & E. A. Rubinstein (Eds.), *Television and social behavior: Vol. 3. Television and adolescent aggressiveness* (pp. 372–382). Washington, D.C.: U.S. Government Printing Office.

Rotter, J. B. (1965). General expectancies for internal versus external control of reinforcement. *Psychological Monographs, 80* (1, Whole No. 609).

Rotter, J. B. (1967). A new scale for the measurement of interpersonal trust. *Journal of Personality, 35,* 651–666.

Rubin, Z., & Peplau, I. A. (1975). Who believes in a just world? *Journal of Social Issues, 31,* 65–89.

Sprafkin, J. N., Rubinstein, E. A., & Stone, A. (1977). The content analysis of four television diets. *Occasional Paper 77-3.* Stony Brook, NY: Brookdale International Institute.

Swanson, C. L. (1967). Patterns of nighttime television viewing. *Proceedings* of the American Marketing Association Conferences. June 1967, Chicago: American Marketing Association, 1967, pp. 143–147.

Wakshlag, J. J., Agostino, D. E., Terry, H. A., Driscoll, P., & Ramsey, B. (1983). Television news viewing and network affiliation changes. *Journal of Broadcasting, 27,* 53–68.

Wells, W. D. (1969). The rise and fall of television programme types. *Journal of Advertising Research, 9,* 21–27.

Wober, J. M. (1978). Televised violence and paranoid perception: The view from Great Britain. *Public Opinion Quarterly, 42,* 315–321.

Wober, J. M. (1981). *A box for all seasons* (Special Report), London: Independent Broadcasting Authority.

Wober, J. M., & Gunter, B. (1982). Television and personal threat: Fact or artifact? A British survey. *British Journal of Social Psychology, 21,* 239–247.

Wober, J. M., & Gunter, B. (1984). *The Winds of War: Audiences, appreciation and opinions for television's most heavily promoted series* (Special Report). London: Independent Broadcasting Authority.

Zillmann, D. (1980). Anatomy of suspense. In P. Tannenbaum (Ed.), *The entertainment functions of television* (pp. 133–163). Hillsdale, NJ: Lawrence Erlbaum Associates.

6 Thought and Action as Determinants of Media Exposure

Allan Fenigstein
Kenyon College

Ronald G. Heyduk
Hartwick College

Several years ago, one of us (R.G.H.) was asked by the parent-teachers organization at his daughter's elementary school to speak on the subject of television and children. The offer was accepted with mixed emotions. On the one hand, it was clear that the discipline of psychology had something of value to communicate on the subject and that the audience would be eager to hear it. On the other hand, previous experience had shown that nonpsychologists often have the uncanny and unnerving ability to identify what psychologists don't know about a topic.

The presentation attempted to survey and summarize what psychological research had uncovered about the varied influences of television, ranging from the early work on aggression to the more recent research on the cognitive development of children. The talk went very well, and the parents responded so enthusiastically during the subsequent discussion that the speaker's confidence had reached unrealistic heights by the time the inevitable question locating the soft spot in our understanding of the media was asked: "It's interesting to find out what TV can do to kids, but what is it about kids that makes them want to watch TV?"

The parent's question had drawn attention to a distinction between two sets of issues in the psychological study of the relationship between the media and behavior. One set of issues concerns the *impact* of the media—that is, what effects television has on the viewer; the other set concerns *attraction* to the media—that is, why viewers watch what they do. Table 6.1 presents selected topics in the psychology of media; for each topic, a sample impact question is paired with a related attraction question.

TABLE 6.1
Impact and Attraction: Two Sets of Issues in the Study
of the Relationship between Media and Behavior

Sample Topics	Sample Issues Concerning the Impact of Media	Sample Issues Concerning the Attraction to Media
Media violence	What are the short-term effects of exposure to a violent television program?	What draws people to violence on television?
Television soap operas	What influences do television soaps have upon values?	What psychological motives attract viewers to television soaps?
News presentations on television	To what extent does television news shape attitudes about political candidates?	Why are television news presentations preferred to other media presentations?
Structural features of the television medium	What effects does exposure to the visual complexity of television have upon reading motivation and skills?	Why is the visual complexity of television so compelling/addictive?

In retrospect, it should have been known that the failure of the presentation to address issues of attraction would be conspicuous to this audience. Not only do attraction questions have logical priority over questions of impact (i.e., without exposure, there can be no effect), but they may also have greater practical significance for parents trying to formulate effective policies regarding television usage by their children. Understanding the potential consequences of one's 5-year-old son watching a violent television program may help one to decide *whether* control over his viewing is desirable, but understanding what draws him and keeps him glued to the show helps one to determine *when and how* to unglue him. In addition, there is an important conceptual sense in which these two issues are closely intertwined. In order to understand how viewers are affected by television, it is useful to know what needs and motives viewers bring to the screen; conversely, knowing how viewers are affected by television may help explain why viewers watch what they do.

In view of these compelling practical and conceptual reasons for not ignoring attraction while trying to understand impact, it was very discomforting to admit to the audience that there was relatively little light to be shed by psychologists on the subject of attraction to the media. Although there are many theories of motivation that can lend themselves to the question of media attraction, there is little experimental data on the subject of what motivates people to expose themselves selectively to the media, especially in comparison to the experimental data concerning the consequences of that exposure.

One likely reason that the psychology of media attraction has lagged behind the psychology of media impact is that the research psychologist's most powerful tool, the experimental method, is more easily adapted to impact than to attraction. Consider, for example, the impact and attraction issues concerning television soap operas posed in Table 6.1. Each issue could generate a number of more specific causal hypotheses, which could only be tested experimentally. In Table 6.2, sample hypotheses concerning the impact and attraction of soap operas are stated in generic terms, and simple experiments to test each hypothesis are presented schematically.

As any survivor of an undergraduate course in research design knows, to be confident of the impact of soap operas upon belief X, one must assign subjects to different "soap" viewing conditions; similarly, to assess the effect of motive Y on attraction to soaps, subjects must be assigned to different levels of motive Y. That is, the hallmark of true experimental research is the unbiased assignment of subjects to experimental conditions created by the experimenter. Television is a readily varied external factor, and it is easy enough for an experimenter to control what and how much a subject views in an experimental setting in order to test the impact hypothesis. But the researcher wishing to test the attraction hypothesis concerning the effects of motive Y is faced with an especially thorny problem: How does one manipulate a presumably internal factor such as the level of a motive? Although the experimental study of motivation has a long and revered history (e.g., Atkinson & McClelland, 1948; Hull, 1943), these procedures have not been readily adapted to the study of exposure to the media, and this may have much to do with why our understanding of media attraction has not kept pace with our understanding of media impact. The present chapter attempts to redress this lag by utilizing an experimental methodology that manipulates some of the psychological states that may underlie different viewing preferences—for example, aggression, sex, affiliation, and achievement—and measures the short-term effects of these situationally induced states upon selective exposure.

The lack of development of viable experimental approaches to the study of how psychological motives influence media preferences may have prevented psychologists from identifying a special kind of interactive relationship between media and behavior. If one of the effects of media exposure is to strengthen a motive which itself plays a causal role in media exposure, an endless feedback loop or "vicious cycle" of impact and attraction may be set up such as the hypothetical one illustrated in Table 6.3. Suppose, for example, that a strong positive correlation was observed between amount of soap opera viewing and strength of affiliative motivation. Aside from the possibility of a third factor causing both viewing and motivation, such a relationship might be produced by a simple impact effect (i.e., watching soaps strengthens the affiliative motive), by a simple attraction effect (i.e., the affiliative motive increases the desire to watch soaps), or by the cycle of impact and attraction shown in Table 6.3. Experiments manipulating soap opera watching would confirm the impact part of the cycle, but in the absence of any experiments manipulating affiliative motivation, there would be no way to confirm the attraction effect. What might actually be an

TABLE 6.2
Applying the Experimental Method to the Study of Media Impact and Attraction

	The Impact of Media	*The Attraction of Media*
Sample issues	What influences do television soaps have upon values?	What psychological motives attract viewers to television soaps?
Sample causal hypotheses	As a result of watching television soaps, one is more likely to hold value X.	As a result of having a strong motive Y, one is more likely to be attracted to television soaps.
Sample true experiments	*Manipulated Experimental Conditions* → *Dependent Variables*. Unbiased assignment of subjects → Watch soaps / Don't watch soaps → Degree of belief in X	*Manipulated Experimental Conditions* → *Dependent Variables*. Unbiased assignment of subjects → High level of motive Y / Low level of motive Y → Degree of interest in watching soaps

TABLE 6.3
Hypothetical Example of a "Vicious Cycle" of Impact and Attraction

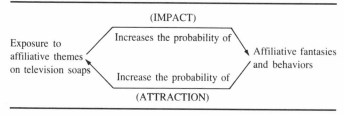

interactive relationship between soap opera viewing and affiliative motivation may therefore be interpreted as a case of pure impact, simply because no experimental evidence is available to document the bidirectional relationship between impact and attraction.

AGGRESSIVE BEHAVIOR
AND ATTRACTION TO MEDIA VIOLENCE

The hypothetical relationship concerning soap operas and affiliation just depicted may, in fact, be an accurate description of the relationship between media violence and aggression. A positive correlation between aggressive behavior and the viewing of violence in the media is a consistent finding in the psychological research, a finding that is virtually beyond challenge at the present time (e.g., Andison, 1977; Bandura, 1973; Belson, 1978; Bogart, 1972; Geen, 1978; Goranson, 1970; Lefkowitz & Huesmann, 1980). The more that persons watch media violence, the more aggressively they behave. Again, this finding may be indicative of several different relationships: Watching violence may increase the likelihood of subsequent aggressive behavior (an impact effect); aggressive behavior may draw persons to media violence (an attraction effect); or there may be a vicious cycle of impact and attraction such that media violence causes aggressive behavior and aggressive persons prefer to watch more violence.

Although in theory any or all of these relationships may be true, the experimental research has been directed *almost exclusively* toward the impact of media violence on aggression. Scores of laboratory and field studies have now found that exposure to certain kinds of media violence results in both an increased likelihood of subsequent aggressive responses and an increased tolerance of aggressive behavior (see reviews by Comstock, 1980; Huesmann, 1982; Pearl, Bouthilet, & Lazar, 1982). Although these findings are not at issue, the research emphasis on those effects caused by viewing violence, to the exclusion of examining why the viewer is watching violence, has served to obscure the possible reciprocal nature of the relationship between the viewer and the media.

It should be reiterated that the causal relationship regarding the impact of viewing violence on aggressive behavior in no way rules out the possibility of a causal link in the opposite direction, a link that has implications for understanding the motives that underlie the viewer's attraction to media violence. Such a relationship would posit that persons who behaved aggressively would be inclined to watch violent acts by others in the media. Furthermore, this attraction effect would have to be demonstrated before one could argue for a circular relationship between media violence and aggression. Despite the apparent value of demonstrating such a relationship, until recently there has been no experimental investigation of the effect of aggression on attraction to media violence. This is even more difficult to understand when one considers the conceptual relationship between the impact and attraction issues: It would seem reasonable to assume that if a consequence of watching media violence is a change in the viewer's aggressive behavior, then aggression would be related to the viewer's reasons for watching media violence.

Correlational Evidence

Although the idea that prior aggressive behavior may predispose persons to seek out television violence was first raised by the Surgeon-General's Scientific Advisory Committee on Television and Social Behavior (1972) and has subsequently been echoed by a number of authors (e.g., Dorr & Kovaric, 1980; Eron, 1982; Kaplan & Singer, 1976), the research evidence in support of this proposition has been largely correlational. Dominick and Greenberg (1972) and Greenberg (1975) have provided evidence that the viewing of violence is associated with attitudes and beliefs favorable to the use of violence, such as a greater belief in its efficacy and a greater expressed willingness to use violence to resolve a conflict. Similarly, a study by Hartnagel, Teevan, and McIntyre (1975) found that those adolescents who perceived the violence portrayed on television as an effective means to a goal (i.e., who may have been somewhat predisposed toward the use of aggression) watched more television violence than those who perceived violence as ineffective. Along these same lines, Diener and DeFour (1978) found that dispositionally aggressive men have a greater preference for viewing violence than do those who are nonaggressive. It has also been reported that low-income and black youths enjoy watching film violence more than their less aggressive, white, middle-class counterparts (Greenberg & Gordon, 1971). Although all of these studies suggest that aggressive persons tend to seek out violent films and programs, the nonexperimental nature of this research leaves the findings open to alternative interpretations and cannot directly address the question of causality.

Several other observational studies have attempted to indirectly assess the causal effects of aggression on the preference for viewing violence, using cross-lagged correlational techniques, with inconclusive results. An early study by Lefkowitz, Eron, Walder, and Huesmann (1972) found no relationship between aggressive behavior at age 9 and the viewing of violence on television 10 years later, and concluded that viewing violence is not caused by prior aggression. Similarly, a 1-year longitudinal study of preschool children provided little indication that aggressive children prefer to watch violent programs (Singer & Singer, 1980). More recently, however, Huesmann (1982) has reported some modest, but significant, correlations between aggressive behavior in first and third graders and the viewing of television violence 1 year later, suggesting that aggression may be a causal antecedent of the viewing of media violence.

Independent of the mixed outcomes of these studies, it must be understood that all observational data are subject to criticism on both statistical and methodological grounds. Many researchers have strong reservations about the analyses used to extract causal inferences from longitudinal data (Comstock, 1978; Kenny, 1972). More generally, correlational studies cannot control the operation of all the relevant third-order variables, making it extremely difficult to establish causal relationships. Thus, the question still remains: Does aggression cause a preference for viewing media violence? The only way to determine cause and effect in a reasonably direct and unambiguous manner is through controlled experimentation, and until recently, questions concerning attraction to the media have resisted experimental investigation.

Experimental Evidence

Part of a recent study by Fenigstein (1979) experimentally tested the hypothesis that persons who acted aggressively toward another would be more interested in viewing media violence than those who were nonaggressive. This study, using male college students, first manipulated the subject's level of aggressive behavior and then determined whether these differences in prior aggression affected the subject's subsequent choice of watching either violent or neutral film segments. After all subjects had given their informed consent to participate in a study involving aggression, some subjects were induced to aggress against another experimental subject (who was actually a confederate of the experimenter). This was achieved by asking the real subjects to press a series of buttons that would deliver loud, somewhat painful bursts of static noise through a headphone that the confederate was wearing, supposedly as a means of evaluating the creativity of the confederate on a free-association task (a paradigm that has been used successfully in previous aggression research; cf. Konecni, 1975).

Although the noises that could be used ranged over 10 levels, subjects were restricted from using either the extremely low or the extremely high end of the range; in effect, these subjects were forced to be moderately aggressive toward the confederate (of course, no noises were actually used, although no subject indicated awareness of this deception). It must be remembered that this experiment was attempting to control aggressive behavior so that its effect on film preferences could be determined. Experimentally controlling the range of responses insured that these subjects would believe that they were acting aggressively toward the other. In comparison, subjects in the nonaggression condition were given the same instructions and used the same apparatus, but did not deliver any physical aggression (in the form of noise) to the confederate. Rather, their button presses simply lit up numbers that conveyed their evaluation of the confederate's responses. Manipulation checks indicated that subjects who thought they were using aversive noise believed they were acting more aggressively than those subjects who were not using noise.

In the next part of the study, which was presumably interested in the cognitive effects of certain visual stimuli, all of the participants were given the opportunity to select 10 different short film clips for viewing, out of a total pool of 26 films. Each clip was described by a brief phrase, such as "a boxing match," "a roller-coaster ride," "an angry mob," or "a speed typist at work." Each film description had previously been rated for its aggressive content, degree of interest, and amount of action. These three dimensions were assessed in an attempt to statistically control a potential confound in the study of attraction to media violence. Any depiction of violence will often involve some action and is also likely to occur in the context of other interesting story elements. Through covariation techniques, it was possible to establish a relatively unconfounded measure of the preference for viewing violence, independent of the effects of interest and action.

The results showed that subjects who earlier had the opportunity to aggress physically, using noise, chose films that were more violent than those chosen by subjects who had no prior opportunity to aggress. It was also found that films chosen by subjects who had aggressed involved more action and were more interesting than those chosen by the nonaggression group. However, covariance analyses indicated that the effect of aggression on the preference for viewing violent films was independent of the films' action and interest levels. Thus, consistent with our hypothesis, the results clearly suggest that males who use aggression are more likely to want to see it used by others in the media.

It should be recognized that these results are completely consistent with the correlational data showing that the viewing of media violence is positively related to aggressive behavior. Furthermore, the findings suggest that the relationship between media violence and aggression is supported by reciprocal causal links: Aggressive behaviors are not only a result of viewing violence, but may also be a cause of viewing violence. As previously suggested, this bidirectional model of influence also argues for the possibility of a vicious cycle in which aggressive acts lead to the viewing of violence, which leads to further acts of aggression, and so on, a position recently supported by others (e.g., Eron, 1982).

AGGRESSIVE THOUGHTS AND
ATTRACTION TO MEDIA VIOLENCE

The previous research demonstrated the effects of aggressive behavior on media viewing preferences. However, the increased desire to view media violence need not be limited only to those who have acted aggressively; it may also apply to those who are cognitively preoccupied with aggression, who fantasize about it, or who simply are motivated to think aggressive thoughts. Consider the following study: Boyanowsky, Newtson, and Walster (1974) found that attendance at a violent movie increased markedly following a brutal local murder, whereas no such increase in attendance occurred for a nonviolent movie. It may be argued that the brutal crime increased the population's concern and curiosity about violence, and one consequence of this heightened awareness of violence was a greater interest in viewing such acts in the media.

Similarly, Gerbner, Gross, Morgan, and Signorielli (1980) have found a positive correlation between exposure to television violence and apprehension about crime. One interpretation of these data, consistent with the present argument, is that persons who are concerned and thinking about crime, compared to those who give little thought to its occurrence, are more inclined to watch television violence. In support of this hypothesis is the finding by Doob and MacDonald (1979) that people in high-crime areas watch more violent television than those in low-crime areas. Here too, it may be suggested that persons who live in constant fear of crime are preoccupied with aggressive thoughts and, as a result, seek out violence in the media.

Experimental Evidence

Although these correlational studies clearly suggest a relationship between aggressive cognitions and an interest in viewing violence, cause and effect have not been established; again, the only way to do so is through controlled experimentation involving the manipulation of aggressive thoughts. One means of experimentally activating such thoughts involves the use of "priming"; that is, by having subjects use a certain concept (e.g., "aggression") during a prior task, that concept becomes more accessible for use in a later task (Higgins, Rholes, & Jones, 1977). Thus, by activating aggressive thoughts (through priming), the effect of those thoughts on viewing preferences can be determined.

The priming manipulation in the present study involved the induction of an aggressive fantasy and examined the question: Do aggressive fantasies increase the preference for viewing violence? The fact that media violence primarily exists in the form of visual images suggests that aggressive fantasies may be particularly relevant to an understanding of television viewing preferences. Previous research has shown that the viewing of violence is positively related to aggressive fantasies (Feshbach, 1976). One causal explanation for this relationship can be found in Feshbach's (1961) research showing that watching violence on television resulted in an increase in fantasy aggression. However, a more recent study by Fenigstein (1979) suggests that the opposite causal relationship is also possible: The existence of aggressive fantasies may lead to a preference for viewing violence. This study, using both males and females, first had subjects express either an aggressive or a nonaggressive fantasy and then, as in the study described earlier, determined whether the fantasy affected the subjects' interest in viewing media violence.

The use of fantasies in the present research has another implication. Singer (1966) has shown that the expression of specific fantasies may arouse corresponding motives; that is, the induction of aggressive fantasies may lead to a heightened motivation toward aggression. Thus, the present research may be construed as testing the effects of aggressive motives on the preference for viewing violence. More generally, the use of fantasy in the series of studies to be reported allows us to examine the effects of different motivational states on attraction to the media.

After giving their informed consent, subjects were asked to create an imaginative story that included each of 24 words in a list supplied by the experimenter. For half the subjects, the list contained 10 words with aggressive connotations, such as *hit, hate, fight,* and *anger;* the remaining subjects were given lists that contained 10 matching nonaggressive words, for example, *hold, love, join* and *joy.* The other 14 words on the list were neutral and the same for both groups (e.g., *walk, car, ball, stop*). Subsequent content analyses confirmed that subjects using the aggressive words did, in fact, write stories that were significantly more aggressive than those written by subjects using the nonaggressive words. Moreover, consistent with our assumptions concerning the relationship between fantasy expression and motivational states, subjects who had used the aggressive words perceived their stories as expressing significantly more fear and anger and as reflecting significantly greater needs for aggression than the nonaggressive-word subjects.

After completing their stories, all subjects were given the same opportunities to choose films as described earlier. It was found that the films chosen by men were significantly more violent than films chosen by women. More important to the present hypothesis, fantasy aggression increased the amount of violence in films chosen by men, although it had no effect on the violent content of women's film choices. Again, these effects were independent of the films' action and interest content.

These results support the conclusion that men who have entertained aggressive thoughts or images have a heightened interest in viewing violence. This again suggests a circular process: Watching violence on television stimulates fantasy aggression, and aggressive fantasies lead to a heightened preference for viewing media violence. A corollary finding of the present research was that men, in general (i.e., independent of any experimentally manipulated aggressive behavior or fantasies), prefer to view violence more than women do. It can be assumed that, due to different socialization pressures, men are more likely than women in our society to act aggressively or to have aggressive fantasies (cf. Bandura, 1973). These sex differences in the preference for viewing violence, then, may be seen as consistent with the argument that those who are more cognitively preoccupied with aggressive thoughts are more likely to want to view violence by others. Women's indifference or antipathy toward media violence in the present study was presumably a reflection of a lifetime's lack of interest or involvement in aggression, a history that could not be overcome by the brief experimental experiences used.

SEXUAL-AGGRESSIVE FANTASIES
AND ATTRACTION TO PORNOGRAPHY

The previous research has established an important antecedent of the preference for viewing violence: aggressive thoughts or images. Does this finding suggest a more general mechanism for exposure to media stimuli, namely that the activation of any thought or motive results in corresponding viewing preferences? We examined this possibility next by using sexually oriented material.

One form of pornography that is becoming increasingly available is that depicting aggression against women. Such portrayals of sexual violence often show the woman as resisting the sexual assault at first, but gradually becoming more and more sexually aroused, until her resistance is completely overwhelmed by passion. These portrayals, though disturbingly out of touch with reality, are readily available in our society and have been the subject of a number of recent experimental investigations. Several studies have now demonstrated that after viewing these stimuli (but not after viewing rape scenes in which the victim is hurt or abused), males (as well as females) tend to become more sexually aroused (Malamuth, 1981a; Malamuth, Heim, & Feshbach, 1980). In addition, they more readily accept the myth that some women actually enjoy rape (Malamuth & Check, 1980b) and they are more likely to act aggressively toward women (Donnerstein, 1980; Donnerstein & Berkowitz, 1981). In general, it may be suggested that as pornographic images become more violent, even "normal" adults become more calloused in their attitudes toward rape and sexual abuse, as reflected in the finding that a disturbing proportion of college males—about 35%—admit to at least a possibility of their committing rape if they were "assured that no one would know" and that they "could in no way be punished" (Malamuth, 1981b).

In view of the detrimental effects of such pornographic stimuli and their proliferation in society, it becomes important to understand why persons seek out sexual-aggressive stimuli. One possibility is suggested by the finding that men who have a relatively high proclivity to aggress against women, as well as those who admit to the possibility of committing rape, are more sexually responsive to rape scenes (including those that portray an unaroused victim) and, presumably, are more attracted to such stimuli (Malamuth & Donnerstein, 1983). Causal inferences, however, remain ambiguous because these correlational data are consistent with at least two different causal hypotheses. Watching violent-sexual events may enhance tendencies toward rape (and, as noted, there is experimental evidence in support of this hypothesis); another causal explanation that has not been investigated is that individuals who have tendencies toward sexual violence—and often have sexual-aggressive fantasies (e.g., Abel, 1983)—may be more attracted to media depictions of rape.

The following study examined whether aggressive and sexual thoughts, activated through fantasy induction, would heighten one's interest in watching rape depictions. Although it has been shown that watching pornographic depictions of rape leads to aggressive-sexual fantasies (Malamuth, 1981a), the opposite causal relationship has not been tested. In the present research, male subjects created either a sexual, an aggressive, a sexual-aggressive, or a neutral fantasy and then were given an opportunity to select films, varying in sexual and aggressive content, for viewing. It was hypothesized that the induction of a fantasy that activated both sexual and aggressive motives would lead to the strongest preference for viewing portrayals of rape.

Prior to their participation, all subjects were forewarned concerning the use of sexual stimuli, were told of their right to withdraw at any time without penalty, and were asked to give their informed consent to participate. In the first part of the study, subjects were given one of four lists and were asked to make up fantasy stories that included each of 20 words provided on their list. For one group of subjects, 10 of the words on the list had sexual connotations (e.g., *body, excite, undress, caress:* for another group, 10 of the words had aggressive connotations (e.g., *hurt, anger, insult, pain;* a third group of subjects received a list containing 5 sexual and 5 aggressive words; and the list given to the fourth group contained neither sexual nor aggressive words. The other 10 words on everyone's list were identical and neutral in content. Thus, four different kinds of fantasies were experimentally induced: sexual, aggressive, sexual-aggressive, and neutral. Preliminary content analyses indicated that the fantasy-induction manipulation was successful.

After this, subjects were told that the next part of the study involved the use of visual stimuli and were presented with a list of descriptions of 13 films (with each film supposedly lasting a few minutes), out of which they were to choose 5 for viewing. Each film description had previously been rated for its interest, action, violence, and sexual content. In accordance with experimental expectations, these ratings confirmed that two of the films could be characterized as erotic-sexual in nature (e.g., "a chance encounter on a beach leads to several glorious hours of lovemaking") two as aggressive (e.g., "a mild disagreement between two business partners slowly escalates into a deadly fight") two as depicting rapes in which the woman is portrayed as sexually aroused (e.g., "a gang of thugs make a young girl submit to repeated rapes and she loves it") and two as rapes in which the woman is clearly victimized (e.g., "a man breaks into a woman's home, and at the point of a gun, viciously forces her to have sex"). Two types of rape depictions involving different outcomes were used because previous research has suggested that normal males respond with considerably more sexual arousal when the rape victim is shown as sexually enjoying the experience than when she is seen as abhorring the assault (Malamuth et al., 1980; Malamuth & Check, 1980a, 1980b); it was assumed that this variable might affect attraction as well. The remaining five films were neither sexual nor aggressive in content.

As with the previous study, few subjects made any explicit connection between the fantasy part of the experiment and the film choices. At the conclusion of the study, an attempt was made to discredit the rape myths that may have been communicated by the film descriptions. Specifically, all participants were told, in part, that "although pornographic material sometimes depicts women as reacting positively to violent or aggressive sexual behavior, there is, in fact, no evidence whatsoever to support this view." Previous research has shown that such debriefing techniques are effective in offsetting the image of a sexually stimulated rape victim (Check & Malamuth, 1984; Donnerstein & Berkowitz, 1981).

Results and Discussion

The major objective of the present study was to determine whether one's interest in viewing portrayals of rape would be heightened by thoughts and images that were sexual, or aggressive, or both. In order to test this possibility, the sex and violence ratings for each film were multiplied to yield a sexual-violence score. The mean sexual-violence scores of the five films chosen by each subject are shown in Table 6.4. Nonorthogonal planned comparisons found that those subjects who had expressed fantasies involving both aggression and sex were more interested in viewing rape scenes than any other group, $F(1, 44) = 11.9$, $p < .003$; the remaining groups did not differ significantly from each other. That is, compared to the neutral fantasy group, neither aggressive fantasies nor sexual fantasies, by themselves, heightened the preference for watching violent pornography; only fantasies that contained elements of both sex and aggression led to an increase in the desire to watch a rape on film.

Although it was expected that subjects who had created a sexual-aggressive fantasy would show a greater preference for rape scenes in which the victim was

TABLE 6.4
Mean Sexual-Violence Scores of Films
Chosen as a Function of Fantasy

Fantasy Conditions	Nonsexual	Sexual
Nonaggressive	11.6	13.5
Aggressive	13.0	20.0

Note. $n = 12$ per cell. Scores ranged from 6 (low) to 31 (high).

portrayed as aroused, these scenes were no more preferred than rape scenes in which the victim was hurt. Part of the reason for this may be the lack of specificity in the fantasies that were induced. The sexual-aggressive fantasies necessarily included elements of sexual activity and harm, but did not have to involve any suggestion of sexual arousal on the part of the victim. Most rape fantasies did not portray a sexually aroused victim, and this may have had the inadvertent effect of creating congruent viewing preferences. Additional content analyses will examine the specific nature of the rape fantasies written, but in general, future research should attempt to control the nature of the fantasy induced more precisely.

The present research suggests that the arousal of sexual-aggressive thoughts or motives in males may predispose them toward seeking out media depictions of sexual violence. This finding is clearly consistent with and helps explain the earlier correlational research showing that men who harbor aggressive feelings toward women or who perceive themselves as capable of committing rape (and who presumably entertain such fantasies) are more attracted to depictions of rape (cf. Malamuth & Spinner, 1980). Moreover, these results suggest an ominous circularity such that inclinations toward sexually abusive behavior result in greater attraction to aggressive-sexual stimuli, while at the same time, exposure to such depictions increases the likelihood of rape.

AFFILIATIVE FANTASIES
AND VIEWING PREFERENCES

Another psychological motive that may play an important role in attraction to a variety of media presentations is affiliation, defined by Atkinson, Heyns, and Veroff (1954) as a concern with "establishing, maintaining, or restoring a positive affective relationship with another person" (p. 455). It seems plausible, for example, that some persons are attracted to the afternoon television soaps because of the multiple opportunities they afford for affiliative fulfillment (see

McGuire, 1974). Group viewing of a television soap opera in a dormitory lounge is itself an attractive, rewarding social event, but even those who watch alone may be provided with potentially interesting topics of conversation for later socializing. In addition, the opportunity for social comparison (Festinger, 1954) with the characters' interpersonal problems on these programs may be a strong inducement for those who are motivated by affiliative concerns. Finally, it may be suggested that long-term viewing of serials is likely to lead to the development of affiliative ties with the screen characters (Esslin, 1981).

The following experiment focused on situationally induced affiliative motivation as a causal antecedent of preference for affiliative themes on television. In the mold of other studies reviewed in this chapter, affiliative fantasies were induced by having subjects write imaginative stories containing words with affiliative connotations. Subsequently, preferences were expressed for program descriptions varying in affiliative content. In addition, this study examined the effects of the previously induced fantasy on subject's interest in and recall for an actual 15-minute video segment involving a strong affiliative theme.

The subjects were 47 female and 30 male undergraduates who participated during a class period as part of a course requirement in introductory psychology. In the initial phase of a four-part procedure, subjects were given a list of words to be used in constructing an "imaginative story describing an event," presumably for the purpose of "investigating the effects of verbal stimuli on thought processes." Subjects in the control condition were given a list of six nouns to be used in their story including, for example, *child, park,* and *dog.* Subjects in the affiliative-fantasy condition received a list of the same six nouns alternating with six additional words relating to affiliation: *help, love, friend, warm, agreement,* and *together.* All subjects were provided with a series of nine questions (developed by Atkinson & McClelland, 1948, in their pioneering work on the projective measurement of motivation) to guide them in their writing and had 10 minutes to complete their stories. Subjectively, there were no significant differences between groups in either length or affective tone of the stories they wrote.

As a check on the success of the fantasy manipulation, 20 randomly selected stories, 10 written by control subjects and the other 10 by subjects in the experimental group, were independently scored for affiliative content by three undergraduates blind to condition and trained in the objective scoring system developed by Atkinson et al. (1954) to measure the "need for affiliation." For each rater independently, as well as for their combined ratings, the stories of the affiliative-fantasy group were scored as significantly more reflective of the need for affiliation than stories written by the control group ($p < .001$ for each rater).

In the second phase of the study, subjects were given six descriptions of program episodes taken from *TV Guide* magazine (with the names of the shows deleted) and were asked to rank order the descriptions according to "how interested you are in watching" the described episodes "based on your current feelings.'' Because the rank ordering was presumably to allow the instructor to decide what would be shown in a subsequent class meeting, subjects did not discern any connection between this and the previous phase of the experiment. The six program descriptions, selected to represent a wide range of affiliative content, had been previously scored for mean affiliative and achievement content based on the ratings of a class of 23 students, working from written descriptions of affiliative and achievement motives (McClelland & Steele, 1972).

After the rank ordering was completed, all subjects in the control group and most of the subjects in the affiliative-fantasy group viewed a 15-minute video-taped segment taken from a television drama selected for its strong affiliative theme and the relative absence of any achievement content. The segment dealt with the vicissitudes of a developing relationship between a fatherless boy and a ''big brother'' adult male, and ended at a critical point when the outcome of the relationship was still in doubt. Subjects were then given a questionnaire that first asked them to rate their interest ''in seeing how things turn out'' between the two persons in the program, and then asked them a series of 11 factual questions pertaining to events in the segment.

Results and Discussion

The top half of Table 6.5 summarizes the major results of the rank-ordering phase of the study. It was hypothesized that subjects in the affiliative-fantasy condition would show greater interest in viewing affiliation-oriented episodes

TABLE 6.5
Effects of Experimental Manipulation of Affiliative Fantasies
on Viewing Behavior

	Fantasy Condition		
Dependent Variable	Affiliative	Control	Significance
Interest in viewing episode with the most affili-	M 3.54	2.87	$F(1, 73) = 5.055$
ative description	N 44	33	$P = .028$
(6 = most interest)			
Affiliation-interest index based on all rankings	M 30.19	28.57	$F(1, 73) = 5.413$
(36 = most interest)	N 44	33	$P = .023$
(20 = least interest)			
Rated interest in how the relationship turned	M 4.53	4.12	$F(1, 63) = 2.348$
out	N 34	33	$P = .130$
(6 = most interest)			
Number of correct answers to questions about	M 8.65	7.94	$F(1, 63) = 4.260$
events	N 34	33	$P = .043$
(11 = maximum)			

than would subjects in the control condition. This was confirmed in two ways. The one episode description that had been rated highest in affiliative content (and coincidentally, lowest in achievement content) received a significantly higher mean ranking of interest from affiliative-fantasy subjects than from control subjects. In addition, an "affiliation-interest index" was derived for each subject by weighting the ranking of interest of each episode description by judges' affiliative-content scores and summing the product; affiliative subjects showed significantly greater average affiliation-interest indices than control subjects.

There were no consistent sex differences in preference for affiliative content, nor was there any significant treatment by sex interactions, either for rankings of the most affiliative episode description or for the affiliation-interest index. Thus, unlike the gender effects found for aggressive fantasies in the study described earlier, both males and females in the affiliative-fantasy condition showed greater interest in viewing affiliation-related programs than did their counterparts in the control condition. Whereas aggression may be a gender-related issue in our society, the present study suggests that affiliative interests and concerns for college-age subjects may be independent of gender.

The bottom half of Table 6.5 presents the major findings concerning subjects' responses to the 15-minute affiliative segment. Compared to the control subjects, subjects whose affiliative motivation had been aroused by the earlier fantasy manipulation showed a greater interest in viewing the outcome of the relationship between the two principal characters, although the difference was not statistically significant. It was also expected that the affiliative-fantasy group would demonstrate greater attention to the video segment as measured by better mean performance on the factual questions, and this effect was confirmed by the analyses. Again, there were no main effects for sex or treatment by sex interactions for either measure.

Additional observations support the conclusion that subjects in the affiliative-fantasy condition were generally more interested in the viewed segment. A team of undergraduates, blind to experimental conditions, observed subjects from behind a one-way mirror during the viewing phase of the experiment. Each observer kept a record of a particular subject's eye contact with the screen while the video tape was on. Although the reliability of the data is questionable, the mean eye-contact time was higher for subjects in the affiliative-fantasy condition than for control subjects.

The results show that situational arousal of affiliative thoughts by means of a simple 10-minute fantasy induction can influence viewing of affiliative themes on television 40 minutes later. It may be suggested that affiliative fantasies in real life or those induced by attentive exposure to certain television programs may have a far more powerful effect on motivation to view further depictions of affiliation, perhaps leading to a cycle of impact and attraction analogous to the interactive, bidirectional relationships discussed earlier.

EXPLANATORY MECHANISMS

A number of different psychological mechanisms may mediate the demonstrated relationships between certain thoughts or actions and the subsequent interest in viewing related events in the media. This speculative discussion focuses largely on the issue of media violence, but the processes proposed here may be more generally applicable to a wide range of media content. Mechanisms concerned with the relationship between aggressive behavior and media violence are discussed first, followed by mechanisms that address the relationship between fantasy aggression and media violence.

Actions and Media Attraction

Social Comparison. Festinger's (1954) influential theory of social comparison argues that persons need to evaluate their opinions and abilities by comparing themselves to others. This need produces a motivation to seek out information about others in an attempt to assess the validity or appropriateness of their own feelings or behavior. Presumably, when a person acts aggressively, questions may be raised concerning the correctness or effectiveness of such action. One means of understanding or gaining some perspective on that behavior would be to observe others behaving that way, and the mass media readily provides such opportunities. In this context, it is interesting to note that exposure to sexually explicit material may also be a function of social-comparison needs; given the difficulty of discussing sexual behavior with others, pornographic stimuli represent an important source of information that helps in the evaluation of one's own sexual behavior (Byrne, 1976). In general, the media may satisfy the need for information concerning one's actions, especially when that behavior is socially prohibited and few other sources of comparison are available.

Justification Processes. Not only do persons want to understand and evaluate their behavior, they may also seek to explain or justify it. Given the occurrence of an act of aggression, along with clear moral and social sanctions against such behavior, it may be assumed that persons need to find some means of rendering such behavior acceptable. Brock and Buss (1962), for example, showed that one means of reducing the dissonance attendant on hurting another is to minimize the amount of pain inflicted. Similarly, Glass (1964) found that persons who were induced to aggress against another person came to derogate their victims, presumably as a means of justifying their aggression.

Media violence may also be an important source of moral reassurance for one's own aggression. One means of justifying behavior that might otherwise be considered wrong is to convince oneself that such behavior is normative (i.e., something that everyone does). Thus, guilt over hurting another may be alleviated by seeking out the message implicit in media violence: Aggression occurs all the time. The sheer ubiquity of media portrayals of violence may certainly add to the perceived legitimacy of such behavior. If one comes to believe that the world is a violent place and that the use of aggression is widespread, then aggressive behavior becomes more defensible—a form of rationalization closely related to the classical defense mechanisms of projection. This may explain why the more aggressive a person is, the more likely he or she is to believe that others are aggressive (Huesmann, 1982).

Does the viewing of violence lead to a distorted view of the world as a violent place where one's own aggression may be necessary and appropriate? Thomas and Drabman (1975) examined how television violence affected children's expectations of other children's aggression. After viewing either a violent or a nonviolent television excerpt, children were asked how they thought other children would deal with a series of conflict situations. Those who had been exposed to the violence were more likely to predict that other children would react aggressively to conflict. This perceived normativeness, presumably, can also ease concerns about one's own behavior. Along similar lines, Gerbner et al. (1980) have argued that the more persons are exposed to the world of television, the more their conceptions of social reality will be congruent with those represented on the screen. They consistently found that heavy television viewers share a relatively homogeneous conception of a mean and dangerous world, a world where they are likely to become involved in real violence. Although Gerbner was primarily concerned with the viewer's increased apprehension and fear of victimization, the perception of the world as a dangerous place could just as well serve as a justification for one's own aggressive behavior.

Media violence may justify prior aggression, not only through the suggestion that such behavior is normative or appropriate, but also by implying that aggressive actions are an effective response to the situation. Previous research has shown that the appropriateness or effectiveness of the violence portrayed in the media is related to the occurrence of aggression (e.g., Berkowitz, 1965; Hoyt, 1970; Meyer, 1972; Slife & Rychlak, 1982). Berkowitz and Powers (1979), for example, found that aggression was enhanced by media violence only when the portrayal was preceded by an introduction making it clear that the aggression to be shown was justified. If the portrayal of justifiable violence establishes conditions conducive to subsequent aggression, those conditions may also support the viewer's prior aggression. A field study by Hartnagel et al. (1975) found a relationship among adolescents between aggressive behavior and the perceived effectiveness of the violence portrayed on television. One interpretation of these results, consistent with the present argument, is that aggressive actions may be justified by seeking out evidence that such acts are successful. Thus, although the mere frequency of violence in the media may be sufficient to change viewers' attitudes toward the acceptability of aggression, to the degree that the portrayal justified violence as useful or appropriate, it is especially likely to be attractive to aggressive persons.

Desensitization. The final explanation to be considered with regard to the effects of aggressive behavior on the viewing of media violence involves the process of desensitization. As persons are exposed to more and more violence, they apparently become less emotionally responsive to such acts (Cline, Croft, & Courrier, 1973; Thomas, Horton, Lippincott, & Drabman, 1977). Similarly, massive viewing of pornography may lead to a loss of sensitivity toward rape victims (Zillmann & Bryant, 1982). It may be argued that persons who aggress will ordinarily experience an emotionally aversive state as a result of the pain they inflict and the attendant guilt and anxiety. If persons are motivated to reduce the emotional consequences of their behavior, they may do so by either cognitively trivializing the pain inflicted (e.g., Brock & Buss, 1962) or, as the desensitization research suggests, by repeated exposure to media violence.

Desensitization, in turn, may alter the viewer's tolerance for aggressive behavior (Drabman & Thomas, 1974a, 1974b; Thomas & Drabman, 1975), thus contributing to the justification processes discussed earlier. In one study, Drabman and Thomas (1974a) showed some fourth-graders a violent movie and then gave them responsibility for monitoring the behavior of two younger children who, over time, became progressively more aggressive toward one another. Relative to a no-film control group, the fourth-graders who had previously seen the aggressive film took longer to report the fighting and were evidently more accepting of the aggressive behavior. This desensitization process leading to increased tolerance can also be used to render one's own aggression more acceptable. Thus, the viewing of media violence can operate in myriad ways to dispel the concerns that aggressive persons may have regarding their behavior.

Thoughts and Media Attraction

Why should persons who are thinking aggressive thoughts, for example, be interested in viewing media violence? A number of different psychological explanations may be offered, some involving mechanisms similar to the ones discussed in the previous section and others drawing on some novel perspectives.

Perceptual Readiness. One explanation of why persons may be interested in viewing whatever is on their minds may be derived from research in cognition. Neisser (1976) argues that imagining an event requires the same cognitive activity as actually perceiving the event. Perceptual activity involves an "anticipatory schema," which directs and prepares the perceiver to seek out and accept certain kinds of information rather than others. On the basis of this model, it may be suggested that thinking about aggression activates an anticipatory aggression schema that creates both a "readiness" to perceive aggression and a tendency to explore the environment for schema-relevant information, that is, aggressive stimuli, which may take the form of attraction to media violence.

This argument may be related to the research on perceptual sets or readiness, showing that a given stimulus may be perceived in different ways depending on the psychological state of the perceiver (Bruner, 1973). In an especially relevant study, Toch and Schulte (1961) explored the notion that police students, because of their experiences and expectancies with respect to the occurrence of violent crime, would be predisposed to perceive ambiguous visual stimuli as depicting violent events. When stereoscopically presented with two different pictures, one showing a violent scene and the other a nonviolent scene, the police students tended to resolve the perceptual ambiguity in favor of the violence twice as often as a control group of university students. In the context of the present research, it may be suggested that this effect may not be limited to imposed stimuli; it may also apply to obtainable stimuli. That is, if as a result of cognitive preoccupation with crime persons are ready to perceive violence, then it may be the case that such cognitive concerns will also lead people to seek out displays of violence.

The same conclusions may be derived from research on availability. A wide range of cognitive judgments may be influenced by the relative availability or salience of objects or events, that is, their accessibility in the processes of perception, memory, or construction from imagination (McArthur, 1980; Nisbett & Ross, 1980; Tversky & Kahneman, 1973). In effect, the more easily an occurrence is imagined, the greater its influence on subsequent thought processes (e.g., Carroll, 1978). Although much of the research on the "availability heuristic" has been concerned with biases in the encoding and recall of information (e.g., Kahneman & Tversky, 1973; Taylor & Fiske, 1978), it may be suggested that salient images also produce biases in attention and exposure to information. Thus, to the extent that the perceiver is imagining an aggressive act, such acts become especially salient to the imaginer, and he or she is more likely not only to attend to other violent stimuli, but also to seek out such events actively.

Social Comparison.   Media violence may have information value concerning the nature of aggressive fantasies. A person engaging in aggressive (or sexual) fantasies may develop an abiding curiosity about the fantasized behaviors. Again, one of the few means available for satisfying that curiosity about behaviors that are very private and largely prohibited is through social comparison with images provided by the media.

Mere Exposure.   As a result of cognitive preoccupation with some idea, one is in a sense repeatedly exposed to that thought or image, and repeated exposure may enhance the attractiveness of the image and increase the desire to seek it out (Zajonc, 1968).

Desensitization.   As discussed earlier, extended exposure to media violence has the effect of trivializing violence and diminishing its emotional impact. Thus, the relationship between exposure to television violence and fear of crime (Gerbner & Gross, 1976a, 1976b) may be understood in terms of the desensitizing effects of continued viewing. Persons who are preoccupied with violence, perhaps because of concerns over their personal safety, may be drawn to media violence as a means of reducing their fear (Zillmann, 1980, 1982).

Fantasies and Motives.   Finally, the expression of specific fantasies can arouse corresponding motives (Singer, 1966). Thus, subjects in the aggression-fantasy condition may have experienced a heightened desire to act aggressively. Under these circumstances, media violence may have become especially attractive, either for its informational value or as a means of vicariously satisfying the aggressive motive (Geen, 1976, 1978; Pytkowicz, Wagner, & Sarason, 1967; Rosenbaum & DeCharms, 1960).

SUMMARY AND CONCLUSIONS

In some early pioneering work on the media, Schramm, Lyle, and Parker (1961) cautioned researchers to get away from "what television does to children" and to be more concerned with "what children do with television." In effect, they were arguing that regardless of how powerful a source of information television may be, that power is only a potential whose realization is necessarily dependent on the internal attributes of the viewer. In a sense, the effects of viewing are very much determined by what program a viewer chooses to watch, what aspects of that program the viewer selects to learn, and what learned behaviors the viewer decides to act on. Their caution was simply that an understanding of media effects requires an understanding of the motives that the viewer brings to the media. This advice has largely gone unheeded: The dominant strategy of most psychologists studying the media has been to examine the media's effects on attitudes and behavior with little regard for the motives of the viewer.

The present chapter describes an experimental methodology that was developed to explore some of the psychological states that may underlie different viewing preferences. The research has shown that aggressive thoughts and behaviors increase the preference for viewing violence, that the arousal of sexual-aggressive fantasies affects the desire to view violent pornography, and that the desirability of viewing affiliation-oriented television programs can be influenced by the experimental manipulation of social motives. In general, this research demonstrates that just as what one watches in the media can have an impact on subsequent behavior, so too can how one thinks and acts affect what one wants to watch.

A number of cautions should be introduced here, specifically with respect to the implications of the present research for attraction to media violence. In view of the enormous amount of violence on television and the fact that some of the most popular programs on TV are among the most violent, it may be reasonable to assume that a large segment of the viewing audience is fascinated by and drawn to programs portraying violence—and so, by implication, large numbers of viewers harbor aggressive thoughts or tendencies. These intuitive assumptions, however, have not been empirically validated. Diener and DeFour (1978) have shown that neither program popularity based on television ratings nor program preferences assessed in a controlled experimental setting were related to the amount of violence on the program. Because themes of physical action, risk, and conflict are often abundant in violent programs, these dramatic factors can easily explain the popularity of the program, independent of its violent content. In addition, numerous surveys and the existence of a number of citizen action groups clearly suggest that many persons consider media violence to be unattractive and even offensive.

However, the fact that violence may be a less important factor in drawing viewers to a program than is generally assumed in no way detracts from the findings of the present research. This research has not been solely or even primarily directed toward explaining the popularity of violence in the media. Rather, these laboratory studies have been concerned with testing the viability of a theoretical causal relationship between aggressive thoughts or actions and a tendency to seek out violent media stimuli. The research does support the contention that such a process may exist, and it may help to explain the frequently observed relationship between the viewing of media violence and aggressive behavior.

The present findings concerning the effects of aggression on the preference for viewing media violence are not necessarily antagonistic to the research demonstrating the aggression-facilitating effects of observed media violence. It is quite possible that aggressive behavior results in congruent viewing preferences, while at the same time exposure to the media shapes subsequent behaviors. This bidirectional flow of effects may provide a more complete understanding, specifically, of the relationship between aggression and media violence and, more generally, of all behavior related to media viewing. Unfortunately, the interactional nature of the relationship between aggression and media violence also suggests a bleak circularity, with already aggressive children watching more violence, which only begets more aggression. In addition, this circularity can easily be abetted by other social factors. For example, aggressive children are likely to have fewer friends, and thus fewer available social activities, and so are likely to spend more of their time watching television (Eron, 1982). The violence they watch may then reassure them of the appropriateness of their own behavior, while at the same time teaching them new aggressive behaviors, which only exacerbates their already problematic peer relationships and keeps the cycle going.

However, the present research also provides cause for optimism and a means out of this circularity. Media violence need not be attractive or have any lasting effect unless the viewer is in some way motivated to view aggressive displays. Slife and Rychlak (1982), for example, found that children who showed no preference for media violence were unlikely to imitate such behavior, despite extended exposure. It may be suggested that children will not be interested in or affected by the viewing of media violence unless or until aggression becomes a meaningful part of their own existence. In principle then, to remove the audience for media violence, we need to construct an environment where people find it unnecessary to think or act aggressively; in reality, this is clearly a formidable problem.

REFERENCES

Abel, G. G.   (1983). Preventing men from becoming rapists. In G. Albee, S. Gordon, & H. Leitenberg (Eds.), *Promoting sexual responsibility and preventing sexual problems* (pp. 238–250). Hanover, NH: University Press of New England.

Andison, F. S.   (1977). TV violence and viewer aggression: A cumulation of study results, 1956–1976. *Public Opinion Quarterly, 41,* 314–331.

Atkinson, J. W., Heyns, R. W., & Veroff, J.   (1954). The effect of experimental arousal of the affiliation motive on thematic apperception. *Journal of Abnormal and Social Psychology, 49,* 455–460.

Atkinson, J. W., & McClelland, D. C.   (1948). The projective expression of needs. *Journal of Experimental Psychology, 38,* 643–658.

Bandura, A.   (1973). *Aggression: A social learning analysis.* Englewood Cliffs, NJ: Prentice-Hall.

Belson, W.   (1978). *Television violence and the adolescent boy.* London: Saxon House.

Berkowitz, L.   (1965). Some aspects of observed aggression. *Journal of Personality and Social Psychology, 2,* 359–369.

Berkowitz, L., & Powers, P.   (1979). Effects of timing and justification of witnessed aggression on observers' punitiveness. *Journal of Research in Personality, 13,* 71–80.

Bogart, L.   (1972). Warning: The surgeon-general has determined that TV violence is moderately dangerous to your child's mental health. *Public Opinion Quarterly, 36,* 391–421.

Boyanowsky, E. O., Newtson, D., & Walster, E.   (1974). Film preferences following murder. *Communications Research, 1,* 32–43.

Brock, T. C., & Buss, A. H.   (1962). Dissonance, aggression, and evaluation of pain. *Journal of Abnormal and Social Psychology, 65,* 197–202.

Bruner, J. S.   (1973). *Beyond the information given: Studies in the psychology of knowing.* New York: Norton.

Byrne, D.   (1976). Sexual imagery. In J. Money & H. Musaph (Eds.), *Handbook of sexology* (pp. 336–345). Amsterdam: Excerpta Medica.

Carroll, J. S.   (1978). The effect of imagining an event on expectations for the event: An interpretation in terms of the availability heuristic. *Journal of Experimental Social Psychology, 14,* 88–96.

Check, J., & Malamuth, N.   (1984). Can there be positive effects of participation in pornography experiments? *Journal of Sex Research, 20,* 14–31.

Cline, V. B., Croft, R. G., & Courrier, S.   (1973). Desensitization of children to television violence. *Journal of Personality and Social Psychology, 27,* 360–365.

Comstock, G.   (1978). A contribution beyond controversy. *Contemporary Psychology, 23,* 807–809.

Comstock, G.   (1980). New emphases in research on the effects of television and film violence. In E. L. Palmer & A. Dorr (Eds.), *Children and the faces of television: Teaching, violence, selling* (pp. 129–148). New York: Academic Press.

Diener, E., & DeFour, D.   (1978). Does television violence enhance program popularity? *Journal of Personality and Social Psychology, 36,* 333–341.

Dominick, J. R., & Greenberg, B. S.   (1972). Attitudes toward violence: The interaction of television exposure, family attitudes, and social class. In G. A. Comstock & E. A. Rubinstein (Eds.), *Television and social behavior* (Vol. 3): *Television and adolescent aggressiveness* (pp. 314–335). Washington, DC: U.S. Government Printing Office.

Donnerstein, E. (1980). Aggressive-erotica and violence against women. *Journal of Personality and Social Psychology, 39,* 269–277.

Donnerstein, E., & Berkowitz, L. (1981). Victim reactions in aggressive erotic films as a factor in violence against women. *Journal of Personality and Social Psychology, 41,* 710–724.

Doob, A. N., & MacDonald, G. E. (1979). Television viewing and fear of victimization: Is the relationship causal? *Journal of Personality and Social Psychology, 37,* 170–179.

Dorr, A., & Kovaric, P. (1980). Televised violence and its effects. In E. L. Palmer & A. Dorr (Eds.), *Children and the faces of television: Teaching, violence, selling* (pp. 183–200). New York: Academic Press.

Drabman, R. S., & Thomas, M. H. (1974a). Does media violence increase children's toleration of real-life aggression? *Developmental Psychology, 10,* 418–421.

Drabman, R. S., & Thomas, M. H. (1974b). Exposure to filmed violence and children's tolerance to real-life aggression. *Personality and Social Psychology Bulletin, 1,* 198–199.

Eron, L. D. (1982). Parent-child interaction, television violence, and aggression of children. *American Psychologist, 37,* 197–211.

Eron, L. D., Lefkowitz, M. M., Huesmann, L. R., & Walder, L. D. (1972). Does television violence cause aggression? *American Psychologist, 27,* 253–263.

Esslin, M. (1981). *The age of television.* Stanford, CA: Stanford Alumni Association.

Fenigstein, A. (1979). Does aggression cause a preference for viewing media violence? *Journal of Personality and Social Psychology, 37,* 2307–2317.

Feshbach, S. (1961). The stimulating versus cathartic effects of a vicarious aggressive activity. *Journal of Abnormal and Social Psychology, 63,* 381–385.

Feshbach, S. (1976). The role of fantasy in the response to television. *Journal of Social Issues, 32,* 71–85.

Festinger, L. (1954). A theory of social comparison processes. *Human Relations, 7,* 117–140.

Geen, R. G. (1976). Observing violence in the mass media: Implications of basic research. In R. G. Geen & E. O'Neal (Eds.), *Perspectives on aggression* (pp. 193–234). New York: Academic Press.

Geen, R. G. (1978). Some effects of observing violence upon the behavior of the observer. In B. A. Maher (Ed.), *Progress in experimental personality research* (Vol. 8, pp. 49–92). New York: Academic Press.

Gerbner, G. & Gross, L. (1976a). Living with television: The violence profile. *Journal of Communication, 26,* 173–179.

Gerbner, G., & Gross, L. (1976b, April). The scary world of TV's heavy viewer. *Psychology Today,* pp. 41–45 89.

Gerbner, G., Gross, L., Morgan, M., & Signorielli, N. (1980). The "mainstreaming of America": Violence profile no. 11. *Journal of Communication, 30,* 10–29.

Glass, D. C. (1964). Changes in liking as a means of reducing cognitive discrepancies between self-esteem and aggression. *Journal of Personality, 32,* 531–549.

Goranson, R. E. (1970). Media violence and aggressive behavior: A review of experimental research. In L. Berkowitz (Ed.), *Advances in experimental social psychology* (Vol. 5, pp. 1–31). New York: Academic Press.

Greenberg, B. S. (1975). British children and televised violence. *Public Opinion Quarterly, 38,* 531–547.

Greenberg, B. S., & Gordon, T. F. (1972). Social class and racial differences in children's perception of televised violence. In G. A. Comstock, E. A. Rubinstein, & J. P. Murray (Eds.), *Television and social behavior* (Vol. 5): *Television's effects: Further exploration* (pp. 231–248). Washington, DC: U.S. Government Printing Office.

Hartnagel, T. F., Teevan, J. J., & McIntyre, J. J. (1975). Television violence and violent behavior. *Social Forces, 54,* 341–351.

Higgins, E. T., Rholes, W. S., & Jones, C. R. (1977). Category accessibility and impression formation. *Journal of Experimental Social Psychology, 13,* 141–154.

Hoyt, J. L. (1970). Effects of media violence "justification" on aggression. *Journal of Broadcasting, 14,* 455–465.

Huesmann, L. R. (1982). Television violence and aggressive behavior. In D. Pearl, L. Bouthilet, & J. Lazar (Eds.), *Television and behavior: Ten years of scientific progress and implications for the eighties* (Vol. 2, pp. 126–137). Washington, DC: U.S. Government Printing Office.

Hull, C. L. (1943). *Principles of behavior: An introduction to behavior therapy.* New York: Appleton-Century-Crofts.

Kahneman, D., & Tversky, A. (1973). On the psychology of prediction. *Psychological Review, 80,* 237–251.

Kaplan, R. M., & Singer, R. D. (1976). Television violence and viewer aggression: A re-examination of the evidence. *Journal of Social Issues, 32,* 35–70.

Kenny, D. A. (1972). Threats to the internal validity of cross-lagged panel inference, as related to "Television violence and child aggression: A follow-up study." In G. A. Comstock & E. A. Rubinstein (Eds.), *Television and social behavior* (Vol. 3): *Television and adolescent aggressiveness* (pp. 136–140). Washington, DC: U.S. Government Printing Office.

Konecni, V. J. (1975). Annoyance, type and duration of post-annoyance activity, and aggression: The "cathartic effect." *Journal of Experimental Psychology: General, 104,* 76–102.

Lefkowitz, M. M., Eron, L. D., Walder, L. D., & Huesmann, L. R. (1972). Television violence and child aggression: A follow-up study. In G. A. Comstock & E. A. Rubinstein (Eds.), *Television and social behavior* (Vol. 3): *Television and adolescent aggressiveness* (pp. 35–135). Washington, DC: U.S. Government Printing Office.

Lefkowitz, M. M., & Huesmann, L. R. (1980). Concomitants of television violence viewing in children. In E. L. Palmer & A. Dorr (Eds.), *Children and the faces of television: Teaching, violence, selling* (pp. 163–182). New York: Academic Press.

Malamuth, N. (1981a). Rape fantasies as a function of exposure to violent sexual stimuli. *Archives of Sexual Behavior, 10,* 33–47.

Malamuth, N. (1981b). Rape proclivity among males. *Journal of Social Issues, 37,* 138–157.

Malamuth, N., & Check, J. V. P. (1980a). Penile tumescence and perceptual responses to rape as a function of victim's perceived reaction. *Journal of Applied Social Psychology, 10,* 528–547.

Malamuth, N., & Check, J. V. P. (1980b). Sexual arousal to rape and consenting depictions: The importance of women's arousal. *Journal of Abnormal Psychology, 89,* 763–766.

Malamuth, N., & Donnerstein, E. (1983). The effects of aggressive-pornographic mass media stimuli. In L. Berkowitz (Ed.), *Advances in experimental social psychology* (Vol. 15, pp. 103–136). New York: Academic Press.

Malamuth, N., Heim, M., & Feshbach, S. (1980). Sexual responsiveness of college students to rape depictions: Inhibitory and disinhibitory effects. *Journal of Personality and Social Psychology, 38,* 399–408.

Malamuth, N., & Spinner, R. A. (1980). A longitudinal content analysis of sexual violence in the best-selling erotic magazines. *Journal of Sex Research, 16,* 226–237.

McArthur, L. Z. (1980). What grabs you? The role of attention in impression formation and causal attribution. In T. Higgins, J. Herman, & M. Zanna (Eds.), *Social cognition: The Ontario Symposium* (pp. 201–246). Hillsdale, NJ: Lawrence Erlbaum Associates.

McClelland, D. C., & Steele, R. S. (1972). *Motivation workshops.* New York: General Learning Corp.

McGuire, W. J. (1974). Psychological motives and communication gratification. In J. G. Blumler & E. Katz (Eds.), *The uses of mass communications* (pp. 167–196). Beverly Hills, CA: Sage.

Meyer, T. P.   (1972). Effects of viewing justified and unjustified real film violence on aggressive behavior. *Journal of Personality and Social Psychology, 23,* 21–29.

Neisser, U.   (1976). *Cognition and reality.* San Francisco: Freeman.

Nisbett, R., & Ross, L.   (1980). *Human inference: Strategies and shortcomings of social judgement.* Englewood Cliffs, NJ: Prentice-Hall.

Pearl, D., Bouthilet, L., & Lazar, J. (Eds.).   (1982). *Television and behavior: Ten years of scientific progress and implications for the eighties* (Vols. 1 & 2). Washington, DC: U.S. Government Printing Office.

Pytkowicz, A., Wagner, N., & Sarason, I. G.   (1967). An experimental study of the reduction of hostility through fantasy. *Journal of Personality and Social Psychology, 5,* 295–303.

Rosenbaum, M., & DeCharms, R.   (1960). Direct and vicarious reduction of hostility. *Journal of Abnormal and Social Psychology, 60,* 105–111.

Schramm, W., Lyle, J., & Parker, E.   (1961). *Television in the lives of our children.* Palo Alto, CA: Stanford University Press.

Singer, J. L.   (1966). *Daydreaming.* New York: Random House.

Singer, J. L., & Singer, D. G.   (1980). *Television, imagination, and aggression: A study of preschoolers* Hillsdale, NJ: Lawrence Erlbaum Associates.

Slife, B. D., & Rychlak, J. F.   (1982). Role of affective assessment in modeling aggressive behavior. *Journal of Personality and Social Psychology, 43,* 861–868.

Surgeon-General's Scientific Advisory Committee on Television and Social Behavior.   (1972). *Television and growing up: The impact of televised violence.* Washington, DC: U.S. Government Printing Office.

Taylor, S. E., & Fiske, S. T.   (1978). Salience, attention, and attribution: Top of the head phenomena. In L. Berkowitz (Ed.), *Advances in experimental social psychology* (Vol. 11, pp. 249–288). New York: Academic Press.

Thomas, M. H., & Drabman, R. S.   (1975). Toleration of real-life aggression as a function of exposure to televised violence and age of subject. *Merrill-Palmer Quarterly, 21,* 227–232.

Thomas, M. H., Horton, R. W., Lippincott, E. C., & Drabman, R. S.   (1977). Desensitization to portrayals of real-life aggression as a function of exposure to television violence. *Journal of Personality and Social Psychology, 35,* 450–458.

Toch, H. H., & Schulte, R.   (1961). Readiness to perceive violence as a result of police training. *British Journal of Psychology, 52,* 389–393.

Tulving, E., & Thomson, D. M.   (1973). Encoding specificity and retrieval processes in episodic memory. *Pscyhological Review, 80,* 352–373.

Tversky, A., & Kahneman, D.   (1973). Availability: A heuristic for judging frequency and probability. *Cognitive Psychology, 5,* 207–232.

Zajonc, R. B.   (1968). Attitudinal effects of mere exposure. *Journal of Personality and Social Psychology Monographs, 9*(1, Pt. 2).

Zillmann, D.   (1980). Anatomy of suspense. In P. H. Tannenbaum (Ed.), *The entertainment functions of television* (pp. 133–163). Hillsdale, NJ: Lawrence Erlbaum Associates.

Zillmann, D.   (1982). Television viewing and arousal. In D. Pearl, L. Bouthilet, & J. Lazar (Eds.), *Television and behavior* (Vol. 2, pp. 53–67). Washington, DC: U.S. Government Printing Office.

Zillmann, D., & Bryant, J.   (1982). Pornography, sexual callousness, and trivialization of rape. *Journal of Communication, 32,* 10–21.

7 Fear of Victimization and the Appeal of Crime Drama

Dolf Zillmann
Jacob Wakshlag
Indiana University

Gerbner and his associates (e.g., Gerbner & Gross, 1976a, 1976b; Gerbner, Gross, Morgan, & Signorielli, 1980) have drawn much attention to the possibility that extensive consumption of television, especially of violence-laden crime drama, leads to exaggerated perceptions of crime in society, to apprehensions about becoming a victim of crime, to interpersonal distrust generally, and to fear of one's fellow citizens. In their theorizing, the heightened sense of risk and insecurity is said to increase the citizen's dependence on established authority and to promote the acceptance of its use of force in accomplishing social pacification. Television's "cultivation" of fear, together with the acceptance of authority that this fear nurses, is considered "the established religion of the industrial order, relating to governance as the church did to the state in earlier times" (Gerbner & Gross, 1976a, p. 194).

To back up such a grand proposal, Gerbner and his associates have presented data that show a significant positive correlation between the magnitude of television consumption, on the one hand, and perceptions of dangers in the environment, interpersonal distrust, and apprehensions about becoming a victim of violent crime, on the other. Specifically, heavy television viewers (defined as persons watching 4 or more hours a day) were found to perceive the world as more dangerous, to report greater distrust, and to be more apprehensive about becoming a victim of crime than were light television viewers (persons watching 2 hours a day or less). This correspondence between heavy television consumption and concern about crime was observed in several social strata.

The interpretation of this simple correspondence as proof of a causal relation between exposure to television and fear of victimization has prompted immediate challenges. Doob and Macdonald (1979) considered the observed relationship spurious and succeeded in showing that experience with crime mediates both heavy television viewing and fear of victimization. Sampling respondents from urban and suburban low- and high-crime neighborhoods, these investigators obtained the correlation reported by Gerbner and his associates when all neighborhoods were pooled. Within neighborhoods, this correspondence was negligible, however. The across-neighborhood correlation apparently resulted mainly from experience with crime and its effect on fear of victimization *and* television viewing. Specifically, people living in high-crime areas stay home more than individuals living elsewhere and when staying home, these people watch more television overall (cf. Jackson-Beeck & Sobal, 1980), and crime drama shows in particular (cf. Doob & Macdonald, 1979). Heavy viewing, then, may not appreciably affect fear of victimization.

Reanalyses of the data originally employed by Gerbner et al. proved equally damaging. Statistically controlling for various extraneous variables rendered the reported relationship between heavy viewing and fear of victimization nonexistent for most relevant strata (Hirsch, 1980, 1981a; Hughes, 1980). Furthermore, the analysis of newly collected data, with numerous extraneous variables being statistically controlled, at times produced findings supportive of a relationship (e.g., Pingree & Hawkins, 1981), though at other times, it failed to do so (e.g., Wober, 1978; Wober & Gunter, 1982). Thus, the correspondence between heavy television consumption and fear of victimization, regardless of what it might mean, can only be characterized as somewhat elusive and fragile.

Gerbner and his associates (e.g., Gerbner et al., 1980; Gerbner, Gross, Morgan, & Signorielli, 1981) proposed subprocesses of cultivation that seem to explain, post facto, the absence of a relationship between heavy television consumption and fear of victimization in situations where such an absence was observed. The problems with their theoretical efforts have been disclosed by Hirsch (1981a, 1981b) and need not be detailed here. Suffice it to indicate that the specific conditions under which the proposed subprocesses (i.e., mainstreaming and resonance) should occur remain rather unclear, as does how they interrelate. Precise predictions are not feasible in the face of these ambiguities.

Despite the fact that Hirsch's assault on the theory and research presented by Gerbner and his associates was furious and laden with vituperative accusations, his criticism is quite incomplete. His efforts concentrated on discrediting the relationship between heavy television consumption and fear of victimization, and it looks as though he would have granted proof of a causal connection if the relationship would have survived the statistical control of extraneous variables that are routinely applied in sociological survey research. We infer from the fact that no concerns were voiced about the research approach as such that correlational proof, if sufficiently sophisticated, would have been accepted as proof of cultivation. In other words, the relation would have been considered nonspurious after statistically controlling for a limited number of extraneous variables, and causation would have been accepted as a result. This, of course, is quite unacceptable. First, spuriousness is difficult to rule out because of an unlimited number of extraneous variables that might produce it. Statistical control is thus insufficient to secure causality. Second, and more important for the purpose of our discussion, evidence of a relationship (i.e., co-relation) is consistent with at least two directional causal hypotheses. The cultivation hypothesis is one of them. But what about the reverse causal chain? Instead of heavy exposure causing fear, fear might cause heavy exposure. And to make matters even more complicated, causation could be bidirectional in that different persons in a social aggregate might respond in opposite ways for specifiable reasons. These obvious causal possibilities, oddly enough, have not been considered in the Gerbner–Hirsch controversy over the television cultivation of fear.

In this chapter, we compensate for this neglect. We first briefly discuss the scarce noncorrelational research efforts aimed at demonstrating the cultivation of fear of victimization by exposure to crime drama. Thereafter, we turn to theoretical proposals that project selective exposure to crime drama on the basis of apprehensions about crime, and we review the available research evidence that pertains to these proposals.

DOES CRIME DRAMA PROMOTE FEAR?

Scary drama may well instill fear of victimization for some time after exposure: for minutes, hours, or in exceptional cases, perhaps days. But such occasional transitory reactions do not constitute cultivation effects. Rather, cultivation refers to a process of forming comparatively stable perceptions, attitudes, and apprehensions through repeated and potentially massive exposure to messages that give impetus to the indicated cognitive and affective changes (cf. Gerbner & Gross, 1976a). The conditions necessary for producing effects of this kind are not easily created, and the experimental exploration of these presumed effects is understandably almost nonexistent. Only one experimental attempt at demonstrating the cultivation of fear has been reported. Bryant, Carveth, and Brown (1981) simulated the conditions of heavy versus light viewership that Gerbner et al. had set and then ascertained fear after controlled exposure. Male and female subjects were tested for manifest anxiety (Taylor, 1953) and, within anxiety conditions, assigned to heavy versus light exposure treatments. Light viewers watched at most 2 hours of drama daily. Heavy viewers watched at least 4 hours daily. The exposure treatments lasted 6 weeks. The condition of heavy viewing was subdivided into exposure to crime drama that featured the restoration of justice versus crime drama that dwelled on injustice. This variation was motivated by the suggestion that perceptions of danger and related affective responses should be most pronounced after exposure to drama that fails to exhibit the disablement of the safety-threatening transgressive forces (Zillmann, 1980).

Following the last day's exposure treatment, subjects were again tested for manifest anxiety. Thereafter, they estimated the likelihood of becoming a victim of violent crime and rated their fearfulness regarding this possibility, among other things. The findings concerning the likelihood of victimization and associated fearfulness were similar, though not entirely parallel. Regardless of gender and initial anxiety levels, subjects showed more concern about their personal safety after heavy exposure to crime drama than after light exposure. Although heavy exposure to injustice-laden drama produced the strongest effects on apprehensions, it failed to exceed significantly the effect of heavy exposure to drama featuring the restoration of justice. Manifest anxiety was affected differently, however. Only heavy exposure to injustice-laden crime drama elevated anxiety levels. Heavy exposure to drama with justice-restoring resolutions, compared to light exposure, had no appreciable effect. Most significantly, subjects who were highly anxious initially and who were heavily exposed to injustice in crime drama exhibited by far the highest levels of and greatest increases in manifest anxiety, whereas those subjects who were highly anxious initially and who were in the light-exposure condition or had been heavily exposed to drama with justice-restoring resolutions dropped to the lowest anxiety levels. These drops yielded levels significantly below those associated with subjects who were comparatively nonanxious initially as well as their own initial levels.

To what extent are these findings supportive of the cultivation hypothesis? The findings on the measures likelihood of victimization and fearfulness certainly show the projected impact. The findings on manifest anxiety are discrepant, however, and show a cultivation effect only for injustice-laden drama. Such drama, needless to say, is rather rare on television. Additionally, and inconsistent with cultivation expectations, the findings show that heavy consumption of crime drama in which justice triumphs and which constitutes the mainstay of television, along with light television consumption, has a beneficial anxiety-alleviating effect on initially anxious persons. But can this somewhat inconsistent pattern of effects be attributed to the longitudinal exposure treatment that was used to simulate the causal conditions of the cultivation process? No, it cannot. Subjects responded to the anxiety and fear questions more or less immediately after their last exposure treatment—that is, in their last experimental session. This circumstance leaves open the possibility that all effects obtained are the result of this single, final exposure. In this last session, heavy viewers were exposed to a higher incidence of crime than were light viewers. Heavy viewers thus may have been *primed* to violence and victimization (cf. Gabrielcik & Fazio, 1984; Wyer & Carlston, 1979; Wyer & Hartwick, 1980; Wyer & Srull, 1981), and their assessments may have been influenced by the temporarily heightened accessibility of concepts pertaining to danger and victimization. This reasoning would also explain the strong effect of injustice in drama on anxiety. Subjects in this exposure condition, unlike those in the others, were not pacified by seeing the threatening conditions removed and the potentiality for violence curbed.

The investigation reported by Bryant et al. (1981), then, does not necessarily demonstrate effects of longitudinal, cultivating exposure, but might demonstrate effects of a single exposure instead. If so, one would expect the effects to be comparatively short-lived. This would be in contrast to what the cultivation hypothesis implies—namely, persisting perceptual and attitudinal changes.

To clarify these matters, Tamborini, Zillmann, and Bryant (1984) conducted an investigation that probed the consequences of a single exposure and the duration of any effects. Subjects were exposed to drama devoid of violence (as a control), crime drama featuring a just resolution, crime drama featuring injustice in the resolution, or a documentary about crime. Immediately after exposure or 3 days later, the subjects' perceptions of the likelihood of crime in various places, their fearfulness concerning victimization in various places, their fearfulness regarding victimization of self and their loved ones, as well as their manifest anxiety were assessed. All these responses were subjected to factor analysis. The emerging factors were: Rural Fear, reflecting concern about safety in rural areas; Urban Fear, reflecting concern about safety in urban areas; Fear for Mate, reflecting concern about the safety of a loved one; Personal Fear, reflecting concern about violent assault upon self; and Perceptions of Crime, reflecting the comparatively nonaffective estimation of crime frequency. Factor scores were used to analyze the data by factor.

The findings reported by Bryant et al. (1981) were replicated on many counts, suggesting that these findings were indeed the result of the last, rather than the entire, exposure treatment. On manifest anxiety, for instance, only exposure to injustice-laden drama produced levels above the control. The effect of single exposure on Personal Fear (i.e., fearfulness) was negligible, however. Fearfulness proved to be specific to region. Rural Fear proved to be unaffected by messages about crime, the crime being mostly urban. Urban Fear, in contrast, was significantly affected: As can be seen from Fig. 7.1, compared to the control condition, it increased significantly immediately after exposure to drama. But the seemingly stronger impact of injustice-laden drama over drama featuring a just resolution was not reliable. This is essentially the effect pattern reported by Bryant et al. for likelihood of victimization and fearfulness. It is worthy of note that exposure to the documentary had by far the strongest effect on Urban Fear. Fear for Mate showed a similar, though weaker, effect pattern. Finally, Perceptions of Crime were also significantly affected by single exposure. Immediately after injustice-laden drama and the crime documentary, crime seemed more ubiquitous than after exposure to crime drama featuring justice or after exposure to drama devoid of crime. Interestingly, exposure to justly resolved drama did not appreciably influence crime perception. Its effect was essentially the same as that of crimefree drama.

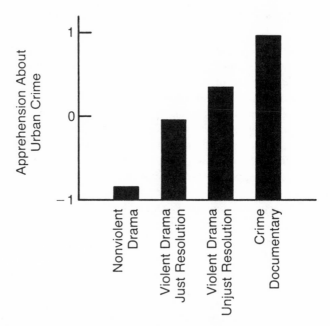

FIG. 7.1. Apprehensions about victimization of self in urban areas after exposure to drama devoid of crime, crime drama featuring the restoration of justice, crime drama ending in injustice, and a crime documentary. Three days after exposure, no appreciable differences in apprehension were found (adapted from Tamborini, Zillmann, & Bryant, 1984).

Regarding the duration of these effects, all but one had vanished within the 3-day delay period. The only one surviving was the impact of exposure to the crime documentary on crime perception.

The upshot of this research is that there is still no compelling demonstration that repeated and potentially extensive exposure to crime drama fosters persisting apprehensions about crime and fear of victimization of self. Though nonsupportive of the cultivation hypothesis in a strict sense, the research we have discussed has numerous constructive elements, and it is certainly not altogether inconsistent with the cultivation proposal. First, the investigations by Bryant et al. (1981) and Tamborini et al. (1984) show that short-term effects of crime drama on the perception of crime and on apprehensions about crime are likely. These short-term effects, if produced and reinstated daily via repeated exposure to crime drama, can be considered to constitute quasi-stable effects—though by no means persisting ones.

Second, the latter study points the way to conceptual refinements regarding what is being affected by media exposure. In past research as well as in the cultivation hypothesis itself, perceptions, attitudes, apprehensions, and acute affective and emotional states have been liberally mixed, and perceptions were treated as manifestations and measures of affect, if not of acute fear. Perceptions need not be linked to emotions, however, and persons can have bleak views on crime but no fear of becoming a victim. This tends to be the case for persons lacking direct experience with victimization. These persons tend to entertain "illusions of invulnerability" (Perloff, 1984). It must also be recognized that apprehensions are situation- and area-specific (Heath, 1984; Heath & Petraitis, 1984). The separation of these all-too-often confounded aspects of concerns with crime would reduce much misconception (cf. Perloff, 1983).

Third, both investigations show that the inducement of apprehensions about crime by crime drama is not uniform. A variable that emerged as critical is the just versus unjust resolution of drama. Drama that fails to present the restoration of justice after the exhibition of violent and other transgressions is likely to produce the strongest apprehensions about crime. The restoration of justice apparently is capable of mitigating much of the effect of witnessing the victimization of others.

CAN APPREHENSIONS ENHANCE
THE APPEAL OF DRAMA?

Gerbner and his associates (e.g., Gerbner & Gross, 1976a, 1976b) based their proposal that heavy television consumption fosters fear of becoming a victim of violent crime on the near omnipresence of violent transgression and victimization in this medium of communication. Surely, criminal victimization is ubiquitous in crime drama; and despite the likelihood that the perception of violent action is mitigated (Gunter, 1983; Gunter & Furnham, 1984) by some genres (e.g., science fiction), by distance of occurrence (e.g., physical or cultural remoteness), or by personality traits of respondents (e.g., their propensity for physical aggression), this type of action is, no doubt, properly recognized as the source of considerable human suffering and a threat to the welfare of many in society. However, if the exhibition of violence consisted solely of the portrayal of the victimization of innocent people with all its grievous consequences, it would be difficult to comprehend the attraction of large audiences to such fare. Exposure to messages that dwell on the brutalization, torment, mutilation, and death of upstanding citizens can only produce annoyance, not enjoyment, in the large majority of viewers. Ignoring sadists and those who begrudge their fellow beings for whatever peculiar reason, exposure to the victimization and the suffering of persons who are obviously undeserving of this fate can only result in empathetic distress, and such distress can hardly be considered a solid foundation for great desires to expose oneself to similar materials for the purpose of entertainment. Especially if it is assumed that exposure to the violent victimization of others causes acute apprehensions about the possibility of becoming a victim of violence oneself, exposure to similar materials should be shunned in order to minimize and control noxious affect (see chap. 8 by Zillmann & Bryant in this volume). The only exception would be exposure to disturbing and terrifying news, as this information may be instrumental in coping with a threat (e.g., a toxin in the city's drinking water or a killer on the loose).

Drama, including violence-laden crime drama, does of course not merely feature the victimization and suffering of innocent people. Though violent transgressions are usually involved and may even be necessary to develop credible antagonists, it is the rare exception that crime drama on television features the torment and annihilation of beloved protagonists and numerous other honorable, law-abiding citizens by hordes of violent transgressors who terrorize society with impunity. It is most important to recognize that television's crime drama *almost always features the triumph of justice*. Transgressors are promptly caught and duly punished. Justice is restored after any wrongdoing. Society is continually freed from its dangerous elements. Rapists, murderers, kidnappers, drug pushers, and child molesters are expediently put away. All this is so obtrusive that it has been proposed (Zillmann, 1980) that television drama "distorts reality more toward security than toward danger" (p. 160). It projects too just and perhaps too safe a world. In real life, molesters, robbers, and killers are less frequently and less promptly brought to justice than in the world of television drama. Such drama continually conveys the message that good forces (i.e., police, private investigators, vigilantes) are out there mopping up the scum of society. Their relentless good efforts make the streets safe again. This kind of message should be music to the ears of troubled citizens, allowing them to relax and put their worries about crime and personal safety to rest.

Troubled citizens, then, can find comfort in the essential message of crime drama. The more troubled they are, the more they should be inclined to seek refuge in such drama. Apprehensive citizens thus should be motivated to consume much crime drama, more than those less apprehensive about victimization. It is this proposal that constitutes an alternative explanation to the fragile correspondence between fear of victimization and heavy television viewing (cf. Zillmann, 1980). It reverses the direction of causality immanent in the cultivation hypothesis.

The seeking out of crime drama for the aforementioned pacifying message is by no means the only drama attractant for the crime-worried person. Several other attractants exist (see Zillmann, 1980, for a more detailed discussion). First, it can be predicted that retaliatory violence (i.e., socially sanctioned violence employed by the good forces in the process of restoring justice) will be the more enjoyed, the more the respondents are motivated to see transgressors punished and rendered innocuous. The stronger motivation of this sort can, of course, be found in persons who are apprehensive about victimization (Zillmann, 1979). Counterintuitive as it may sound, scared persons can get more out of crime drama that features plenty of retaliatory violence (and television drama does this with regularity) and, hence, should seek it out more than others do.

Second, and equally counterintuitive, it is conceivable that crime-apprehensive persons are attracted to crime drama because it reduces their apprehensions. This outcome is predictable not only from the main theme of crime drama (i.e., good forces weeding out the forces of evil) but also from behavior-modification theory (cf. Bandura, 1969). Analogous to the extinction of phobias, which in its initial stages is accomplished by repeated exposure to representations of a phobia-inducing entity under conditions guaranteeing personal safety, repeated exposure to the stimuli associated with crime apprehension in the safety of the home should weaken these apprehensions. Anxiety reactions to transgressive events in drama and to the perpetrators of transgressive actions are bound to grow weaker as their excitatory component habituates (cf. Zillmann, 1982). Crime-phobic persons' selective exposure to crime drama could thus be characterized as a self-administered behavior-modification program, a program aiming at mastery of scary situations.

Finally, and related to the foregoing, persons who are apprehensive about victimization should be more distressed than others by scenes in which others are victimized. Their greater distress is associated with greater sympathetic activity, and residues of that activity are likely to persist through the restoration of justice in the dramatic resolution (or in the analogous resolution of minor plots midway through a drama). The respondent's euphoric reaction to these resolutions is then intensified by the residues of excitation from distress (Zillmann, 1980, 1983). Nonapprehensive persons, because of their less intense response to victimization, will experience less euphoria upon resolutions. Their lesser cheering should ultimately result in a smaller appetite for crime drama.

Taken together then, there is ample reason for expecting crime-apprehensive persons to be more strongly drawn to crime drama than are persons with little or no concern about crime. But what about research evidence?

FEAR OF VICTIMIZATION
AND SELECTIVE EXPOSURE

An early study on this relationship was conducted by Boyanowsky, Newtson, and Walster (1974). These investigators explored attendance at movie theaters in a community that was terrorized by a killer who had just brutally murdered a student. After much publicity of the killing that must have created considerable apprehensions concerning victimization of self, attendance at a highly violent movie rose compared to attendance at a nonviolent movie. This finding may be considered suggestive, but it is certainly not compelling proof that fear fosters an appetite for violence. It is possible, of course, that word got out that the nonviolent film was a flop and the other a blast, so that moviegoers went to the more interesting film despite its violence rather than because of it.

Boyanowsky (1977) reported a rare, controlled experiment on the effects of acute fear of victimization. Through elaborate deception, female students were led to believe that a girl had just been attacked either nearby on campus (a condition of high threat) or on another campus across town (low threat). The information was provided by a uniformed campus guard who also told them to be especially alert and careful when walking home after the experiment in which they were to participate and which was run at night. No threatening conditions were disclosed in a control condition. In what to the students appeared to be the experiment, the females were given a choice among various films they could watch, and they rated the desirability of viewing these films. The materials, described in synopses, were: (a) a romantic comedy, (b) a romantic interlude, (c) an instructional film about women's self-defense against men, (d) a drama featuring male violence toward females, (e) a drama featuring intermale violence, and (f) a sexual orgy. The apprehension treatment had no appreciable effect on the desirability of seeing any of the first four offerings. Although the self-defense information was useful under the circumstances, fearful females exhibited no greater appetite for it than did their more relaxed counterparts. Also, the fearful women did not display any higher disdain for the film that promised the victimization of women by men, as might have been expected (see chap. 8 by Zillmann & Bryant in this volume). The last two choices were significantly affected by apprehension, however. Compared with the control, the desirability of seeing intermale violence tripled in both threat conditions and the eagerness to watch an orgy doubled.

What could make intermale violence and sex devoid of violence so attractive? The obvious, common element is that *female* victimization is *not* an issue. But this issue is equally nonexistent in the romantic pieces, yet these failed to become more attractive. Other explanatory possibilities are similarly contrived. It could be argued, for instance, that intermale aggression becomes attractive to females who are apprehensive about aggression by men because it shows the decimation of men, as some are being victimized. And it could be speculated that these females are attracted to sexual themes because men making love are rendered innocuous. But a more prudent stand is to admit bewilderment and to consider the findings not supportive of any single, coherent selective-exposure rationale.

The previously discussed investigation of exposure effects by Bryant et al. (1981) also involved an assessment of selective exposure. Starting no earlier than 1 week after the conclusion of the extended exposure treatment and the measurement of its immediate impact on perceptions of and attitudes about crime, subjects were assigned two tasks. First, to insure that an upcoming class discussion about television drama would be stimulating, subjects were encouraged to watch further drama. Several pieces were placed on reserve in the library, and consumption was unobtrusively recorded. Second, subjects were instructed to keep a diary of their consumption of television fare over the next 4 weeks. Following the collection of these data, subjects were ostensibly approached by a marketing firm and offered payment for keeping a television diary for 3 weeks. A sufficient number of subjects responded to this request.

The findings show that, compared to light prior exposure, heavy prior exposure to drama featuring justice enhances the consumption of crime drama, whereas heavy prior exposure to drama depicting injustice in its resolution reduces consumption. The use of drama on reserve produced a significant differentiation of this kind. The diaries showed the same pattern. However, for the instructor-solicited diaries, the consumption-depressing effect of drama depicting injustice fell short of significance, and for the commercially solicited diaries, the consumption-enhancing effect of drama dwelling on justice fell short.

These findings would be most informative if it could be assumed that, weeks after the longitudinal exposure treatment, the effect of heavy exposure to crime drama, especially to injustice-laden crime drama, on fear of victimization would still persist. But in light of our earlier discussion of the likely short-lived nature of any facilitation of crime apprehensions by exposure to crime drama, such an assumption is simply unwarranted. Also worthy of note is that the initial levels of manifest anxiety, to which—weeks after the exposure treatment—subjects should have returned, were without consequence for selective exposure. No main effect of anxiety was observed, nor an interaction with anxiety.

As the findings cannot be considered to establish consequences of fear of victimization or manifest anxiety, what do they demonstrate? The most parsimonious account of the process that produced them is this: Subjects who were massively exposed to drama featuring justice found such drama satisfying and developed a taste for television drama; in contrast, subjects who were massively exposed to drama resulting in injustice found it unsatisfying, if not disturbing, and thus developed a disdain for television drama. In this sense, the findings once again point to the significance of the justice–injustice variable in the enjoyment of and selective exposure to crime drama.

The strongest support for the proposed influence of crime apprehension on selective exposure to crime drama comes from an investigation by Wakshlag, Vial, and Tamborini (1983). These investigators placed both male and female subjects in a state of apprehension about victimization by exposure to a documentary on crime. Such exposure is known to make victimization salient and thereby produce acute apprehensions about particular crimes, though only for a limited period of time (Tamborini et al., 1984). In a control condition, subjects were shown an innocuous documentary about the Himalayas. This manipulation resulted in a significant differentiation of victimization apprehension. Following this treatment, the subjects were led to believe that they could choose what to watch next. They were given a list of synopses of films and asked to indicate their preference by selecting films to be seen. The synopses had been pretested to obtain scores for the degree to which a film was perceived as featuring violent victimization and/or punitive restoration of justice. Measures of the appeal of these two pertinent themes were attained by summing the victimization scores and the justice-restoration scores for the films selected from the list.

The findings concerning the appeal of violent victimization are presented in Fig. 7.2. Strong gender differences are apparent. Violence in drama appealed to the males much more than to the females. Or stated differently, the females showed a greater disdain for violence in drama. However, irrespective of these gender differences, the appeal of violent victimization dropped significantly (and equally for both males and females) for subjects who were acutely apprehensive about the possibility of violent victimization. This finding indicates that violence per se is *not* an attractive element of entertainment for persons who are fearful of victimization. To these persons, violent victimization in drama is the opposite: a deterrent to watching.

The findings concerning the appeal of justice restoration are presented in Fig. 7.3. They also show strong gender differences. Overall, the restoration of justice held more appeal to females than to males. Irrespective of this main effect of gender, however, crime-apprehensive subjects exhibited great sensitivity to the crucial theme of justice restoration. The appeal of drama featuring this theme grew significantly with such apprehensions. This finding leaves little doubt about the fact that persons who are worried about crime seek comfort in entertaining messages that promise justice and, hence, safety. Crime-apprehensive persons, then, do get more out of the crime drama that abounds on television (i.e., drama emphasizing justice) than do those who are oblivious to the threat of crime.

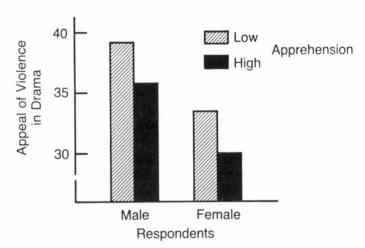

FIG. 7.2.   Appeal of violent victimization in crime drama as a function of ap-prehensions about becoming a victim of violent crime (adapted from Wakshlag, Vial, & Tamborini, 1983).

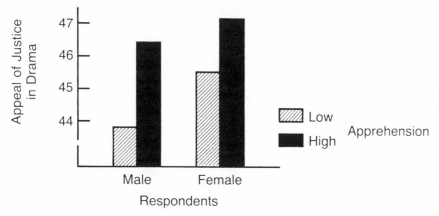

FIG. 7.3. Appeal of retaliatory justice in crime drama as a function of apprehensions about becoming a victim of violent crime (adapted from Wakshlag, Vial, & Tamborini, 1983).

An investigation exploring the previously discussed mechanics of excitement and the enjoyment of crime drama by persons apprehensive about crime has been reported by Wakshlag, Bart, Dudley, Groth, McCutcheon, and Rolla (1983). Subjects' fear of victimization was assessed, and on the basis of these data, they were placed in conditions of low versus high apprehension. Two weeks later, these subjects were recruited for an ostensibly unrelated study. Within apprehension levels, they were assigned to two drama conditions. They saw an excerpt from violent crime drama in which either the protagonist or the antagonist was ultimately killed. Various measures of sympathetic excitation were recorded. Evaluations of the program were obtained as well.

The physiological measures consistently indicated that apprehensive persons respond more strongly to victimization in drama than do nonapprehensive persons. Apprehensive subjects exhibited, for instance, greater increases in heart rate and diastolic blood pressure during exposure. This difference in response was specific to crime drama, as no difference could be found in the response to other materials. Evaluations of the programs' ending were also different in the two apprehension groups. Apprehensive subjects tended to be more disturbed by the violent endings, and they consequently tended to enjoy them less than did their less apprehensive counterparts.

The investigation discloses critical individual differences in the response to crime drama. Excitatory reactions are a function of fearfulness. So are experiential assessments. As proposed earlier, apprehensive persons should have more intense excitatory responses, and this should mediate a greater intensity of affect—whatever this affect may be. The observed chain of events confirms just that. However, the study failed to show the greater enjoyment of the just resolution (i.e., the antagonist being shot) by apprehensive persons that was expected. This failure is probably the result of efforts to create the two drama versions through editing, in the process of which the necessary dispositional development of the characters may have suffered considerably.

CONCLUDING REMARKS

The research addressing the association between fear of crime and crime-drama consumption has established that apprehensions can foster increased selective exposure. The drama variable that emerged as most significant in this connection is that of justice–injustice. Drama that features the restoration of justice after the commission of criminal transgressions appears to hold great appeal to crime-apprehensive persons. As justice restoration commonly relies on violent action, the appeal of the justice theme entails the acceptance and appreciation of some degree of violence: the violence needed to achieve the punitive objectives involved in the restoration of justice. Violence in and of itself does not appear to be an attractant (cf. Diener & De Four, 1978). For crime-apprehensive persons, it seems to function as a deterrent to exposure. And comparatively speaking, violence resulting in injustice emerged as an unattractive formula for crime drama.

The research also provides some evidence that crime-apprehensive persons obtain greater excitement from crime drama than others do and that emotional responses to drama, including enjoyment of favorable resolutions, are accordingly more intense.

It should be recognized, however, that all of this does not preclude cultivation effects such as perceptions of crime in society that fail to correspond with reality, esteem for those instrumental in restoring justice and safety for citizens, and an acceptance of violence in the service of justice and security. But it would seem that these effects of exposure result more from coping with crime apprehensions that are based on pertinent experience and reliable information (cf. Baumer, 1978; Skogan & Maxfield, 1981) than from incidental and seemingly involuntary exposure to crime drama and the maladaptive anxieties it produces—as some have insinuated.

REFERENCES

Bandura, A. (1969). *Principles of behavior modification*. New York: Holt, Rinehart & Winston.

Baumer, T. L. (1978). Research on fear of crime in the United States. *Victimology: An International Journal, 3*, 254–264.

Boyanowsky, E. O. (1977). Film preferences under conditions of threat: Whetting the appetite for violence, information, or excitement? *Communication Research, 4*, 133–145.

Boyanowsky, E. O., Newtson, D., & Walster, E. (1974). Film preferences following a murder. *Communication Research, 1,* 32–43.

Bryant, J., Carveth, R. A., & Brown, D. (1981). Television viewing and anxiety: An experimental examination. *Journal of Communication, 31,* 106–119.

Diener, E., & DeFour, D. (1978). Does television violence enhance program popularity? *Journal of Personality and Social Psychology, 36,* 333–341.

Doob, A. W., & Macdonald, G. E. (1979). Television viewing and fear of victimization: Is the relationship causal? *Journal of Personality and Social Psychology, 37,* 170–179.

Gabrielcik, A., & Fazio, R. H. (1984). Priming and frequency estimation: A strict test of the availability heuristic. *Personality and Social Psychology Bulletin, 10,* 85–89.

Gerbner, G., & Gross, L. (1976a). Living with television: The violence profile. *Journal of Communication, 26*(2), 173–199.

Gerbner, G., & Gross, L. (1976b, April). The scary world of TV's heavy viewer. *Psychology Today,* pp. 41–45, 89.

Gerbner, G., Gross, L., Morgan, M., & Signorielli, N. (1980). The "mainstreaming" of America: Violence profile no. 11. *Journal of Communication, 30*(3), 19–29.

Gerbner, G., Gross, L., Morgan, M., & Signorielli, N. (1981). A curious journey into the scary world of Paul Hirsch. *Communication Research, 8,* 39–72.

Gunter, B. (1983). Personality and perceptions of harmful and harmless TV violence. *Personality and Individual Differences, 4,* 665–670.

Gunter, B., & Furnham, A. (1984). Perceptions of television violence: Effects of programme genre and type of violence on viewers' judgements of violent portrayals. *British Journal of Social Psychology, 23,* 155–164.

Heath, L. (1984). The impact of newspaper crime reports on fear of crime: A multi-methodological investigation. *Journal of Personality and Social Psychology, 47,* 263–276.

Heath, L., & Petraitis, J. (1984, May). *Television viewing and fear of crime: Where is the mean world?* Paper presented at the meeting of the Midwestern Psychological Association, Chicago.

Hirsch, P. M. (1980). The "scary world" of the non-viewer and other anomalies: A reanalysis of Gerbner et al.'s findings on cultivation analysis, part 1. *Communication Research, 7,* 403–456.

Hirsch, P. M. (1981a). Distinguishing good speculation from bad theory: Rejoinder to Gerbner et al. *Communication Research, 8,* 73–95.

Hirsch, P. M. (1981b). On not learning from one's own mistakes: A reanalysis of Gerbner et al.'s findings on cultivation analysis, part 2. *Communication Research, 8,* 3–37.

Hughes, M. (1980). The faults of cultivation analysis: A re-examination of some effects of television watching. *Public Opinion Quarterly, 44,* 287–302.

Jackson-Beeck, M., & Sobal, J. (1980). The social world of heavy television viewers. *Journal of Broadcasting 24,* 5–11.

Perloff, L. S. (1983). Perceptions of vulnerability of victimization. *Journal of Social Issues, 39*(2), 41–61.

Perloff, L. S. (1984, May). *The effect of indirect experience on perceived vulnerability to victimization.* Paper presented at the meeting of the Midwestern Psychological Association, Chicago.

Pingree, S., & Hawkins, R. (1981). U.S. programs on Australian television: The cultivation effect. *Journal of Communication, 31*(1), 97–105.

Skogan, W. G., & Maxfield, M. G. (1981). *Coping with crime.* Beverly Hills, CA: Sage.

Tamborini, R., Zillmann, D., & Bryant, J. (1984). Fear and victimization: Exposure to television and perceptions of crime and fear. In R. Bostrom (Ed.), *Communication yearbook 8* (pp. 492–513). Beverly Hills, CA: Sage.

Taylor, J. A. (1953). A personality scale of manifest anxiety. *Journal of Abnormal and Social Psychology, 41,* 285–290.

Wakshlag, J., Bart, L., Dudley, J., Groth, G., McCutcheon, J., & Rolla, C. (1983). Viewer apprehension about victimization and crime drama programs. *Communication Research, 10,* 195–217.

Wakshlag, J., Vial, V., & Tamborini, R. (1983). Selecting crime drama and apprehension about crime. *Human Communication Research, 10*, 227–242.

Wober, J. M. (1978). Televised violence and paranoid perception: The view from Great Britain. *Public Opinion Quarterly, 42*, 315–321.

Wober, M., & Gunter, B. (1982). Impressions of old people on TV and in real life. *British Journal of Social Psychology, 21*, 335–336.

Wyer, R. S., Jr., & Carlston, D. (1979). *Social cognition, inference and attribution.* Hillsdale, NJ: Lawrence Erlbaum Associates.

Wyer, R. S., Jr., & Hartwick, J. (1980). The role of information retrieval and conditional inference processes in belief formation and change. In L. Berkowitz (Ed.), *Advances in experimental social psychology* (Vol. 13, pp. 241–284). New York: Academic Press.

Wyer, R. S., Jr., & Srull, T. K. (1981). Category accessibility: Some theoretical and empirical issues concerning the processing of social stimulus information. In E. T. Higgins, C. P. Herman, & M. P. Zanna (Eds.), *Social cognition: The Ontario Symposium* (Vol. 1, pp. 161–197). Hillsdale, NJ: Lawrence Erlbaum Associates.

Zillmann, D. (1979). *Hostility and aggression.* Hillsdale, NJ: Lawrence Erlbaum Associates.

Zillmann, D. (1980). Anatomy of suspense. In P. H. Tannenbaum (Ed.), *The entertainment functions of television* (pp. 133–163). Hillsdale, NJ: Lawrence Erlbaum Associates.

Zillmann, D. (1982). Television viewing and arousal. In D. Pearl, L. Bouthilet, & J. Lazar (Eds.), *Television and behavior: Ten years of scientific progress and implications for the eighties: Vol. 2. Technical reviews* (pp. 53–67) (U.S. Public Health Service Document No. ADM 82-1196). Washington, DC: U.S. Government Printing Office.

Zillmann, D. (1983). Transfer of excitation in emotional behavior. In J. T. Cacioppo & R. E. Petty (Eds.), *Social psychophysiology: A sourcebook* (pp. 215–240). New York: Guilford Press.

8 Affect, Mood, and Emotion as Determinants of Selective Exposure

Dolf Zillmann
Indiana University

Jennings Bryant
University of Houston

Upon cursory reflection, most people seem to agree that when it comes to consuming entertainment, individuals have distinctive tastes. These tastes tend to be thought of as comparatively stable, lasting preferences for certain kinds of music, comedy, drama, sports, and the like. The formation of these tastes is usually deemed a mystery, however. Regarding good taste or bad taste, people are said to have it or not. Attributions such as these certainly give the impression that taste is mainly a hereditary trait and minimally, if at all, affected by experience.

The suggestion that entertainment preferences might vary with affects, moods, and emotions generally evokes considerable skepticism. It seems to be counterintuitive because people tend to believe that, if they are free to choose, they usually select whatever best meets their seemingly never changing taste. And if, on occasion, they watch or listen to something above or below their taste, they believe that they would be aware of it. Such beliefs further support the conviction that taste manifests itself in a stable set of choice criteria that tell the respondent which selections are good, right, or appropriate and which are not.

In this chapter, we challenge the colloquial wisdom on taste and reverse the presumed sequence of events. Instead of accepting the idea that taste, as a trait of unknown origin, governs entertainment choices throughout all conceivable emotions, we attempt to show that the choice behavior in question grows from a situational context and that affective and emotional states and reactions play a key role in the formation of rather stable content preferences. We first present our theoretical proposals concerning the formation of these preferences and then discuss the research evidence that pertains to them.

A THEORY OF AFFECT-DEPENDENT
STIMULUS ARRANGEMENT

The essentials and particular aspects of the proposals detailed in the following paragraphs have been discussed elsewhere by Zillmann (1982). As earlier expositions have been limited to exposure to mass media entertainment, an effort is made here to show the generality of the model and only then to apply it to entertainment consumption specifically.

1. It is proposed that individuals are motivated to terminate noxious, aversive stimulation of any kind and to reduce the intensity of such stimulation at any time. It is further proposed that individuals are motivated to perpetuate and increase the intensity of gratifying, pleasurable experiential states.

Extreme understimulation (boredom) and extreme overstimulation (stress) constitute aversive states. So does any threat to the welfare of individuals, in both a most direct and broader sense (cf. Zillmann, 1979). The experience of gratification, on the other hand, is conservatively defined by the absence of aversive stimulation. It is characterized by the temporary nonexistence of acute, action-instigating needs. Stimulation is nonextreme.

2. Based on this hedonistic premise, it is proposed that individuals are inclined to arrange—to the extent that they are capable—internal and external stimulus conditions so as to minimize aversion and maximize gratification. Both minimization and maximization are in terms of time and intensity.

3. To the extent that the control of stimulation is limited to environmental stimuli, individuals are inclined to arrange and rearrange their environment so as to best accomplish the stipulated ends.

4. To the extent that the control of external stimulation is reduced to entertainment fare, individuals are inclined to arrange and rearrange their exposure so as to best accomplish the stipulated ends—or to influence this arrangement to the extent that they can without jeopardizing the hedonistically defined objectives.

This proposition can be applied to the consumption of entertainment generally or to listening to music or watching television specifically. Whereas Proposition 3 entails the choice among actions such as traveling (the "change of scenery" as an arranged environment, with hopes for beneficial effects on moods and emotions), going fishing, or playing cards, Proposition 4 seeks to address the choice among so-called "passive" forms of entertainment. In contrast to potentially highly active entertainment behavior, the consumption of "entertainment fare" refers to reading books, listening to records, watching movies, and the like. The decision to consume such fare, at home or elsewhere, is usually deliberate. But it need not be, as individuals—due to illness or for economic or other reasons—may be confined to a particular locale. Also, the degree of control over stimulus exposure may vary and be severely limited at times. Group consumption of entertainment fare (consumption in the family context, with friends) is the most common choice-reducing condition.

5. Individuals are assumed capable, within limits, of arranging and rearranging environmental stimulation, through action and/or comparatively passive selection, so as to minimize aversion and maximize gratification. This capability or skill is presumed to develop as follows:

a. Initially, individuals in states of aversion or gratification act on and select stimulus environments in a random fashion.

b. Actions incidentally taken and selections incidentally made during states of aversion that terminate or reduce the hedonically negative experience will leave a memory trace that will increase the likelihood for similar actions and selections under similar circumstances. In Thorndikean (1911, 1932) terms, *relief stamps in the preference;* or in more contemporary language, the actions or selections that provide relief from aversion are negatively reinforced (e.g., Nevin, 1973; Skinner, 1969) and thus placed in a superior position for reenactment under similar conditions of aversion.

c. Actions incidentally taken and selections incidentally made during states of gratification that extend or enhance the hedonically positive experience will analogously leave a memory trace that will increase the likelihood for similar actions and selections under similar circumstances. In this case, the reinforcement is positive, and *pleasure stamps in the preference.*

6. Although the preferences for entertainment options that are thus formed—and once formed, further reinforced—may exhibit strong individual variation, they cannot be fully idiosyncratic or overly esoteric because particular actions or selections consistently alter affective states in unique ways. Actions and selections can be grouped in terms of stimulus properties, and these groupings allow predictions of effects on affect.

In the following, the stimulus variables that seem most likely to exert a degree of control over moods and emotions are detailed. The mechanics of their influence on affect are indicated. However, it is not claimed that this listing is exhaustive.

a. It is proposed that persons in states of extreme understimulation that are construed as aversive will act on their environment so as to increase stimulation. If the rearrangement of environmental stimulation is accomplished by passive selection (rather than by energetic, environment-altering action), persons will choose highly varied, potentially arousing stimuli over poorly varied, potentially calming ones. Analogously, it is proposed that persons in states of extreme overstimulation that are construed as aversive will act on their environment so as to decrease stimulation. If the rearrangement of environmental stimulation is accomplished by selection, persons will choose poorly varied, potentially calming stimuli over highly varied, potentially arousing ones.

The stipulated selections obviously serve the normalization of excitatory activity. As normalizing choices are reinforced (with relief stamping in the preference), the affect-specific preference that is being formed can be said to serve excitatory homeostasis.

b. On the premise that persons in acutely aversive states seek alleviation, it is porposed that such persons will display a preference for the most engaging and most absorbing types of stimulation available. However, on the premise that persons experiencing gratification seek to perpetuate that state, it is proposed that such persons will exhibit the opposite preference for stimulation.

Both projections are based on the fact that the cognitive accompaniment of acute affect tends to facilitate and extend the affective experience and that any stimulus intervention tends to disrupt and impair the affect-maintaining looping in and rehearsing of cognitions pertaining to the particular affective experience (cf. Kendall & Hollon, 1979). The more engaging and absorbing any intervening stimulation, the more likely it becomes that the affective state in which it intervenes will diminish in intensity and terminate rapidly. This potential effect (i.e., relief from aversion) should stamp in the preference specific to negative affect. Persons in states of positive affect should, of course, want to revel in the cognitions pertaining to their experience of gratification and avoid or minimize intervening stimulation. The inclination to avoid potentially distracting stimulation altogether should be strongest in extreme states of positive affect, such as elation and triumph.

c. It is proposed that persons in acutely aversive states will display a preference for stimuli that exhibit minimal, if any, behavioral affinity with their experiential state. In contrast, persons experiencing gratification are expected to prefer stimuli of high behavioral affinity, should they elect to expose themselves to distracting stimulation at all.

These proposals derive from the observation that behavioral affinity between an experiential state and intervening stimuli tends to impair or remove the experience-diminishing or experience-terminating effect of stimulus intervention. Intervening stimulation of high behavioral affinity is likely to perpetuate prior affect because it revives affect-maintaining cognitions (Zillmann, 1979). Such revival is due to the fact that behaviorally related affective reactions share associative networks (Anderson & Bower, 1973; Landman & Manis, 1983; Lang, 1979) and that cortical excitation is capable of spreading so as to bridge minor associative discrepancies (Collins & Loftus, 1975). Only engaging and absorbing intervening stimulation that is devoid of any affinity with the experience in which it intervenes, or whose affinity is minimal, can manifest its full impact in disrupting and thus diminishing an emotional experience.

d. It is proposed that persons in acutely aversive states will prefer hedonically positive stimuli over hedonically negative stimuli. Persons experiencing gratification are expected to display this preference to a lesser degree, if at all.

These expectations are based on the proposal that the hedonic valence of intervening stimulation eventually will come to dominate affect and supersede earlier affective experience. At the very least, hedonically positive stimulation is expected to impair the maintenance of hedonically negative affect and to reduce the intensity of negative affect that might persist (Baron, 1977).

Again, the listing of stimulus variables that seem to control selective exposure to some degree is not meant to be exhaustive. In this initial exploration, we choose to concentrate on those variables that are most likely to play a significant part in selective exposure. Also, although some degree of covariation in the effect of the variables discussed is apparent (e.g., the strongest aversion breakers being stimuli that combine high absorption, low behavioral affinity, and positive hedonic valence; the weakest would be stimuli with opposite properties), the projected effects of the variables are obviously not entirely parallel (e.g., aversion can be broken effectively by both low and high excitatory response, but only by one extreme of any other property). We do not exhaustively specify the interactive pattern of effects. Such specification seems unnecessary, as all interactions are implicitly defined. Additionally, we address the critical interactions later in the discussion of research findings.

Selective Exposure and Cognition

The theory of affect-dependent stimulus arrangement does not stipulate that respondents need be aware of the determinants of their environment-altering choices nor that they comprehend the ends served by their choices. Although some individuals may well recognize that their environment-altering actions and selections influence their moods and emotions, even that they seek to attain particular effects dependent on particular moods and emotions, it is considered the rule that persons have poor comprehension both of the causes of their choices and of the ends that these choices serve. Consistent with reinforcement theory generally (cf. Glaser, 1971), it is assumed that individuals execute choices rather "mindlessly," that is, without awareness of choice criteria and without deliberate consideration of desirable effects. Often—though by no means always—persons will simply do things or make selections spontaneously or on impulse. The fact that they are capable of producing elaborate "explanations" for their choice of actions or selection when queried, and usually do so, does not invalidate this assessment.

Applied to selection among available offerings, especially entertainment offerings, this choice model projects the following operations:

1. An arbitrary selection is made. A particular program is encountered by chance or by mindless probing. In the latter case, basic (or primitive) attentional processes, such as the orienting reflex, may determine the initial selection.

2. If the encountered program is pleasing, it is *accepted. If it is displeasing, it is rejected.* Being pleased or displeased is considered an immediate affective reaction that does not rely on elaborate cognitive deliberations. It is, so to speak,

a gut reaction. The program either "feels good," or it doesn't. The affective response to an encountered program is a function of prevailing moods and emotions. The implications for acceptance and rejection are those specified in the theory of affect-dependent stimulus arrangement.

3. If the encountered program is accepted, respondents refrain from further program sampling. Should dissatisfaction set in, acceptance is withdrawn, and the inclination to reject will grow to the point where the program is abandoned and program sampling recurs. If the encountered program is rejected, program sampling continues.

4. Rejected available programs are entered into short-term memory. In continued program sampling, the sampled program is compared with those in memory. Essentially, this comparison is between the affective reactions that were evoked by the compared programs, and it takes the form of *better* or *worse*. Respondents will return to recalled programs that are deemed better than present ones. This return to better offerings can be applied successively until the program deemed best is reached. More likely, however, respondents will cease making comparisons (i.e., they will discontinue the sampling process) once a satisfying program has been found. Obviously, respondents should not be inclined to return to recalled programs that are deemed worse than present ones.

5. If programs or program components are known (i.e., stored in long-term memory), the anticipation of pleasure or displeasure that is based on prior responding to the programs (e.g., episodes of a series) or program components (e.g., actors with particular roles) enters into the comparison process. It expedites this process in the sense that little exposure to sampled programs is needed to render a verdict of accept–reject or better–worse.

The outlined choice model for selective exposure differs considerably from choice models that assume complex cognitive operations in the framework of sophisticated evaluation criteria (for a discussion of such models, see chap. 10 by Heeter & Greenberg in this volume). The construction of complex choice models has been greatly influenced by survey data on program evaluations. As respondents seem at ease evaluating stimulus materials on numerous value dimensions and as the analysis of the respondents' evaluations tends to yield multidimensional systems for evaluations, it has been assumed—if not taken for granted—that the selection of materials is similarly multifaceted. The assumption that evaluations after message consumption must be structurally identical with, or at least highly similar to, choice-precipitating evaluations is untenable, however. First of all, the justification of a choice is obviously based on far more information about the subject of the choice than is available at the time the choice is made. Moreover, choices tend to be made during exposure to stimuli that are to be judged, not upon recall at leisure in distraction-free postexposure periods. The fact that complex evaluations are prestructured on questionnaires and that respondents manage to respond to all the items listed is probably most directly responsible for visions of complex cognitive deliberations in models of program choice. But even if postconsumption evaluations had been less prestructured and more spontaneous, it cannot be assumed that the justification of program choice entails essentially the same cognitive processes as does the actual behavioral choice.

We take the position that people usually pay little attention to why they choose what they choose when they choose it. As stated earlier, however, they may well be cognizant of some reason for their choice. Some individuals may clearly recognize the actual determinants of their choice. But many others, and presumably the large majority of people, are likely to attribute their choice to factors other than the actual determinants. Within any cultural community, persons learn to explain their behavior—including the causation of their actions—in certain terms to themselves and to others (Festinger, 1954; Schachter, 1964; Zillmann, 1978). These explanations tend to be roundabout and need not be correct in order to be accepted. Many correct explanations (e.g., statements to the effect that, say, a piece of classical music was consumed to help alleviate the pains stemming from desertion by a loved one) might, in fact, prove unacceptable and bewildering.

All this is not to say that choice among options—in particular, among entertainment options—is never precipitated by elaborate evaluation of the options. Surely, respondents can and do apply informal, quasi-formal, and formal criteria and weigh, more or less rigorously, the options and their components on several dimensions of relevance. And sometimes, especially when exposure decisions are made in and by groups, such deliberations will have a critical influence on choice behavior. It is suggested, however, that this is the exception, even the rare exception. The new communication technology is likely to make it rarer yet, as social conflict about exposure can readily be resolved by individualized access to all entertainment options. In view of this, it appears that the analysis of introspective data on selective exposure to communication has inspired unnecessarily complicated choice models. If these models would be recognized as models of what people say their criteria for choice are (or put more negatively, as models of choice rationalization), objections are misplaced. But these models are characteristically offered as models of actual choice behavior, and as such, they appear to violate parsimony of explanation. If parsimony of explanation is to be served, basic models of *selective behavior*—such as the one we have proposed—are to be adhered to until it is shown that their predictive power is wanting and complicating amendments are necessary.

EXPOSURE EFFECTS ON AFFECT, MOODS, AND EMOTIONS

In the theory of affect-dependent stimulus arrangement, it has been assumed that certain stimulus types have particular effects and that they have these effects with consistency. Without such consistency, stable selective-exposure patterns could neither develop nor be maintained. It would seem crucial, then, to establish that specifiable stimulus properties reliably produce specifiable affect-modifying effects. Fortunately, many of the effects in question can be considered well established. The relevant research evidence has been discussed elsewhere in considerable detail (e.g., Zillmann, 1982, 1983a). Suffice it here to indicate the nature of the evidence and to point out the research findings that pertain to the postulated response patterns most directly.

There can be no doubt about the fact that messages, both informative and entertaining ones, can differ greatly in their capacity to arouse respondents. Arousal reactions are usually conceptualized as sympathetic dominance in the autonomic nervous system, and they have been measured in peripheral manifestations (mainly in increased cardiovascular activity) or in their endocrine concomitants (mainly in traces of catecholamine release). Such assessment of the excitatory response to messages has led to the emergence of stimulus categories and stimulus hierarchies from nonarousing to arousing. Nonvaried, monotonous stimuli form the bottom of the implicit continuum (Bryant & Zillmann, 1977). Nature films that emphasize the grandeur of things (rather than those that show predation, etc.) are to be placed similarly. Not only have they been found not to arouse respondents, but they actually reduce excitedness in those who had been somewhat aroused (Levi, 1965; Wadeson, Mason, Hamburg, & Handlon, 1963). Action drama, comedy, and game shows tend to be moderately arousing. Depending on the respondents' affective dispositions toward the interacting parties (cf. Zillmann, 1980), such fare can become highly arousing, however (Bryant & Zillmann, 1977; Carruthers & Taggart, 1973; Levi, 1965). Highly violent and potentially fear-evoking drama assumes a position close to the top of the continuum (e.g., Zillmann, Hoyt, & Day, 1974). Nonfictional materials of this kind (as in sports, documentaries, and newscasts) produce even stronger excitatory reactions (Bryant & Zillmann, 1977; Geen, 1975; Geen & Rakosky, 1973). Materials need not feature threats to well-being and destructiveness, however. Sexual themes rank among the strongest arousers available (e.g., Donnerstein & Hallam, 1978; Levi, 1969; Zillmann, 1971; Zillmann et al., 1974). Research on the affect-altering effect of the intervention potential, the behavioral affinity, and the hedonic valence of messages is less abundant, but quite sufficient in establishing particular response patterns.

The intervention effects of entertainment stimuli of different intervention potential on acute affect have been explored in an investigation by Bryant and Zillmann (1977). Subjects were placed in a state of annoyance and anger. They were then exposed to messages that differed sharply in their capacity to engage and absorb the respondents. This capacity had been determined through pretesting with nonannoyed subjects. After exposure to the materials in the main experiment, the subjects were provided with an opportunity to express their remaining anger in aggressive actions against their annoyer.

As was expected, minimally engaging messages—presumably because of their inability to disrupt the subjects' cognitive preoccupation with the experience of annoyance and anger—proved minimally effective in altering affective state, affective dispositions, and affective behavior. The more engaging messages, in contrast, led to diminished anger and aggression—apparently because subjects were less able to maintain affect-perpetuating cognitions. The most engaging message of those devoid of contents pertaining to provocation, anger, and retaliation (i.e., the behavioral components of the subjects' affect) had the strongest intervention effect; that is, it diminished the experience of anger and reduced aggression. The linear relationship between the capacity of messages to engage and absorb respondents (their so-called intervention potential) and the affect-diminishing effect of intervening exposure is evident from Fig. 8.1. As can be seen, a quiz show proved most engaging and consequently reduced aggressiveness most strongly. It also most effectively reduced sympathetic excitation, which can be taken to be the most reliable indicator of the intensity of affect (in this case, anger). Nonaggressive sports (i.e., figure skating) and come-

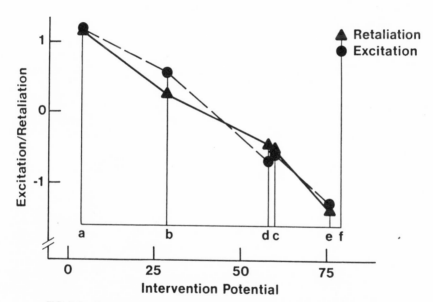

FIG. 8.1. Level of excitation and retaliatory behavior as a function of the intervention potential of entertaining television programs. The greater the capacity of contents to absorb respondents (points connected by gradients), the greater the recovery from annoyance-produced excitation (circles), and the less severe the postexposure retaliation against the annoyer (triangles). Contents featuring hostilities were absorbing to nonannoyed subjects but failed to induce efficient recovery from excitation and failed to lower the level of retaliatory behavior in annoyed subjects (isolated points on coordinate f). The programs were: (a) a monotonous stimulus, (b) a nature film, (c) a comedy show, (d) nonaggressive sport, (e) a quiz show, and (f) contact sport entailing aggressive actions beyond the legitimate sport activity. Excitation and retaliation are expressed in z scores for ease of comparison (from Zillmann, 1979).

dy were somewhat less engaging and, accordingly, had a somewhat weaker impact. Despite the aforementioned fact that nature films tend to be calming, exposure to such a stimulus was found to have little intervention power.

The investigation by Bryant and Zillmann (1977) also provided a test of the proposal that messages featuring behaviors of great affinity to the affective state during which they are received have only minor affect-diminishing strength. The angry subjects' exposure to violent sports (specifically, rough ice hockey with extracurricular aggressive activities) failed to reduce arousal, anger, or aggressiveness, despite the fact that the program had been found to be highly absorbing for nonannoyed persons. The effect of behavioral affinity is obtrusive in Fig. 8.1 (Point f). Similar findings have been reported for fictional violence by Zillmann and Johnson (1973).

Further corroboration of the proposal that the behavioral affinity between message and affect prevailing during reception removes much or all intervention power comes from research on the effects of humor and comedy. In an investigation conducted by Berkowitz (1970), subjects were provoked or not provoked by a peer, exposed to hostile or nonhostile comedy, and then allowed to express hostility toward their peer. After hostile comedy, provoked subjects retaliated more strongly than their counterparts who had been exposed to nonhostile comedy. No such effect was found in unprovoked subjects. The materials that featured actions closely related to the subjects' state (i.e., belittlement, degradation) apparently failed to let them forget about their own mistreatment. But materials devoid of such relatedness, which in the absence of acute affect were similarly funny and similarly absorbing, accomplished the intervention necessary for affect diminution.

The effects of the hedonic valence of messages on affect prevailing during reception have been explored with different types of stimuli: humor, music, and mainly erotica. Baron and Ball (1974) conducted an investigation in which subjects were provoked or not provoked, exposed to entirely nonhostile cartoons or to pictures of scenery, furniture, and abstract paintings in a control condition, and then provided with an opportunity to vent their emotions in actions against their provoker. Cartoon-elicited amusement, compared against the impact of no amusement in the control condition, led to diminished retaliatory inclinations of provoked subjects. Amusement was of no consequence for unprovoked subjects, however. For persons in an acutely negative affective state, then, exposure to material that triggers a positive affective state, if only temporarily, appears to cut into the initial negative state and reduce its intensity. Day (1980) demonstrated that exposure to pleasant music is similarly capable of reducing negative affect.

Moreover, exposure to pleasant but nonarousing erotic materials has been shown to alleviate negative affect. Baron (1974) reported an experiment in which males were provoked or not provoked by a male peer, exposed to photographs of beautiful female nudes or to innocuous nonerotic control stimuli, and then given an opportunity to behave aggressively toward their peer. Paralleling Baron's findings on the effect of amusement, the mild erotic stimulation, compared against the control, led to decreased aggressiveness in provoked subjects but was of no consequence for unprovoked subjects. This finding has been replicated repeatedly (e.g., Ramirez, Bryant, & Zillmann, 1982).

Exposure to pleasant erotica does not necessarily reduce prevailing negative affect, however. In fact, such exposure may facilitate negative affect that recurs after exposure. If erotic materials are both pleasant and arousing, the aversion-alleviating effect of positive hedonic valence tends to be counteracted by the emotion-enhancing effect of residual excitation from exposure (cf. Zillmann, 1983b). Strongly arousing stimuli are likely to intesify negative affect in the postexposure period despite the positive valence of the erotica. Moderately

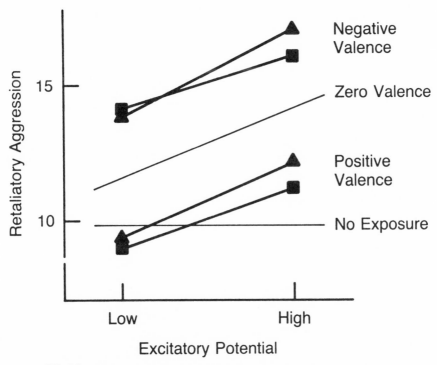

FIG. 8.2.   Effects of stimulus intervention in acute anger. The horizontal line defines retaliation without intervention. The zero-valence gradient indicates the hypothetical effect of hedonically neutral materials as a function of residual excitation. The heavy lines specify the joint operation of excitatory and hedonic properties of messages in the modification of retaliatory behavior. Triangles denote erotic materials, squares nonerotic fare. Retaliation was measured in the frequency of noxious noise delivered to punish the tormentor (adapted from Zillmann, Bryant, Comisky, & Medoff, 1981).

arousing stimuli may have no particular effect on prevailing affect, as positive and negative influences tend to neutralize and cancel each other out.

It should also be clear that exposure to displeasing stimuli, whether erotic or not, is likely to aggravate aggravated persons further. Preexposure annoyance should combine with annoyance from exposure, with the combination constituting postexposure annoyance. Negative affect is thus expected to sum. Insult is added to injury, so to speak. By the same token, positive affect of stimulus intervention can be considered to sum with prevailing negative affect, the positive component being subtracted out of the negative.

Zillmann, Bryant, Comisky, and Medoff (1981) explored all these expectations in an investigation that varied both the hedonic valence of intervening stimuli and their excitatory potential. Additionally, erotica were matched with nonerotic stimuli in terms of both hedonic and excitatory properties. As in other investigations of this kind, subjects were annoyed, exposed to communication,

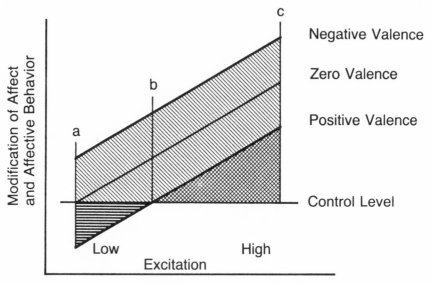

FIG. 8.3.   A two-component model of stimulus intervention in negative affective states. Compared against the control level (zero effect), stimuli with low excitatory potential and positive hedonic valence reduce initial affect (horizontally hatched area). The reduction effect is nil at Point b because affect reduction due to positive valence is neutralized by affect enhancement due to excitation. Stimuli with high excitatory potential and positive hedonic valence increase initial affect (cross-hatched area), owing to the dominant effect of excitation. Stimuli with negative hedonic valence increase initial affect; and they do so more, the higher their excitatory potential (diagonally hatched area). In all cases, the effect of residual excitation and hedonic valence combines additively. The model extends to one of intervention effects in positive affect by reversal of positiveness and negativeness of valence.

and then allowed to vent their remaining annoyance by retaliating against their annoyer. It was found that both the hedonic valence and the excitatory potential of intervening messages exerted a degree of control over aggressive behavior and, apparently, over the affective experience (anger) that mediates this behavior. Aggressiveness was at significantly higher levels after exposure to negatively valenced stimuli than after exposure to positively valenced ones. Likewise, aggressiveness was at significantly higher levels after exposure to arousing stimuli than after exposure to nonarousing ones. Both affect-modifying influences were independent (i.e., they were additive). Moreover, there was no difference whatsoever in the effect of erotic and nonerotic materials. The findings, summarized in Fig. 8.2, gave rise to a two-component model of stimulus intervention, which is presented in Fig. 8.3. This model is developed more completely elsewhere (Zillmann, 1984; Zillmann & Bryant, 1984). Suffice it here to point to the model's critical projection that intervention in negative affective experiences is likely to be effective if the intervening stimuli have positive valence and/or low excitatory potential and that it is likely to be ineffective, even counterproductive, if the stimuli have negative valence and/or high excitatory potential. The combination of stimulus properties with parallel effects is essentially additive. So is the combination of properties of opposite effects, except that the summative combination now operates toward neutralization— that is, toward zero impact.

TESTING SELECTIVE-EXPOSURE HYPOTHESES

Experimental research on selective exposure to entertainment offerings was initially exploratory (e.g., Zillmann, Hezel, & Medoff, 1980). Procedures for the behavioral assessment of selective exposure had to be developed, and their usefulness determined. In the design of procedures, both for the measurement of exposure and the types of material available for selection, a high degree of ecological validity was sought. Such intentions worked against achieving maximum control over the properties of the messages from among which respondents could choose. Various critical message properties (e.g., hedonic valence, excitatory potential, absorption capacity) tended to be confounded, making rigorous tests of hypotheses unfeasible. Tests of specific proposals have been reported only recently (e.g., Bryant & Zillmann, 1984b). In part, this is due to the fact that the earlier exploratory work inspired refinements in the formulation of selective-exposure hypotheses (Zillmann, 1982).

In this discussion of the available selective-exposure research, we follow conceptual guidelines rather than trace historical developments. We begin with research on the exposure implications of boredom and stress and then procede to that on the implications of good and bad moods. Finally, we inspect recent work on the selective-exposure consequences of apprehensions and fear of victimization. In all of this, we point to likely stimulus confoundings and interpret them vis-à-vis the various posited hypotheses concerning stimulus properties that have been stated earlier.

Overcoming Boredom and Stress

To test the proposal that persons in states of acute under- or overstimulation that are construed as aversions (i.e., as boredom vs. as stress) tend to arrange their environment—their television environment, in particular—so as to maximize their chances for prompt relief, Bryant and Zillmann (1984b) conducted an investigation in which subjects were placed into a state of boredom or stress and then allowed to watch television, ostensibly while they were waiting for the experiment to continue. Boredom was accomplished by having the subjects perform monotonous tasks, such as threading washers onto a lace without any performance pressures being applied, for an extended period of time. Stress was induced by the administration of GRE/SAT type exams, and performance pressures were constantly applied. As the subjects waited for a second study to begin, they could, but did not have to, watch television. The experimenter enticed them to watch, however. He pointed out that various programs could be received from a new cable service, and he sampled from six available programs before leaving the individually tested subjects alone for 15 minutes. Actually, the programs that were available on the monitor were received from playbacks in the adjacent room. The subjects' selections were ascertained in this room, too. Choice of channel and time of exposure to each channel were recorded for the entire test period.

Six programs were simultaneously available. In a pretest with subjects who were neither bored nor under stress, these programs had been evaluated on a battery of scales. The analysis of the ratings yielded three programs that were considered exciting and three that were considered relaxing. The exciting ones presented an action-packed adventure drama, a professional football game, and a play-off quiz show; the relaxing ones presented underwater nature scenes, classical lullabies from a concert, and a travelogue on restful vacationing.

It was expected, of course, that bored subjects would choose exposure to exciting materials over exposure to relaxing ones and that stressed subjects would exhibit the opposite preference. These are the choices that would serve excitatory homeostasis.

As there was no theoretical interest in exposure to the individual programs, exposure times were accumulated across programs within the categories of the exciting–relaxing dichotomy. These aggregate data were subjected to analysis. The findings, which apply to both genders equally, are shown in Fig. 8.4. As can be seen, bored subjects very much avoided exposure to relaxing programs and showed a strong inclination to watch exciting materials. This is exactly as expected. Stressed subjects conformed less closely to expectations. They elected to expose themselves as much to exciting as to relaxing fare. An explanation for

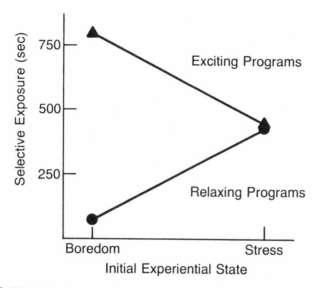

FIG. 8.4. Selective exposure to exciting and relaxing television programs as a function of prior boredom and stress. Respondents chose from among six available offerings. Three were exciting, three relaxing. Selective exposure was measured in accumulated time of channel selection (adapted from Bryant & Zillmann, 1984b).

this might be a strong disdain for nonexciting, "dull" programs by young people. The distaste might be strong enough to prevent the selection of such materials in situations where the selection has benefits. However, although an ideal transverse interaction pattern was not obtained, the divergent interaction displayed in Fig. 8.4 gives ample evidence of selective-exposure behavior as predicted from the consideration of excitatory homeostasis. After all, bored subjects elected to expose themselves significantly more to exciting programs than did stressed subjects, and stressed subjects elected to expose themselves significantly more to relaxing programs than did bored subjects.

In addition to the selective-exposure assessment, subjects' excitatory responding was monitored prior to and after exposure to television. As can be seen from Fig. 8.5, the boredom manipulation resulted in low arousal levels. The stress treatment, in contrast, produced acute excitedness. More important, the findings show that the few bored subjects who elected to expose themselves to relaxing fare remained in a state of low arousal. The large majority of bored subjects managed to alter their excitatory state, however. Through exposure to exciting materials, their arousal level increased significantly. Furthermore, the data show that exposure to the different types of programs was of no consequence for stressed subjects. Regardless of specific contents, exposure led to a reduction of arousal in the stressed subjects, or perhaps more accurately, it allowed stress-

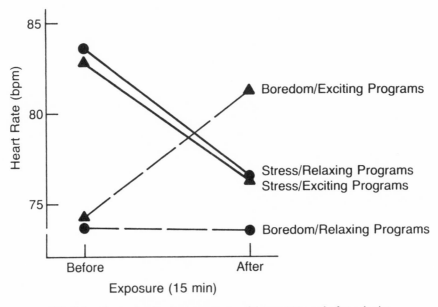

FIG. 8.5. Heart rate after boring and stressful treatments and after selective exposure to exciting and relaxing programs (adapted from Bryant & Zillmann, 1984b).

induced arousal to dissipate. The choice of programs with relaxing contents apparently served excitatory homeostasis well. But so did the choice of programs with exciting contents. The latter can be explained in at least two ways. First, stress may foster levels of arousal that are generally above those that common television fare can accomplish. Stressed persons, hence, can only calm down when watching television—regardless of exactly what they are watching. Still, it must be expected that some types of programs will do better in providing this relaxation than will others. Second, it can be argued that somewhat exciting programs are effective stress-combating choices because of their comparatively high absorption potential. If absorption were not a factor, exciting programs might well be less effective in lowering arousal levels than relaxing programs. But if a confounding of excitatory capacity and intervention potential is assumed, it can be suggested that exciting programs are capable of calming the hyperexcited individual because their distraction effect may outweigh opposing forces.

Notwithstanding the likely confounding in the capability to arouse and absorb (or distract) in some of the stimuli, the findings certainly support the proposal that individuals tend to select exposure to programs that effectively normalize levels of prevailing arousal. The data indicate that such "corrective" behavior might actually overcorrect a nonhomeostatic state. Figure 8.5 shows that subjects tended to overshoot the excitatory middle ground. This overcorrection is likely to be transitory, however.

Excitatory homeostasis is, of course, not the only condition served by stimulus selection. In fact, such selection often serves the evocation of positive affect of the greatest possible intensity (cf. Zillmann, 1980). It is most unfortunate for this pursuit of high emotions that the excitatory reaction habituates with repeated exposure to particular stimuli. The processes in question have been explored in considerable detail for erotica (cf. Zillmann & Bryant, 1984). Erotic stimuli initially produce strong sympathetic reactions, but with massive exposure to the stimuli, these reactions tend to become modest, if not negligible. However, intense excitatory reactions are necessary, though not sufficient, for intensely felt pleasantness. As these reactions become shallow, the hedonic response becomes shallow along with them.

The consequences of such excitatory habituation for selective exposure are obvious: The evocation of intense affect-pleasant sexual excitedness, in this case, requires exposure to novel stimuli to which individuals have not yet habituated. Selectivity in the erotic realm predictably leads away from the common and into the so-called bizarre.

Selectivity of this kind has recently been demonstrated in an investigation by Bryant and Zillmann (1984a). Both male and female subjects underwent massive exposure to common, nonviolent erotic films or experienced no such exposure. Ostensibly while waiting, they were given a private opportunity to watch videos. They could choose from among G- and R-rated materials as well as from among X-rated fare. Explicit erotica were standard (i.e., material to which massively exposed subjects had excitationally habituated) or not standard. The latter type offered sadomasochism in which males dominated females, sadomasochism in which females dominated males, and bestiality with human females. Use of videos was unobtrusively recorded.

The findings show that both women and men, but especially men, who had excitationally habituated to common erotic fare selected and consumed (in terms of time of exposure) significantly more of the uncommon erotic materials than did nonhabituated women and men. Loss of excitatory responding, then, fosters selective exposure to materials that hold the greatest promise of providing intense excitatory reactions as accompaniments of positive affect.

Breaking Out of Bad Moods

The first experimental investigation that explored selective-exposure behavior in an unobtrusive fashion was conducted by Zillmann et al. (1980). It was designed to determine whether mood states influenced selective exposure to broad content categories, such as drama, comedy, and sports. It aimed for a high degree of ecological validity not only in the exposure situation (where programs in such categories competed against one another, and subjects were free not to watch or to watch whatever they pleased), but also in the selection of stimulus materials. A week's prime time offerings had been recorded. All programs were classified by content, and from the pools of content classes, program combinations were randomly drawn (within defined limits). This was done to assure that every subject was confronted with a unique—yet in terms of content classes, identical—choice situation.

The first part of the experiment served to induce a bad, a good, or no particular mood state. Subjects performed an emotion-recognition test. After proper recognition of emotion was emphasized as an important social skill, they were exposed to a series of slides showing ambiguous facial expressions. They chose one of four emotions and stated their solution. The experimenter informed them whether it was right or wrong and recorded their responses. In the bad-mood condition, he failed the subjects and asserted that they got almost all expressions wrong. He also insinuated that the subjects were lacking in a critical skill. By contrast, in the good-mood condition, the experimenter led subjects to believe that they got almost everything right. He also praised them as being highly sensitive to facial expressions. The subjects' performance in the no-mood condition was mixed and said to be at the level of most other persons.

Following this induction of mood, subjects were informed of a delay and invited to pass the time watching television in the experimenter's room. The experimenter explained that, thanks to a new cable service, prime time programs could now be received. He flipped through the channels, stopped at an empty one, and left the subject. As described earlier (Bryant & Zillmann, 1984b), playbacks in the adjacent room fed the monitor, and the subjects' choices were recorded there. The available programs were a situation comedy, an action drama, and a game show. All were parts of series with which the subjects were familiar. As each subject was confronted with a unique triplet drawn from these program categories, the findings can readily be generalized to prime time comedy, drama, and game shows per se.

What exposure behavior can be expected under these circumstances? The programs' excitatory potentials hardly allow specific predictions. Comedy, drama, and game shows can all be highly arousing, and clear-cut differences do not exist. The same is the case for the programs' absorption or intervention potentials. The situation is slightly different for behavioral affinity. Game shows pertain to performance. Contestants succeed and fail, are praised or consoled. However, these shows tend to mix success and failure, and this admixture makes for a stimulus in which behavioral affinity tends to exist as often as it is counteracted. Persons in a bad mood because of failure might find some relief in the exhibition of others' success (although envy might make this unlikely), but they are probably reminded of their own dilemma when seeing others fail. Mixtures of success and failure, then, do not seem to offer a good way out of bad mood.

Only the consideration of hedonic valence seems to allow specific predictions. Both action drama and game shows offer suspense, tension, and many sad moments along with a few happy ones. Comedy, in contrast, is designed to induce laughter, merriment, and euphoria. In short, it is designed to place viewers into a positive, good mood. Based on these considerations, it may be expected that persons in a bad mood should prefer situation comedy over action drama and game shows. Persons in a good mood obviously are less in need of being cheered up. Persons in no particular mood can be expected to have an intermediate appetite for comedy. Their consumption can be considered normative.

The findings concerning the effect of mood on selective exposure are presented in Fig. 8.6. As can be seen, moods exerted a considerable degree of control over selective exposure to the available program types. The influence was not entirely consistent with expectations, however. Whereas exposure to comedy was, as expected, lower for subjects in a good mood than for those in the no-mood condition, subjects in a bad mood did not exhibit the strong preference for comedy they were expected to display. Not only did they not prefer comedy, they shunned it—and very strongly so.

The data on drama and game shows are of interest in that they show significant changes over time. Those subjects in a good mood who had initially elected to watch game shows apparently became increasingly disenchanted with this type of program. They eventually deserted game shows in favor of drama. Subjects in

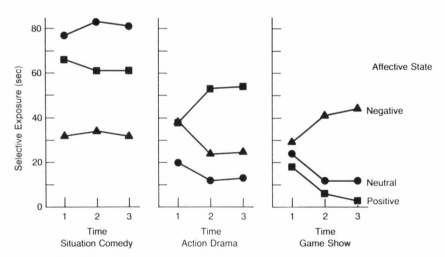

FIG. 8.6.   Selective exposure to situation comedies, action dramas, and game shows as a function of mood. The programs competed against each other. Exposure was unobtrusively recorded over time. Each time block is comprised of 150 seconds (adapted from Zillmann, Hezel, & Medoff, 1980).

a bad mood who had initially chosen drama went the opposite route: They eventually deserted drama in favor of game shows.

How can these shifts and shunts be explained? Program format offers one solution. If it is assumed that upset persons are less patient than relaxed people, it can be argued that the bad-mood subjects who elected to watch drama were too impatient (perhaps still too preoccupied with their mood state) to make sense of the slowly unfolding dramatic events—slowly because the plots of serial action drama span an hour. Game shows, in contrast, are short-formatted. They are composed of numerous rather autonomous segments, and viewers can quickly and without too much cognitive effort catch onto the events and become absorbed by them. Subjects in a good mood, on the other hand, apparently had the needed patience to stick with drama. However, this reasoning leaves unexplained why, over time, they deserted game shows.

The unexpected finding that bad-mood subjects avoided comedy, comparatively speaking, becomes less puzzling when the nature of situation comedy in prime time is considered. It has been established, through content analysis (Stocking, Sapolsky, & Zillmann, 1977; Zillmann, 1977), that the predominant form of humor in prime time comedy is hostile humor, which thrives on teasing and put-downs, on belittlement and demeaning treatment. Given such salience of hostility in prime time comedy, the behavior of the subjects in a bad mood can be understood in terms of the reasoning on behavioral affinity. These subjects had just suffered failure and belittlement themselves, and exposure to others' belittlement, though humorous, was likely to perpetuate their annoyance. The avoidance of such material, then, might constitute intelligent behavior in that it facilitated their breaking out of a bad mood.

This reasoning was put to the test in a follow-up study by Medoff (1979, 1982; see also Zillmann et al., 1980). Behavioral affinity was manipulated in two ways. First, subjects were placed into a bad mood either by frustration only or by frustration and provocation. Subjects were neither frustrated nor provoked in a control condition. Second, subjects were confronted with a choice situation in which either hostile or nonhostile comedy competed against drama. Under these circumstances, affinity is pronounced only for the choice of hostile comedy by provoked subjects. Only in this case can humorous debasement reinstate experienced debasement. Only these subjects should shun hostile comedy. Subjects who were merely frustrated (i.e., unable to complete a task, this being of no social consequence) should be free to seek out hostile comedy, as affinity between contents and experience is rather poor. Nonhostile comedy, finally, should appeal to both frustrated and provoked subjects.

The manipulation of mood states was analogous to that already described (Zillmann et al., 1980). The original procedure confounded failure (i.e., frustration) and insult (i.e., attack, provocation). This confounding was now undone, and frustration was produced by failure and provocation by failure plus insult. Also, subjects could choose between drama and comedy only. The drama was

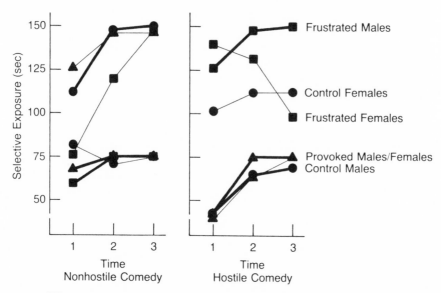

FIG. 8.7.   Selective exposure to hostile and nonhostile comedy as a function of mood. Comedy competed against drama. Exposure was unobtrusively recorded over time. Each time block is comprised of 150 seconds (adapted from Medoff, 1979).

kept constant. Comedy was either hostile or not. All other aspects of the procedure were as before.

The findings are presented in Fig. 8.7. As can be seen, enormous gender differences emerged. In the earlier investigation, apparently due to the discussed confoundings, gender differences had been negligible.

The behavior of female respondents accords rather well with expectations. First, these respondents consumed nonhostile comedy as expected. Selective exposure to nonhostile comedy by provoked females is above the level of frustrated females, and that level, in turn, is above that of females in the no-mood control condition. Second, frustrated females did not avoid hostile comedy, but provoked females clearly did. All this is in line with affinity considerations.

The behavior of male respondents, in contrast, accords well with expectations on one point only: Frustrated men were drawn to hostile comedy. Provoked men tended to avoid comedy, but no more so than the men in the control condition. However, the troubling findings that run counter to expectations concern the consumption of nonhostile comedy. Both frustrated and provoked males, compared to no-mood males, should have sought out nonhostile comedy, but instead they exhibited a strong disdain for it. Could it be that frustrated and angry men are so preoccupied with the circumstances of their experience, especially with what to do about it, that they don't feel like laughing—at least not for some time? Research on gender differences in the response to provocation would support such an account (cf. Sapolsky, Stocking, & Zillmann, 1977; Zillmann, 1979). However, this research also suggests that gender differences vanish as provocation becomes severe. It is conceivable that both males and females, if sufficiently agitated, would find it difficult to escape into merriment by exposure to comedy of any kind—or to entertainment generally. Counter to the contention that watching televised entertainment offers an escape from acute problems, if not from reality (e.g., van den Haag, 1960), severely annoyed persons would probably avoid distraction altogether and concentrate on what they can do about their predicament. The recent observation by Christ and Medoff (1984) that acutely annoyed women elected to watch less televised entertainment overall than did their good-mood counterparts seems supportive of such a proposal.

Gender differences in selective exposure seem to be most pronounced in the area of hostility and aggression. Compared to men, women exhibit less liking for violent entertainment fare altogether (cf. Gunter, 1983). More important, however, there are some research findings that can be taken as suggesting that angry women avoid exposure to such fare, whereas angry men seek it out. The latter points to the possibility that, when it comes to hostile and aggressive behavior, men are not eager to discontinue a presumably noxious preparatory mood state. In fact, they would seem to want to perpetuate it—as if to maintain an emotional readiness for consummatory responses (i.e., retaliatory action).

Freedman and Newtson (1975) conducted an investigation in which males were annoyed or not and then given a choice between films to watch. Annoyed subjects chose significantly more films with violent contents than did nonannoyed subjects. But as Goldstein (1972) had observed similar preferences after subjects had merely read aggressive versus nonaggressive prose passages, the preference for violent fare might be explained as the result of salience and priming (cf. Wyer & Srull, 1981). Subjects are set to engage in violent imagery, and hence, they continue with that activity rather than switch to another. Still, this would mean that such activity is not noxious to men.

The gender difference in question has been shown most clearly in an investigation by Fenigstein (1979). Both males and females were enticed to engage in aggressive, nonaggressive, or no fantasies and then given a choice among numerous film clips for viewing. The choice was made on the basis of brief descriptions of the films' content. These descriptions promised different degrees of violence. Under these choice conditions, it was found that males selected films with significantly greater amounts of violence than did females. But more important, males who had initially engaged in aggressive fantasies exhibited a greater taste for violence than did males who had engaged in nonaggressive fantasies. Females who had engaged in aggressive fantasies, in contrast, did not show a greater appetite for violence than females who had engaged in nonaggressive fantasies. If anything, they were less inclined to watch violence. In a follow-up study with males only, it was further observed that the performance of aggressive acts (i.e., the administration of noxious noise to a peer) enhanced the desire to watch violent films.

Taken together, this research is most suggestive of gender differences in the use of depictions of hostile and aggressive behaviors. Women show little fondness for such materials. Men appear to like them, especially after being enticed by aggressive fantasies or by behaviors that have such a fantasy component. The research does not tell us, however, whether acutely angry men have an appetite for violent entertainment fare, whether acutely angry women have none, or whether that of acutely angry men exceeds that of acutely angry women. Because the subjects were never placed into a state of acute aversion, the data cannot tell us what men or women would do—through selective exposure, in particular—to rid themselves of this state. It is conceivable that provoked men would elect to keep themselves preoccupied with thoughts of retaliation until they accomplished their objective and that provoked women would respond quite differently (cf. Zillmann, 1979). But such possible differences in coping with aversion through deliberate stimulus arrangements cannot be considered to have been demonstrated as yet.

Research on selective exposure as a function of acute fear is similarly inconclusive, though for different reasons. Boyanowsky, Newtson, and Walster (1974) proposed that fearful persons, as a form of mastery training (cf. Fenichel, 1939), should seek out fear-evoking but safe situations. They thought to have provided evidence to that effect by showing that in a university community attendance at a highly violent movie, compared to that of a nonviolent one, rose after the much publicized brutal murder of a student. This observation is open to any number of alternative explanations, however, and cannot be considered to prove anything about selective exposure.

A more controlled investigation was conducted by Boyanowsky (1977). Female subjects were placed into a state of apprehension about their safety and then provided with a choice among various informative and entertaining offerings. They were led to believe, and convincingly so, that another female student had just been attacked close to their locale (high fear) or across town (low fear). No such apprehensions were created in a control condition. The subjects were eventually given a list of film synopses to read, and they were asked to rate their desire to see the described materials. The six films offered were a romantic comedy, a romantic interlude, a documentary on female self-defense, a thriller about an insane girl-hunting murderer, a dramatic episode in which a man attacks another man, and an erotic venture.

If consumption were motivated by mastery ambitions, one would expect the material of greatest behavioral affinity (i.e., the thriller) to be selected by the fearful women. No such preference emerged, however. Useful information (i.e., the documentary on self-defense) was not in increased demand either. It might be speculated that the choice of such material, because of the affinity with fear, would have done little to diminish apprehensions. It can, of course, be argued that the two films of great affinity with prevailing affect should have been avoided by fearful women. This was not the case either, however.

Comedy and romance received high ratings, but their appeal did not differ as a function of fearfulness. Surely, such materials offer little opportunity for mastery training. On the other hand, their gaiety might have turned away the fearful women who could have benefited from exposure (because of absorption and positive valence).

Where, then, was selective exposure affected by fear? Strangely enough, fearful women (in both the low- and high-fear conditions) were attracted to male-male violence and erotic fare. This outcome is puzzling and fails to fit or support any of the rationales under consideration. It cannot be explained as serving a need for mastery training. Nor is it adequately explained as an effort to cut aversion. Whereas the erotic stimulus (i.e., a sexual orgy) can be considered a potent mood changer (because of its great absorption capacity and positive hedonic valence), the clip of intermale violence (because of its affinity with fear as aggression-apprehension) cannot.

The research on selective exposure under conditions of acute fear thus leaves us bewildered, and it can only be hoped that clarifying work is forthcoming in the near future. Research on selective exposure during acute, intensely suffered annoyance—whether it be anger, fear, or an admixture thereof—confronts the problem that individuals in such a state are likely to prepare and engage in actions capable of removing the basis of their annoyance (cf. Zillmann, 1979). Only if evasive and destructive actions fail, are inconceivable, or inadvisable (i.e., associated with punitive contingencies) can individuals be expected to resort to curbing their emotions by arranging their stimulus environment in a way that leaves the causes for their emotions unaltered. In the face of likely assault, for instance, persons are unlikely to resolve their fears by watching television. If, as in the study by Boyanowsky (1977), acutely fearful persons are forced into making entertainment selections, they surely will accommodate the experimenter by choosing something. But such selections might prove a poor simulation of what they would do in duress if they were free in their actions. Entertainment thus seems unlikely to play a critical role in the control of human emotions whose causes can be influenced by direct action—most directly, through avoidance or modifying attack. By the same token, aversive emotions that invite coping through stimulus arrangement that does not alter the causes are those emotions whose causes cannot be altered, at least not through immediate action.

One of these aversive experiences is the premenstrual syndrome in menstruating women. Aversion can be reduced somewhat by appropriate medication, but the experience remains one from which there is no escape and which has to be waited out and suffered through. As women cannot rid themselves of the somatic conditions that create their misery, they should seek alleviation through stimulus arrangement.

Meadowcroft and Zillmann (1984) tested the implications of this proposal for the consumption of entertaining television fare. Female undergraduates, excluding those on oral contraceptives as well as those apparently pregnant, were given a list of familiar prime time offerings (comedies, dramas, game shows) and asked to put together an evening's worth of enjoyable programs for themselves. According to the subjects' report of the onset of their last and next-to-last menstrual bleeding, they were placed into seven 4-day groups throughout the cycle.

Following the suggestion by Hamburg (1966) and Melges and Hamburg (1976) that the premenstrual syndrome is created mainly by the rapid withdrawal of progesterone and estrogen that afforded anesthetizing protection earlier (cf. Zillmann, 1984), it was argued that premenstrual and menstrual women should feel most depressed and, hence, experience the greatest need for being cheered up. This need should not exist, or should exist to a smaller degree, midway through the cycle when estrogen levels are elevated and progesterone levels rise. Comedy was expected to offer the best way out—that is, to serve the desirable mood change most effectively. This prediction is based, of course, on the consideration of hedonic valence.

The findings are presented in Fig. 8.8. As can be seen, the choice of comedy programs was at a maximum prior to and during menses, and it was at a low point midway through the cycle. This is exactly as expected. The only data point that is not perfectly in line with what can be expected on the basis of hormonal conditions is that of days 16 through 20. At this point, both progesterone and estrogen levels are comparatively high, and one would have expected a lower demand for comedy. The women behaved as if their mood was influenced by the

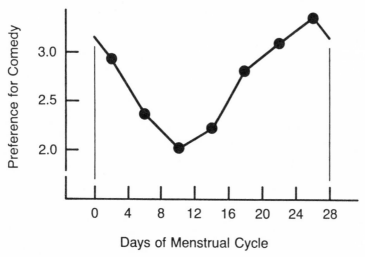

Days of Menstrual Cycle

FIG. 8.8. Selection of comedy for consumption as a function of menstrual conditions. Point 0 defines the onset of menses. The left-most data point (between 0 and 4) indicates selections during menses. The right-most data point (between 24 and 28) indicates selections prior to menstruation. Midcycle selections are given between points 8 and 16 (adapted from Meadowcroft & Zillmann, 1984).

knowledge of forthcoming aversion. But taken together, the findings show that women are quite capable of choosing entertainment programs that hold the greatest promise of alleviating their negative moods. As these choices serve their well-being, they certainly qualify as intelligent behavior—despite the likelihood that most women, if not all, are not cognizant of the causal circumstances of their actions.

On Being Comforted

There appear to exist conditions under which negative affective states are overcome by informative elements of entertaining messages rather than by the intervention of stimuli that make the maintenance of the initial affect difficult, if not impossible. This is to say that exposure to messages may be sought not so much because of expectations regarding particular excitatory and hedonic reactions, but primarily because they contain soothing, comforting information. Those who just confronted a hostile social environment, for instance, might find comfort in presentations that depict kindness in social exchanges. And those who are apprehensive about crime should find appeasement in features that emphasize its effective curtailment. The assumption is that persons who are disturbed about specific conditions that jeopardize their well-being are able to reduce their apprehensions, and along with them their noxious affective accompaniments, by exposure to information that shows their concerns to be unwarranted and groundless. Hence, they should seek exposure to such information. Additionally, they should avoid information that confirms their apprehensions, as exposure could only worsen their negative affective states.

The proposal is reminiscent of dissonance theory (Festinger, 1957, 1964; see also chap. 2 by Cotton in this volume) in that it projects the seeking out of belief-supporting information and the avoidance of belief-challenging messages. The motivational basis for the proposed selectivity is quite different, however. Dissonance theory has concentrated on postdecisional conflict and its implications. The choice of a particular belief can, of course, be considered a decision that gives rise to particular dissonance pressures, these pressures motivating the seeking of confirmatory information and the avoidance of challenging messages. But is it meaningful to assume that similar pressures arise when information is received that challenges what persons would like to believe, not what they actually believe? After all, selective exposure is thought to be motivated by information that is supportive of what could be labeled "wishful thinking." Support for beliefs such as those that nurse apprehensions is actually thought to foster avoidance. The usefulness of stretching the dissonance concept to include implicit beliefs concerning the goodness of personal comfort and safety may thus be questioned. In particular, it seems moot to postulate dissonance forces where aversions as basic emotional experiences are known to provide great motivational power. Be this as it may, the projection stands that comforting information holds appeal to the distressed, whereas discomforting information does not, and that exposure to comforting information should be sought and extended, and exposure to discomforting information avoided and minimized.

In a rare exposure study with children, Masters, Ford, and Arend (1983) provided strong evidence for this kind of selectivity. Four- and five-year-old boys and girls were placed into a nurturant, neutral, or hostile social environment and then provided with an opportunity to watch children's television fare. More specifically, the subjects were always treated neutrally, but a same-gender companion of theirs was not. In the condition of neutral affect, an adult supervisor treated this companion the same way he treated the subject. He repeatedly criticized and belittled the companion in the positive affect condition (i.e., in the nurturant environment). In the condition of negative affect (i.e., in the nonnurturant, hostile environment), in contrast, he admired and praised the companion repeatedly. He admired the child's clothing, for instance, and told the child that he or she was "the most fun of any person I've ever been with" (p. 107). The subjects' affective reactions were thus indirectly produced through the treatment of the companion. Following the induction of affect, subjects were allowed to watch television as long as they liked. They were free to push a button to shut off the monitor and to have the supervisor return. Only one program could be watched. It was either nurturant or neutral. The nurturant program was composed of segments from *Mister Rogers' Neighborhood*. Mister Rogers is highly nonthreatening and supportive at all times, and he makes nurturant comments like "I really like you," and "You know, you are a nice person" (p. 108). The neutral program consisted of clips from news shows for children and featured such items as the sugar cane harvest in Hawaii. The time the children elected to watch television served as the measure of selective exposure.

The findings are summarized in Fig. 8.9. As can be seen, the expected effect materialized for boys only. Boys who had suffered from the nonnurturant, hostile social conditions exposed themselves for significantly longer periods to the nurturant program, compared to boys with nonaversive experience. There were no corresponding differences in exposure to the neutral program.

Why did girls not show the need to substitute a nurturant television environment for their immediate social environment when it was so flagrantly nonsupportive? The data suggest that they were not in great need for nurturance because they may have averted the full impact of the nonnurturant treatment by effectively distracting themselves from it. They apparently resorted to solving puzzles that were available during the aversive treatment. Findings such as these point once again to striking gender differences in coping with aversion.

Although the experiment conducted by Masters et al. (1983) can be considered to have been ineffective in inducing aversion in girls and, therefore, to have produced meaningful exposure data for boys only, it leaves no doubt about the fact that strategies for the aversion-reducing arrangement of environmental stim-

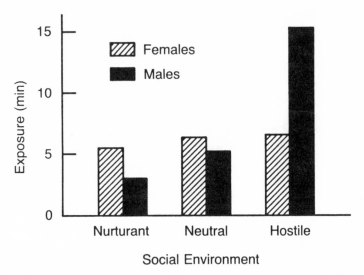

FIG. 8.9.   Exposure to a nurturant television program as a function of affect produced by social experience (adapted from Masters, Ford, & Arend, 1983).

uli, including the selection of television materials, are established quite early in childhood.

Research on the partiality of adults for comforting information has been aggregated in the area of concern with crime. Gerbner and his associates (e.g., Gerbner & Gross, 1976; Gerbner, Gross, Jackson-Beeck, Jeffries-Fox, & Signorielli, 1978) reported a positive relationship between consumption of television and apprehensions about personal safety. They interpreted these data as indicating that heavy viewing of television fare, because of the high degree of violence and victimization it contains, causes these apprehensions about personal safety (see chap. 7 by Zillmann & Wakshlag for a more detailed discussion of this issue). The relationship, should it exist (cf. Hirsch, 1980; Hughes, 1980), can be interpreted quite differently, however. In fact, it has been suggested that any causal linkage might be the opposite of that proposed by Gerbner et al. (Zillmann, 1980). Instead of exposure breeding fear, it could be that fear promotes exposure. Such a reverse projection makes little sense as long as the premise is accepted that television—crime drama, in particular—is laden with nothing but atrocious violent transgressions. If this were so, heavy viewers should indeed get the impression that ''it's dangerous out there''; and given that impression together with a vested interest in believing that the streets are safe, it is difficult to see how these programs could hold any appeal to large audiences. But the message in crime drama is somewhat different. Yes, violent transgressions are plentiful. But they tend to be rectified. Unlike in the real world, the transgressors are promptly apprehended, brought to justice, and duly punished. The overall message in crime drama is that the criminals are put away and that the streets are made safer. Crime drama, by and large, is not a celebration of violent chaos, but rather, a celebration of justice because transgressors are met with punishment. This triumph of good over evil should, of course, hold considerable appeal for those who are apprehensive about crime. It is the type of message capable of providing comfort.

Gunter and Wober (1983) probed the relationship between the strength of beliefs in a just world and consumption of action-adventure drama and found it to be positive. The fact that heavy viewers believed the world to be a just place clashes with the contention that heavy viewing creates fears of becoming the victim of violent crime. But the findings leave open the possibility that exposure may have cultivated the perception of a just world. Nonetheless, the findings can also be interpreted as showing that persons who believe in a just world seek to confirm their beliefs by exposing themselves to drama more frequently than do others. The findings are inconsistent, however, with the view that persons who fail to detect much justice in the world would be particularly eager to consume fiction that projects justice.

Wakshlag, Vial, and Tamborini (1983) provided a more direct test of the selective-exposure hypothesis regarding fear of crime. In a laboratory experiment, these investigators placed male and female subjects in a state of apprehension and later gave them entertainment choices. Apprehensions were made manifest and created by exposure to a police documentary on crime. In a control condition, subjects watched a documentary about the Himalayas. Entertainment choices were made from a list of film synopses. These synopses had been pretested and received scores for the degree to which a film was perceived to feature violent victimization and/or punitive restoration of justice. Measures of

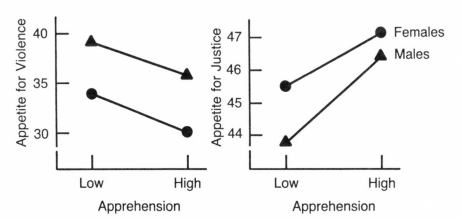

FIG. 8.10.   Selection of drama that emphasizes violent victimization or the punitive restoration of justice as a function of apprehensions about crime (adapted from Wakshlag, Vial, & Tamborini, 1983).

the appeal of violence and justice could thus be attained by summing the scores across selected films.

The findings are presented in Fig. 8.10. Clear-cut gender differences emerged in the appeal of violent victimization. Females exhibited less appetite for violent drama than did males. Additionally, a greater tendency for females to select drama that promises just resolutions is apparent. Notwithstanding these gender differences, however, both apprehensive males and apprehensive females are equally sensitive to the aspects of drama that have been discussed. Persons who were apprehensive about crime selected drama that was comparatively low in violent victimization and comparatively high in justice restoration. This is, of course, exactly what is expected on the basis of the proposed selectivity model. Persons apparently minimize exposure to entertainment that contains disquieting information, and they apparently maximize exposure to entertainment that carries a comforting message.

CONCLUDING REMARKS

From inspection of the available research, it can be safely concluded that affects, moods, and emotions do influence selective exposure to communication. Individuals are apparently sensitive to the effects of a variety of properties of available messages, and they apparently employ this sensitivity to select exposure to messages that are more capable than others of achieving desirable ends. Generally speaking, these ends are excitatory homeostasis, the maximization of positive affect, and the minimization of aversion.

In light of the research evidence, it can be considered established that persons select entertainment: (a) to facilitate excitatory homeostasis, (b) to maximize pleasant excitement, and (c) to reduce aversion. The consumption of entertainment for the purpose of aversion reduction—the self-administered therapeutic scheduling of entertainment, so to speak—has received the most attention. According to the research findings, such aversion reduction can be accomplished by exposure to: (a) arousing materials (in the case of boredom), (b) calming materials (in the case of stress), (c) distracting materials, (d) materials of low behavioral affinity, (e) materials of positive hedonic valence, and (f) materials that contain comforting information.

Gender differences in coping with aversion complicate generalizations to some degree. In particular, coping with anger and fear through selective exposure to entertaining messages remains an unresolved issue that is in need of further exploration.

Taken together, the focus on selection of entertainment under different conditions of affect draws attention to negative affect and our coping with it. This focus shows individuals' selective behavior to be intelligent in that messages are exploited for their therapeutic value. But it becomes clear at the same time that the consumption of entertaining fare has limited aversion-diminishing powers and does not offer a solution to anybody's acute emotional problems.

Finally, it should be clear that what the research has established are certain effects of affect on selectivity. Most of these effects are predictable from the operant-conditioning model that we proposed at the outset of this chapter. This model is parsimonious and useful in the sense that it projects effects with a reasonable degree of accuracy. The model disregards, however, many cognitive processes that presumably accompany and possibly influence selective behavior. The integration of these processes into models with greater predictive accuracy is obviously desirable. Also, many stimulus properties that influence choice behavior may have gone entirely unnoticed. They need to be uncovered and their effects eventually integrated into the models, too. The search for refined explanation must go on!

REFERENCES

Anderson, J. R., & Bower, G. H. (1973). *Human associative memory*. Washington, DC: Winston.

Baron, R. A. (1974). The aggression-inhibiting influence of heightened sexual arousal. *Journal of Personality and Social Psychology, 30*, 318–322.

Baron, R. A. (1977). *Human aggression*. New York: Plenum Press.

Baron, R. A., & Ball, R. L. (1974). The aggression-inhibiting influence of nonhostile humor. *Journal of Experimental Social Psychology, 10*, 23–33.

Berkowitz, L. (1970). Aggressive humor as a stimulus to aggressive responses. *Journal of Personality and Social Psychology, 16*, 710–717.

Boyanowsky, E. O. (1977). Film preferences under conditions of threat: Whetting the appetite for violence, information, or excitement? *Communication Research, 4*, 133–145.

Boyanowsky, E. O., Newtson, D., & Walster, E. (1974). Film preferences following a murder. *Communication Research, 1*, 32–43.

Bryant, J., & Zillmann, D. (1977). The mediating effect of the intervention potential of communications on displaced aggressiveness and retaliatory behavior. In B. D. Ruben (Ed.), *Communication yearbook 1* (pp. 291–306). New Brunswick, NJ: ICA-Transaction Press.

Bryant, J., & Zillmann, D. (1984a). *Erotic appetites after massive exposure to common erotica*. Unpublished manuscript.

Bryant, J., & Zillmann, D. (1984b). Using television to alleviate boredom and.stress: Selective exposure as a function of induced excitational states. *Journal of Broadcasting, 28*(1), 1–20.

Carruthers, M., & Taggart, P. (1973). Vagotonicity of violence: Biochemical and cardiac responses to violent films and television programmes. *British Medical Journal, 3*, 384–389.

Christ, W. G., & Medoff, N. J. (1984). Affective state and selective exposure to and use of television. *Journal of Broadcasting, 28*(1), 51–63.

Collins, A., & Loftus, E. (1975). A spreading-activation theory of semantic memory. *Psychological Review, 82*, 407–428.

Day, K. D. (1980). *The effect of music differing in excitatory potential and hedonic valence on provoked aggression*. Unpublished doctoral dissertation, Indiana University.

Donnerstein, E., & Hallam, J. (1978). Facilitating effects of erotica on aggression against women. *Journal of Personality and Social Psychology, 36*, 1270–1277.

Fenichel, O. (1939). The counterphobic attitude. *International Journal of Psychoanalysis, 20*, 263–274.

Fenigstein, A. (1979). Does aggression cause a preference for viewing media violence? *Journal of Personality and Social Psychology, 37,* 2307–2317.

Festinger, L. (1954). A theory of social comparison processes. *Human Relations, 7,* 117–140.

Festinger, L. (1957). *A theory of cognitive dissonance.* Evanston, IL: Row, Peterson.

Festinger, L. (1964). *Conflict, decision, and dissonance.* Stanford, CA: Stanford University Press.

Freedman, J., & Newtson, R. (1975). *The effect of anger on preference for filmed violence.* Paper presented at the annual conference of the American Psychological Association, Chicago.

Geen, R. G. (1975). The meaning of observed violence: Real vs. fictional violence and consequent effects on aggression and emotional arousal. *Journal of Research in Personality, 9,* 270–281.

Geen, R. G., & Rakosky, J. J. (1973). Interpretations of observed violence and their effects on GSR. *Journal of Experimental Research in Personality, 6,* 289–292.

Gerbner, G., & Gross, L. (1976). Living with television: The violence profile. *Journal of Communication, 26*(2), 173–199.

Gerbner, G., Gross, L., Jackson-Beeck, M., Jeffries-Fox, S., & Signorielli, N. (1978). Cultural indicators: Violence profile no. 9. *Journal of Communication, 28*(3), 176–207.

Glaser, R. (Ed.). (1971). *The nature of reinforcement.* New York: Academic Press.

Goldstein, J. H. (1972). *Preference for aggressive movie content: The effects of cognitive salience.* Unpublished manuscript, Temple University, Philadelphia.

Gunter, B. (1983). Do aggressive people prefer violent television? *Bulletin of the British Psychological Society, 36,* 166–168.

Gunter, B., & Wober, M. (1983). Television viewing and public trust. *British Journal of Social Psychology, 22,* 174–176.

Hamburg, D. A. (1966). Effects of progesterone on behavior. In Association for Research in Nervous and Mental Disease, *Research Publications: Vol. 43. Endocrines and the central nervous system* (pp. 251–265). Baltimore: Williams & Wilkins.

Hirsch, P. M. (1980). The "scary world" of the non-viewer and other anomalies: A reanalysis of Gerbner et al.'s findings on cultivation analyses. *Communication Research, 7,* 403–456.

Hughes, M. (1980). The faults of cultivation analysis: A re-examination of some effects of television watching. *Public Opinion Quarterly, 44,* 287–302.

Kendall, P. C., & Hollon, S. D. (Eds.). (1979). *Cognitive-behavioral interventions: Theory, research, and procedures.* New York: Academic Press.

Landman, J., & Manis, M. (1983). Social cognition: Some historical and theoretical perspectives. In L. Berkowitz (Ed.), *Advances in experimental social psychology* (Vol. 16, pp. 49–123). San Francisco: Academic Press.

Lang, P. J. (1979). A bio-informational theory of emotional imagery. *Psychophysiology, 16,* 495–512.

Levi, L. (1965). The urinary output of adrenalin and noradrenalin during pleasant and unpleasant emotional states: A preliminary report. *Psychosomatic Medicine, 27,* 80–85.

Levi, L. (1969). Sympatho-adrenomedullary activity, diuresis, and emotional reactions during visual sexual stimulation in human females and males. *Psychosomatic Medicine, 31,* 251–268.

Masters, J. C., Ford, M. E., & Arend, R. A. (1983). Children's strategies for controlling affective responses to aversive social experience. *Motivation and Emotion, 7,* 103–116.

Meadowcroft, J., & Zillmann, D. (1984). *Choice of television programs during the menstrual cycle.* Unpublished manuscript.

Medoff, N. J. (1979). *The avoidance of comedy by persons in a negative affective state: A further study in selective exposure.* Unpublished doctoral dissertation, Indiana University.

Medoff, N. J. (1982). Selective exposure to televised comedy programs. *Journal of Applied Communication Research, 10*(2), 117–132.

Melges, F. T., & Hamburg, D. A. (1976). Psychological effects of hormonal changes in women. In F. A. Beach (Ed.), *Human sexuality in four perspectives* (pp. 269–295). Baltimore, MD: Johns Hopkins University Press.

Nevin, J. A. (Ed.). (1973). *The study of behavior: Learning, motivation, emotion, and instinct.* Glenview, IL: Scott, Foresman.

Ramirez, J., Bryant, J., & Zillmann, D. (1982). Effects of erotica on retaliatory behavior as a function of level of prior provocation. *Journal of Personality and Social Psychology, 43,* 971–978.

Sapolsky, B. S., Stocking, S. H., & Zillmann, D. (1977). Immediate vs delayed retaliation in male and female adults. *Psychological Reports, 40,* 197–198.

Schachter, S. (1964). The interaction of cognitive and physiological determinants of emotional state. In L. Berkowitz (Ed.), *Advances in experimental social psychology* (Vol. 1, pp. 49–80). New York: Academic Press.

Skinner, B. F. (1969). *Contingencies of reinforcement: A theoretical analysis.* New York: Appleton-Century-Crofts.

Stocking, S. H., Sapolsky, B. S., & Zillmann, D. (1977). Sex discrimination in prime time humor. *Journal of Broadcasting, 21,* 447–457.

Thorndike, E. L. (1911). *Animal intelligence.* New York: Macmillan.

Thorndike, E. L. (1932). *The fundamentals of learning.* New York: Columbia University, Teachers College, Bureau of Publications.

van den Haag, E. (Spring, 1960). A dissent from the consensual society. *Daedalus,* pp. 315–324.

Wadeson, R. W., Mason, J. W., Hamburg, D. A., & Handlon, J. H. (1963). Plasma and urinary 17-OHCS responses to motion pictures. *Archives of General Psychiatry, 9,* 146–156.

Wakshlag, J., Vial, V., & Tamborini, R. (1983). Selecting crime drama and apprehension about crime. *Human Communication Research, 10,* 227–242.

Wyer, R. S., Jr., & Srull, T. K. (1981). Category accessibility: Some theoretical and empirical issues concerning the processing of social stimulus information. In E. T. Higgins, C. P. Herman, & M. P. Zanna (Eds.), *Social cognition: The Ontario Symposium* (Vol. 1, pp. 161–197). Hillsdale, NJ: Lawrence Erlbaum Associates.

Zillmann, D. (1971). Excitation transfer in communication-mediated aggressive behavior. *Journal of Experimental Social Psychology, 7,* 419–434.

Zillmann, D. (1977). Humor and communication. In A. J. Chapman & H. C. Foot (Eds.), *It's a funny thing, humour* (pp. 291–301). Oxford, England: Pergamon Press.

Zillmann, D. (1978). Attribution and misattribution of excitatory reactions. In J. H. Harvey, W. J. Ickes, & R. F. Kidd (Eds.), *New directions in attribution research* (Vol. 2, pp. 335–368). Hillsdale, NJ: Lawrence Erlbaum Associates.

Zillmann, D. (1979). *Hostility and aggression.* Hillsdale, NJ: Lawrence Erlbaum Associates.

Zillmann, D. (1980). Anatomy of suspense. In P. H. Tannenbaum (Ed.), *The entertainment functions of television* (pp. 133–163). Hillsdale, NJ: Lawrence Erlbaum Associates.

Zillmann, D. (1982). Television viewing and arousal. In D. Pearl, L. Bouthilet, & J. Lazar (Eds.), *Television and behavior: Ten years of scientific progress and implications for the eighties: Vol. 2. Technical reviews* (pp. 53–67) (U.S. Public Health Service Publication No. ADM 82-1196). Washington, DC: U.S. Government Printing Office.

Zillmann, D. (1983a). Arousal and aggression. In R. G. Geen & E. I. Donnerstein (Eds.), *Aggression: Theoretical and empirical reviews: Vol. 1. Theoretical and methodological issues* (pp. 75–101). New York: Academic Press.

Zillmann, D. (1983b). Transfer of excitation in emotional behavior. In J. T. Cacioppo & R. E. Petty (Eds.), *Social psychophysiology: A sourcebook* (pp. 215–240). New York: Guilford Press.

Zillmann, D. (1984). *Connections between sex and aggression.* Hillsdale, NJ: Lawrence Erlbaum Associates.

Zillmann, D., & Bryant, J. (1984). Effects of massive exposure to pornography. In N. M. Malamuth & E. Donnerstein (Eds.), *Pornography and sexual aggression* (pp. 115–139). New York: Academic Press.

Zillmann, D., Bryant, J., Comisky, P. W., & Medoff, N. J. (1981). Excitation and hedonic valence in the effect of erotica on motivated intermale aggression. *European Journal of Social Psychology, 11,* 233–252.

Zillmann, D., Hezel, R. T., & Medoff, N. J. (1980). The effect of affective states on selective exposure to televised entertainment fare. *Journal of Applied Social Psychology, 10,* 323–339.

Zillmann, D., Hoyt, J. L., & Day, K. D. (1974). Strength and duration of the effect of aggressive, violent, and erotic communications on subsequent aggressive behavior. *Communication Research, 1,* 286–306.

Zillmann, D., & Johnson, R. C. (1973). Motivated aggressiveness perpetuated by exposure to aggressive films and reduced by exposure to nonaggressive films. *Journal of Research in Personality, 7,* 261–276.

9 Selective Exposure to Educational Television

Jacob Wakshlag
Indiana University

For many years, educational television has incorporated entertainment to attract young viewers. Capturing and holding an audience in the face of an increasingly attractive and diverse set of entertaining alternatives has been and remains a major concern of producers and distributors of educational material (cf. Lesser, 1974; Mielke, 1983). After all, what good comes from the finest in educational programming if it is not viewed by those who stand to gain from it?

The concern with attracting an audience to education would appear to be a relatively recent phenomenon. Education has traditionally been something done in captive surroundings (classrooms) where exposure has been taken for granted. But the television audience, unlike that in the classroom, is not captive. Any member of the audience is free to choose as he or she wishes from among the diverse set of material available at any given time. And today, one is not restricted to the offerings of a few local broadcasters. One may have basic and pay television channels available via cable, as well as one's own library of video cassettes and discs.

Unlike persons in the classroom, who may be motivated by long-range goals or a teacher's supervision, the in-home television viewer can choose to gratify more mundane and immediate desires. The noncaptive television viewer is free, and apparently uses this freedom, to maximize gratification from exposure. For some viewers, the informational content, in and of itself, may be of sufficient interest to attract exposure. However, for the vast majority of viewers, and for children in particular, the information itself does not seem to be sufficiently gratifying to attract and hold attention. Apparently, most viewers prefer the gratifications offered by entertainment programs most of the time. Viewers may (and apparently do, if the ratings are any indication) ignore the offerings of

191

educational television or, after watching such shows for a short while, decide to switch to the comedy, drama, or sports available on competing channels. Informational shows that do attract more than a handful of viewers contain dramatic or entertaining features. Except for the Sunday morning interview shows like *Meet the Press,* one would be hard pressed to identify any programs, including daily news programs, that are devoid of entertaining embellishments. Thus, for the most part, it would appear that producers and creators of educational and informational fare have embraced the marriage of information and entertainment. The prevailing belief appears to be that such a marriage can only help the cause of education (Zillmann & Bryant, 1983).

EXPOSURE AND ATTENTION

Exposure and attention are highly related phenomena. Exposure is clearly a prerequisite for attention. One must be exposed to something before being able to pay attention to it. Just as clearly, however, attention has something to do with the exposure decision. Inasmuch as one does pay attention to programs when evaluating various options, attention is critical as one explores these various program options and selects the program of choice. No doubt, the maintenance of attention to the program is important for continued exposure as well. The program that fails to hold one's attention is unlikely to be one's exposure choice for long.

By paying attention, the viewer discovers whether the content is sufficiently gratifying to justify initial exposure choice and continued exposure. If a show is sufficiently gratifying, the viewer has no reason to discontinue exposure. If not, the viewer actively engages in efforts to end exposure to the program and may switch to another channel or turn the television set off.

It is the anticipation of gratification rather than the gratification itself that probably drives exposure. After all, if one were watching a program and knew that the "good stuff" was over, one would not be likely to stay and watch the rest. The continuing anticipation of gratification is what holds the viewer to the screen. This anticipation is derived from past experience with the program, with similar programs, or with program elements or characters enjoyed in the past, and the like. It can be assumed that if earlier samplings of the content have proven gratifying, the viewer anticipates similar gratification to result from the future consumption of such content. Thus, a program that provides the right cues will be more likely to attract exposure, at least initially. Research evidence suggests, however, that the use of some such cues (e.g., puppets or clowns, presumably because of their continual presence to which children become accustomed) may not hold young viewers to a program if other expected gratifications are not forthcoming (see Wakshlag, 1981, cited in Bryant, Zillmann, & Brown, 1983). The anticipation of gratification should be affected by gratifying *experiences* encountered during exposure to the program, especially when prior experiences fail to produce clear anticipations.

What types of cues are likely to yield such anticipation? Whereas the theory of gratifiers and the law of affect are explicitly understood (see chap. 8 by Zillmann & Bryant in this volume), little is known about which televised cues are sufficiently gratifying to produce positive effects on exposure. But the recent and parallel emergence of research on factors that enhance or inhibit visual attention is highly suggestive (e.g., Anderson & Lorch, 1983; Rice, Huston, & Wright, 1982). Many attributes have been identified which attract visual attention (i.e., motion, cuts, sound effects, laughter, women's and children's voices, instrumental music) or inhibit it (i.e., long zooms, men's voices, slow music). Such variables are likely candidates for research on factors that facilitate exposure to educational television as well.

SELECTIVE EXPOSURE CUES

Given the importance of attracting an audience to educational television, one would expect a large body of literature probing for variables that could aid in this effort. There is only conventional wisdom, however, to guide expectations. Entertaining elements such as humor, special effects, and auditory features seem to be prime targets for inquiry. Although a large number of studies have investigated the relationship between such formal attributes of television programs and visual attention (Anderson & Lorch, 1983; Rice et al., 1982), very few have looked at their effects on selective exposure. Wright, Calvert, Huston-Stein, and Watkins (1980) related the occurrence rates of such features to national audience ratings for Saturday morning children's programs. High action and violent content were predictors of viewership for preschool children. Among 6–11-year-old children, however, viewership was best predicted by variability and tempo. Thus, some variables that control children's attraction to particular entertainment programs have emerged. But the role of these features on exposure to educational programs has only recently become the subject of empirical examination.

Humor and Selective Exposure

The first study that directly addressed the relationship between formal attributes and exposure to educational programming (Wakshlag, Day, & Zillmann, 1981) experimentally manipulated the involvement of humor. In this investigation, educational programs were manipulated to produce a version without humor and versions with humor in a slow, intermediate, and fast pace. The amount of humor in the humor conditions was held constant. Humorous episodes were combined into blocks (12 individual episodes in the fast-paced versions; six blocks of 2 episodes in the intermediate versions; three blocks of 4 episodes in the slow-paced versions). The variation could thus be described as distributed versus clustered humor in an educational program. The humorous episodes were semantically unrelated to the content of the programs. These manipulated messages competed against two others that were simultaneously available on different channels of a television monitor. While in a waiting period, first- and second-grade school children could watch any of these programs for as long as they chose, or they could turn off the set if they so desired. The children were unaware that their program selections were mechanically recorded (see chap. 3 by Webster & Wakshlag in this volume for a detailed description of this measurement procedure).

It was found that exposure to these educational programs was substantially longer when they contained humor. Subjects of both grades and sexes spent far more time watching the programs when they contained humorous episodes than when they did not. The study thus demonstrates that children, when left alone to watch what they please, will favor educational programs that contain humorous entertainment.

Looked at in another way, the findings suggest that nonentertaining educational television programs are not likely to compete very well with other educational programs, such as *Sesame Street,* which contain humor and other embellishments. Furthermore, when faced with programs whose principal function is entertainment, such as those typically available from the networks, nonentertaining educational programs would probably fare even worse. Thus, when faced with several program choices and when not coerced or supervised by parents or other sources of authority or guidance, children choose to view entertaining television. Educational programs that do not contain such material are likely to compete very poorly with those that do, at least as far as attracting child audiences is concerned.

Equally important, and perhaps even more so to the designer of educational television, the study found that the distribution or pacing of humorous episodes had a substantial effect on duration of exposure to the programs. Presumably because humorous stimuli were more frequently available during the initial sampling of programs and because more frequent encounters with humor discouraged the sampling of competing programs, the fast pacing of humorous stimuli attracted viewers more rapidly and held them longer to the program. This effect can be seen in Fig. 9.1.

During the first 2 minutes, subjects spent about 33% of their time with the program containing humor. Given that they were confronted with three unfamiliar programs, this is exactly what one would expect in terms of random sampling. The use of humorous inserts at a slow pace failed to increase exposure beyond this initial level. In the relatively long time periods without humor, the children apparently sampled other programs and stayed with them. In sharp contrast, the use of humorous inserts at an intermediate and particularly at a fast pace produced considerable increases in exposure. Furthermore, once these high-

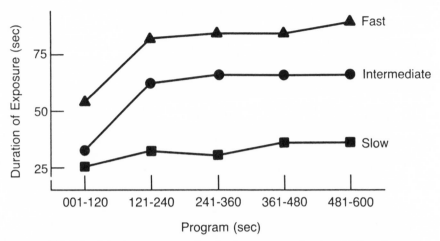

FIG. 9.1.   Selective exposure to educational programs as a function of differently paced humorous inserts. The programs competed, one at a time, against two others that were simultaneously available on a television monitor. The fast-paced interspersion of humor (triangles) proved more effective at attracting and sustaining an audience than the interspersion of the same humorous materials at an intermediate pace (circles); the latter, in turn, proved more effective than the interspersion of humor at a slow pace (squares) (adapted from Wakshlag, Day, & Zillmann, 1981).

er levels of exposure were reached, they were maintained. The fast-paced condition proved most effective at quickly attracting viewers to the program and maintaining high levels of exposure.

Based on these results, presenting humorous stimuli in a rapid fire of short bursts appears to be the winning formula for attracting viewers. As long as exposure alone is the objective, there would seem to be no reason to limit the use of humor: The more that humor is employed, and the faster its pace, the better. If the sole objective of a televised show is to attract the largest possible audience, the "rapid fire of short bursts" formula might be used without reservation. However, this formula may not serve a program's educational objectives very well. Taking numerous, brief "timeouts" for humor may be effective in attracting and holding viewers, but it also disrupts the continuity of the educational message. There must be some point at which such disruptions become too numerous and have a detrimental effect on learning. Thus, limits for the use of humorous stimuli must be recognized. For young children, however, demands on attention have to be kept to a minimum anyway. They are easily distracted and might pay even less attention to the educational material—and consequently, may learn less—without the interspersed humor.

Apparently cognizant of their audience's short attention span, creators of television fare for children often design their programs using short, self-contained segments. Humor can easily be inserted around these segments, so that they can be employed to their fullest advantage for attracting exposure and attention while minimizing the risks associated with disruptions of the educational message. Notwithstanding arguments about rapid-fire presentations and their potentially negative impact on the development of rehearsal processes considered essential for learning (Singer, 1980), it appears that as long as the essential elements of an educational message are not disrupted, the frequent use of short humorous segments is effective in attracting and sustaining viewers' exposure and would appear to be a desirable strategy. Distributing the humorous segments throughout the show is much more effective than clustering the humor into longer timeouts as far as exposure is concerned. Other research suggests that the same is true for attention and information acquisition as well (Zillmann, Williams, Bryant, Boynton, & Wolf, 1980). Although there certainly must be limits to the nature and number of interruptions in an educational message, empirical research has yet to identify these limits.

The audience-drawing capacity of the frequent use of short humorous segments does not appear to be restricted to young school children. High school students were the subjects of an investigation by Schleicher, Bryant, and Zillmann (cited in Bryant et al., 1983). In this study, it was found that the frequent interspersion of humorous stimuli within an educational program attracted more students, and attracted them longer, than did the interspersion of the same stimuli at a slower pace.

Background Music and Selective Exposure

It is unlikely that humorous gratifiers are the only type capable of enticing viewers to a program. According to Lesser (1974), appealing music is one production element used to attract viewers and hold them once they have been attracted. One need only look at, and listen to, the introductions of *Sesame Street* and *The Electric Company* to see how this formula is applied.

According to a review of the literature by Seidman (1981), fast melodic music tends to elicit happiness, gaiety, excitement, and so forth, whereas slow music tends to elicit less positive and less arousing affective states. If fast music does, in fact, elicit more active and positive moods, educational programs containing such music should prove to be more immediately gratifying than the same programs without such music. The anticipation of such gratifications drives exposure as well. Thus, children hearing positive and rousing music should expect a program to be more gratifying than a similar show without such music. Fast melodic music, then, because it is gratifying in itself and/or because it cues the child to expect a program that is likely to be gratifying, should entice exposure.

A recent experiment designed to assess the effects of background music on selective exposure (Wakshlag, Reitz, & Zillmann, 1982) did find that certain kinds of music increased exposure. In this study, educational films were manipulated to produce versions that contained either fast-liked, slow-disliked, or no background music. The music was pretested using subjects of the same age as those in the main experiment (first- and second-grade school children) in order to be sure that the musical pieces were, in fact, differentiated in terms of appeal. One of the two experimental programs competed against two others, one of which contained music typical of that employed in such films. The experimental films were systematically rotated to increase generalizability. As with the study on humor, the children, ostensibly during a waiting period, were allowed to view any of the three available programs by changing the channel on the monitor. They were unaware that their choices were being mechanically recorded. Earlier experience with the procedure indicated that program choices were made quickly. Consequently, selective exposure was monitored only for the first 2 minutes.

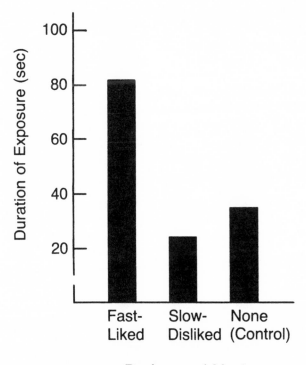

Background Music

FIG. 9.2.   Selective exposure to educational programs as a function of background music. The programs competed, one at a time, against two others that were simultaneously available on a television monitor. Selective exposure to the programs was greatly enhanced when they contained fast-liked music. Selective exposure to the programs was somewhat reduced when they contained slow-disliked music, when compared to the control condition (no background music) (adapted from Wakshlag, Reitz, & Zillmann, 1982).

Subjects of both sexes and grades responded strongly to the background-music manipulation. As can be seen from Fig. 9.2, selective exposure to the educational programs was greatly enhanced when they contained fast-liked background music; it was somewhat reduced when the background music was slow and disliked. In the fast-liked background music condition, subjects spent about 67% of their time with the program. Given that they could choose from three available programs, this is twice what would be expected from random viewing behavior. The other two conditions fell close to or somewhat below chance expectations. Thus, the educational programs competed far more effectively when they had fast-liked background music than when they had slower and less appealing music or no background music at all.

Analyses of exposure choices over time indicated that any exposure drawing power of the music emerged within 30 seconds. However, only the fast and appealing music was effective in attracting viewers to the program and at maintaining, at least for the 2-minute period, the exposure gained.

As far as exposure is concerned, gratifying music acts as does gratifying humor in attracting young viewers to a program. Programs that contain such gratifications appear to compete far more effectively for viewers than those devoid of them. The findings also show that exposure choices are long lasting. Once an exposure choice is made, children tend to stay with the chosen channel. The fact that this is the case for educational television programs that are not principally entertaining is encouraging. It suggests that once a program becomes a person's initial choice, it is likely to remain the choice for an extended period of time. For a program to be successful at attracting viewers, it must, therefore, attract them quickly. The findings indicate that there is an exposure inertia not unlike the attentional inertia identified by Anderson, Alwitt, Lorch, and Levin (1979). The longer a child views a program, the less likely he or she is to change the channel and view another.

CONCLUDING REMARKS

A substantial amount of work remains to be done if we are to develop a sound understanding of the factors that influence exposure to educational programs. The influences of music and humor have been identified for younger viewers. Nothing is known about how these factors influence exposure by adults or the effects of other cues on the selective exposure choices of children.

Relatively little is known about how the factors that influence exposure affect later steps in the learning process. The use of humorous episodes at a fast pace has been shown to exert a positive influence on visual attention and information acquisition (Zillmann et al., 1980) as well as on selective exposure. Thus, there appears to be little reservation about the use of humor as a generally effective and desirable ingredient in educational television. With the exception of irony and similarly confusing forms of humor (Zillmann et al., 1984), humor seems to aid greatly in delivering televised education to children.

Such a generalization cannot be made, however, for background music. Fast rhythmic background music has been found to reduce visual attention to educational programs. More important, it has also been observed to reduce information acquisition (Wakshlag et al., 1982). Thus, pleasant and/or fast rhythmic background music, which is heard as the educational message is being delivered (unlike interspersed humorous episodes), may distract viewers from the educational message even though it attracts exposure to the program as a whole. This important and subtle difference between the episodic use of humor versus the continuous use of background music has yet to be adequately unraveled. It would appear, however, that the continued presence of gratifiers, when they are unrelated to the message, may attract people to a program but interfere with the delivery of information. Gratifiers that are related or incorporated into the message may be preferable (Smith, 1984), but may be difficult or expensive to incorporate. The use of intermittent timeouts for humor (or perhaps, a brief musical interlude) may be far more easily and inexpensively incorporated when needed to enhance exposure and attention to, or learning from, televised messages.

Extensions to other areas of information dissemination by television are readily apparent. Accounts of both successful and unsuccessful information campaigns across a slew of areas abound (cf. Rice & Paisley, 1981). In such cases, it is easy to see that those who most need the information being disseminated are often those who are the least motivated to obtain or pay attention to it. If these individuals were already motivated to obtain the information, they would probably already have it. Thus, information campaigns often foster knowledge gaps between the haves and the have-nots or produce little or no effect on the knowledge levels of their targets. If one cannot instill a utilitarian motivation to foster attention to messages (i.e., "watch, this is good for you"), perhaps one can resort to more mundane or immediate inducements (i.e., "watch, this is entertaining").

The incorporation of entertaining elements in informational messages would appear to be worthwhile. As has been pointed out elsewhere (cf. Atkin, 1981), the use of entertainment can enhance the effectiveness of information campaigns. But many of the elements of entertainment that might be effective have yet to be isolated and specified.

As research in this area expands, one should take note of the fact that those features that are useful at attracting exposure may not have the same facilitative effects on attention, learning, attitude change, or behavior modification. Similarly, message features that have positive effects at these levels may have differing effects on exposure. Thus, a variable that has little utility for gaining exposure may, in fact, be highly effective at enhancing information acquisition. Likewise, a variable that is ineffective at facilitating information acquisition from a program which one is forced to view—as is the case for television shown in the classroom or in typical formative evaluations of educational programs—may be quite effective at inducing exposure. As more programs become simultaneously available, knowledge of the cues that enhance selective exposure becomes even more crucial. The detection of cues that enhance exposure without impeding other communication objectives remains an important area for future inquiry.

REFERENCES

Anderson, D. R., Alwitt, L. F., Lorch, E. P., & Levin, S. R. (1979). Watching children watch television. In G. Hale & M. Lewis (Eds.), *Attention and cognitive development* (pp. 331–361). New York: Plenum.

Anderson, D. R., & Lorch, E. P. (1983). Looking at television: Action or reaction? In J. Bryant & D. R. Anderson (Eds.), *Children's understanding of television: Research on attention and comprehension* (pp. 1–33). New York: Academic Press.

Atkin, C. K. (1981). Mass media information campaign effectiveness. In R. E. Rice & W. J. Paisley (Eds.), *Public communication campaigns* (pp. 265–279). Beverly Hills, CA: Sage.

Bryant, J., Zillmann, D., & Brown, D. (1983). Entertainment features in children's educational television: Effects on attention and information acquisition. In J. Bryant & D. R. Anderson (Eds.), *Children's understanding of television: Research on attention and comprehension* (pp. 221–240). New York: Academic Press.

Lesser, G. S. (1974). *Children and television: Lessons from Sesame Street.* New York: Random House.

Mielke, K. W. (1983). Formative research on appeal and comprehension in 3–2–1 CONTACT. In J. Bryant & D. R. Anderson (Eds.), *Children's understanding of television: Research on attention and comprehension* (pp. 241–263). New York: Academic Press.

Rice, M. L., Huston, A. C., & Wright, J. C. (1982). The forms of television: Effects on children's attention, comprehension, and social behavior. In D. Pearl, L. Bouthilet, & J. Lazar (Eds.), *Television and behavior: Ten years of scientific progress and implications for the eighties: Vol. 2. Technical reviews* (pp. 24–38) (U.S. Department of Health and Human Services Publication No. ADM 82-1196). Washington, DC: U.S. Government Printing Office.

Rice, R. E., & Paisley, W. J. (Eds.). (1981). *Public communication campaigns.* Beverly Hills, CA: Sage.

Seidman, S. A. (1981). On the contributions of music to media productions. *Educational Communication & Technology Journal, 19,* 49–61.

Singer, J. L. (1980). The power and limitations of television: A cognitive-affective analysis. In P. H. Tannenbaum (Ed.), *The entertainment functions of television* (pp. 31–65). Hillsdale, NJ: Lawrence Erlbaum Associates.

Smith, S. M. (1984). *Use of background music to induce context-dependent memory.* Paper presented at the meeting of the Midwest Psychological Association, Chicago.

Wakshlag, J. J., Day, K. D., & Zillmann, D. (1981). Selective exposure to educational television programs as a function of differently paced humorous inserts. *Journal of Educational Psychology, 73,* 27–32.

Wakshlag, J. J., Reitz, R. J., & Zillmann, D. (1982). Selective exposure to and acquisition of information from educational television programs as a function of appeal and tempo of background music. *Journal of Educational Psychology, 74,* 666–677.

Wright, J. C., Calvert, S., Huston-Stein, A., & Watkins, B. (1980). *Children's selective attention to television forms: Effects of salient and informative production features as a function of age and viewing experience.* Paper presented at the meeting of the International Communication Association, Acapulco, Mexico.

Zillmann, D., & Bryant, J. (1983). Uses and effects of humor in educational ventures. In P. E. McGhee & J. H. Goldstein (Eds.), *Handbook of humor research: Vol. 2. Applied studies* (pp. 173–193). New York: Springer-Verlag.

Zillmann, D., Masland, J. L., Weaver, J. B., Lacey, L. A., Jacobs, N. E., Dow, J. H., Klein, C. A., & Banker, S. R. (1984). Effects of humorous distortions on children's learning from educational television. *Journal of Educational Psychology, 76,* 802–812.

Zillmann, D., Williams, B., Bryant, J., Boynton, K. R., & Wolf, M. A. (1980). Acquisition of information from educational television programs as a function of differently paced humorous inserts. *Journal of Educational Psychology, 72,* 170–180.

10 Cable and Program Choice

Carrie Heeter
Bradley Greenberg
Michigan State University

The most pervasive assumption of research on program choice has been that when viewers select a program to watch, they evaluate all program options available at the time and select the one that best fits some criterion. In a television environment where only three networks are available, this assumption rarely has been questioned. However, in cable television environments, as the number of program options increases vastly, the assumption becomes less plausible. One implication of the cable environment for selective-exposure research is to suggest that the actual choice process needs better articulation.

Many different approaches, both theoretical and atheoretical, have been advanced to predict program choice. Most of them move directly from predictor factors to choice outcome on the basis of a program-choice maximizing assumption. Articulation of a choice process could help identify conditions under which a predicted outcome would be most likely to occur. For example, a number of studies have found a relationship between aggressive predisposition and the amount of television violence viewed (e.g., Atkin, Greenberg, Korzenny & McDermott, 1979; Lefkowitz, Eron, Walder, & Huesmann, 1972; Stein & Friedrich, 1972). Subjects whose process of choice does involve evaluation of all alternatives and selection of the best program will be aware of all violent and nonviolent program options. Those who check only a few options may not be aware that nonviolent (or violent) program options exist, and therefore, they might not select the program they most prefer. Thus, subjects who evaluate all program alternatives should demonstrate the strongest relationship between aggressive predisposition and exposure to violent shows. Similarly, Zillmann and colleagues are finding evidence of a relationship between affective state and program choice (e.g., Zillmann, 1982; Zillmann, Hezel, & Medoff, 1980).

203

When viewers turn on television to relax or unwind, they are expected to seek absorbing content that can serve to disrupt their internal rehearsal of aversive situations, which motivated them to seek relaxation, and content that will not remind them of these situations. However, when viewers watch for excitement, they seek arousing fare. Here again, those viewers who use a maximizing choice process should best demonstrate this relationship. In contrast, those who do not screen the full set of available options may have their needs less satisfied.

Marketing research models of program choice also ignore the choice process in their attempts to predict viewership patterns from program-type preferences. Program-type preferences have been defined, measured, and used to differentiate consistently among different subgroups of viewers (Gensch & Ranganathan, 1974). However, attempts to predict viewing from preferences and liking for shows have met with little success. Scheduling factors (e.g., program-type availability at any given time, program length, channel, and day of week; e.g., Bowman & Farley, 1972; Bruno, 1973; Frank, Becknell, & Clokey, 1971) as well as viewer availability to watch television when preferred show types are on (Gensch & Shaman, 1980) appear to confound any observed relationships between preferences and viewership. Scheduling factors confound program-preference models in broadcast television environments. Cable television may improve prediction by offering a more consistent and larger array of program options.

Webster and Wakshlag (1983) integrate many of the divergent program-choice research approaches into a single model of program choice. They identify the following components: viewer availability, viewer awareness of program options, program and program-type preferences, viewer needs, viewing group, and the structure of available programming. The approaches they bring together were conceived of and studied in the context of network-dominated broadcast television. The present chapter uses Webster and Wakshlag's framework to detail changes and additions to those components when the television environment is cable television instead of broadcast. A model of the actual choice process with cable is advanced, which may also have utility in broadcast situations. Research on cable and programming to date is limited, but where available, preliminary findings are reported. Finally, a research agenda is suggested.

VIEWER AVAILABILITY
AND PROGRAM STRUCTURE

Gensch and Shaman (1980) suggest that viewer availability may be the best predictor of viewership. Using a trigonomic network share timeseries model, they were able to explain 85% of the variance in network viewing share across a year at 7:30 p.m., 50% of the variance at 9:30 p.m., and 44% of the variance at 10:00 p.m. The annual component parallels changes in the amount of daylight. They propose that nontelevision activities determine the size of total network viewing and that behavioral assumptions about how viewers determine what to watch may require a subtle change. Rather than first selecting programs and then organizing other activities, individuals may first determine whether or not to watch television and then decide what to watch.

Structural programming factors have consistently confounded attempts to predict network viewing behavior on the basis of content or program-type preferences. Factor analytic attempts to isolate program types from viewing data find scheduling factors (e.g., day of the week, time of day, network channel, etc.) exerting more influence than program type on the resultant groupings of programs. Webster and Wakshlag (1983) argue that viewer availability to watch television "is the single factor most responsible for the absence of content-based patterns of viewing, as well as, the presence of structually defined viewing patterns" (p. 438).

All the studies that have sought to define program types or predict actual viewership on the basis of preferences have thus far considered broadcast viewing situations, normally concentrating entirely on the major networks. Thus, three different programs are available at any given point in time. It is the limited and variable structure of program options that makes predictions of network viewership so sensitive to structural factors. Cable television alters the available structure, expands program options, and provides more consistently available content types. In doing so, cable reduces the importance of viewer availability in terms of both time and content.

Cable's Program Option Structure

Cable channels tend to specialize (to different degrees) in some type of content, often making it available 24 hours a day. For example, ESPN insures that sports programming is always a viewing option; Reuters' Stock Channel permits constant exercise of the preference for watching stock news; Nickelodeon devotes itself to children's programming. Unlike broadcast viewing, where those who prefer sports must wait until it is offered, much of cable's content structure is constant.

Channels available over cable can be aligned on a continuum of program predictability by content specificity. The networks, independent stations, superstations, and other general-appeal channels would be the least predictable, offering different types of content that is often different from day to day and from time slot to time slot among days. Then there are generic content-typed channels, such as ESPN or the movie channels, where a broadly defined program type is always available, although there is uncertainty whether the viewer will like the specific program being shown (e.g., rugby vs. baseball, *The Clockwork Orange* vs. *Mary Poppins*). MTV, offering short clips of rock music with accompanying video, and CNN, with a repeating cycle of newscasts, are more specialized. A viewer who likes news or rock music is fairly certain to find some preferred content quite quickly. Finally, there are channels so predictable, with repetitive, continuous content, that all they offer might be the time of day or local weather.

Because of the greater variety and fixed structure of available content with cable, program choice should better reflect viewers' content preferences, particularly among those viewers who take advantage of cable's diversity and among those who have content preferences for which specialized channels exist. Cable may provide a better environment for assessing the impact of program-type preferences.

Another structural impact of cable, which has more implications for *how* television is viewed than *what* is viewed, is program length. The networks traditionally offer hour and half-hour programs, and even the movies and sports events that exceed this tend to start and end on the hour or half-hour. On cable, some of the channels run programs with very different lengths. MTV provides short clips of 5–7 minutes. CNN goes through a 45-minute news cycle. Text channels have cycles of varying length. Sporting event and movie channel programs consistently have variable end times. The weather channel is meant to be viewed for very short periods. This structural variation may alter the practice of watching in half-hour blocks. Viewers may join and leave programs at different points, in part on the basis of their own availability, having just completed viewing something else. Also, there is program content available during commercial breaks, when with only the networks to choose from, there are only other commercials to turn to.

An analysis of interactive cable viewing data found that these cable channels are watched in different ways (Heeter, D'Alessio, Greenberg, & McVoy, 1983). One third of all channel changes to the networks resulted in a viewing stretch longer than 15 minutes. The average time per network stretch was 1 hour. MTV, on the other hand, resulted in stretch viewing from only one tenth of all changes to that channel. MTV stretch-viewing periods lasted about 50 minutes. CNN was in between: One-fifth of changes resulted in stretches, lasting an average of 30 minutes.

Similarly, an examination of *when* viewers change channels throughout a composite hour cycle (each of the 24 hours of the viewing day collapsed into a single hour) identified peaks of channel changing at the hour and half-hour. Slight increases were also observed near quarter-hour marks, conforming to expectations of the network program and commercial structure. However, channel changing was spread across the hour cycle and was by no means limited to those predictable peaks. Rarely did changing for any minute in the hour drop below 70% of the rate expected by chance, if changes were evenly spread across all minutes of the hour.

Channel Loyalty

Channel loyalty is cited by Webster and Wakshlag (1983) as one of the routinely observed features of viewing behavior in broadcast studies, and it appears to predict a significant amount of the variance in viewership. They define channel

loyalty as "the tendency of programs on the same channel to have a dispropor-
tionately large duplicated audience" (p. 434).

Channel loyalty takes several forms in models of broadcast network viewing.
The "inheritance effect," also labeled "audience inertia," where viewers of one
show on a channel are likely to continue watching the next show on that channel,
has been one of the strongest predictors. Inheritance effects have been found to
occur primarily between adjacent programs, with effects ranging in size but
accounting for less than 50% of the second show's total audience (Goodhart,
Ehrenberg, & Collins, 1975). For programs on the same channel separated by
more than one other program, effects are generally negligible.

Another way of defining channel loyalty has been as the tendency for viewers
to watch a particular channel, even when a program that used to be on it has been
replaced. In a study of the impact of network affiliation change by local stations,
Wakshlag, Agostino, Terry, Driscoll, and Ramsey (1983) found that most viewers continue to watch news on the same *channel* even though the network news
they were accustomed to watching had moved to a new channel.

In broadcast models, channel loyalty has been considered relatively content
free (in part because the adjacent or replacement program may be totally different
from the original show). Instead, channel loyalty is interpreted to be an outcome
of stochastic or "as if random" processes (Goodhart et al., 1975). An alternative
or additional conceptualization of channel loyalty would be a "tendency to
watch programs on one channel in preference to others" (Wakshlag et al., 1983,
p. 53). With cable, there are three reasons to expect channel loyalty to be more
pronounced. First, many of the cable channels specialize in particular program
content. Thus, we would expect channel loyalty to cease to be a content-free
function and, in fact, to become confounded with program-type loyalty. Second,
with commercial television, programs have been traditionally considered a "free
public good," with no direct cost to the viewer. With cable, special pay services
(for the most part, movie channels) and tiers of special channels are available for
an extra monthly fee. Viewers who are conscious of paying for certain channels
may watch those channels more than they would were those channels available at
no cost. Third, because of the large number of cable channels, identification of
favorite or usual channels may be a means of simplifying the choice process,
avoiding the need to evaluate all channels and instead concentrating on a subset
of channels that are regularly considered. In fact, viewers have been found to
watch a subset of channels regularly (Nielsen Newscast, 1983), which has been
labeled an individual's "channel repertoire" (Heeter et al., 1983).

Channel Repertoire

Cable television's impact on broadcast television is often reported in terms of
differences in viewership to channel types (e.g., Webster, 1983). The channel
types reported tend to be based on channel source rather than on channel content

(e.g., network channels, independent, pay movie, PBS, and basic cable). Webster presents an analysis of viewing shares with and without cable across 24 markets. Weekly viewing shares among cable viewers are lower for local network affiliates and public television stations. Pay cable channels attract a 14–20% share in pay cable homes. Distant stations draw a 10% share in the largest market and as much as 46% in smaller markets. The remaining cable-only channels account for very little viewing time (less than 10%). These kinds of aggregate comparisons do not address the impact of cable on individual viewers. They demonstrate that networks still attract the plurality of the viewing share and that the individual basic cable channels do not attract appreciable aggregate viewing shares. Therefore, to conclude that cable does not alter viewing-choice process or outcome may eventually be warranted, but studies of individual and household use of cable suggest that cable has substantial impacts. For example, although viewing shares (percentage of overall viewing time) of public television and independent and network stations are lower among cable households, the cumes (percentage of households that watch the channel) are higher for cable (Webster, 1983). Cable viewers watch more different channels, if for less time per channel.

Cable viewers may watch more different channels, but they watch far fewer than the total number of available channels. In cable systems with 20 or more channels available, an average of about 10 different channels is watched regularly (Heeter et al., 1983; Nielsen 1983). Other studies report fewer significantly viewed channels, often in cable systems with lower channel capacities, but in each case, cable viewers do watch more different channels (Webster & Agostino, 1982; Television Audience Assessment, Inc., 1983; Webster, 1983).

Individual use of each channel in a 35-channel system was assessed in a study by Heeter (1984). Of 35 channels carried, only the 3 local network affiliates were regularly watched by 50% or more of the cable subscribers surveyed. HBO, WTBS, and a local independent were watched by 40–50%. Nine of the 22 other channels available only with cable (ESPN, MTV, CNN, Nashville, Cinemax, USA, CHN, Nickelodeon, and an "inspirational" channel) were watched by one tenth to one third of the viewers. Thirteen cable channels were watched by less than one tenth of the subscribers. This pattern suggests that one individual's repertoire of 10 regular channels may be very different from another's repertoire.

Cable viewers have a limited set of channels that they watch regularly. The broadcast networks (or at least one or two of the networks) tend to be common across channel repertoires. But specialized cable channels are watched by highly fragmented audiences. About 10% of the cable viewers surveyed had channel repertoires of 2 or fewer channels (Heeter, 1984). For 11%, the repertoire consisted of 12 or more channels. Viewers with small channel repertoires and viewers whose repertoires include only broadcast channels are not likely to be taking full advantage of the content available on cable that would appeal to them. Conversely, a viewer whose repertoire consists of CNN, Reuters' Stock Channel, and AP News is using cable to specialize in highly preferred content, but possibly misses out on other preferred options.

We have suggested that cable's expanded and more consistent program availability structure decreases the importance of viewer availability to watch television and should increase the importance of channel loyalty and program-type preferences in predicting program choice. Next we turn to viewer awareness and the actual choice process.

VIEWER AWARENESS
AND PROGRAM-CHOICE PROCESS

Although the broader and more constant program structure of cable decreases the importance of viewer availability in predicting program choice, it increases the importance of viewer awareness. Webster and Wakshlag (1983) point out that both uses and gratifications models and the program-type preference models of selective exposure assume perfect viewer awareness of program alternatives. Similarly, predictions that certain affective or arousal states will lead to exposure to certain content presuppose awareness or willingness to search for unknown program content. With cable, the assumption that each time viewers select a program they are aware of and weigh all program alternatives to select a most preferred option is untenable. There are simply too many options. Even on a general basis, cable subscribers are not very aware of the different channels available to them over cable, let alone the different programs.

Arbitron (1983) reports that "cable focus groups conducted in June, 1981 revealed that cable subscribers are not aware of all the services available to them, or even of what service they're watching at any given time" (p. 13). In door-to-door interviews, viewers were able to correctly identify an average of 9 of 35 available channels by number or location on the channel selector, and they were aware of one additional service of uncertain location (Heeter, 1984). Twenty-three percent of respondents were able to identify only 0–3 channels. A common response was, "I don't know, I just watch TV;" they had little knowledge of which local broadcast channels existed, let alone the specialty of cable offerings. Another 23% correctly named 14–27 channels, and the remainder identified between 4 and 13. The number of channels viewers could identify was highly correlated (.60) with the size of their channel repertoire. Respondents generally were familiar with more channels than they watched regularly.

To begin to explain the differences in viewer awareness of alternatives and the differences in channel repertoire, we turn to an information-processing model of program choice. Heeter (1984) posits that program choice follows the progression of a "well structured problem with indefinite goals." Greeno (1976) defines this type of problem as one where viewers "adopt a goal that is indefinite in the sense that it is satisfied by any of several alternatives, and the selection of an alternative is based on information generated within the process of problem solving'' (p. 479). Applying this model to program choice, viewers are assumed to approach a viewing situation with a variety of overt and covert potential goals (or needs) that might be satisfied by watching any number of different available programs. For example, a viewer's affective state may suggest certain needs (e.g., a need for arousal, a need for arousal reduction) in addition to his or her general content and program preferences. More than one program may satisfy portions of the viewer's needs to some extent. Thus, the goal is indefinite in terms of specific content. The program options are arrayed on structured channels. Although many cable channel options are more content consistent than broadcast channels, both media provide a relatively fixed, formatted set of channel options, all easily accessible, making the program-selection task well-structured and routine in comparison to many other choice tasks (e.g., selecting a book to read or a restaurant for lunch). Greeno (1976) suggests that ''when a problem-solver sets an indefinite goal [e.g., satisfying some combination of needs], the ensuing process often involves a search for information in the situation, without knowledge of how the information will be used'' (p. 480). In program choice, the search for information is an examination of program options, accompanied by a covert matching of needs with programs that fulfill them, resulting eventually in selection of a matched needs-program option. The nature of this orienting search for information will be a function of information-processing abilities and preferences of the individual viewer, as well as various system factors. For each channel alternative checked, a viewer must make a judgment. There are three possible outcomes of the option evaluation: reject, accept, or consider and check other options. Accepting or rejecting are the less taxing information-processing evaluations. Holding a program option in memory for consideration and searching for additional desirable options induce greater uncertainty and, as more possible options are identified, require greater information-processing effort and skill in terms of sheer memory as well as weighing options that meet different needs to different extents.

It is important to note that not all television viewing invokes this model of program choice. About half of the time, cable viewers know what they will watch before they approach the viewing situation (Heeter, 1984), whereas the other half of the time, programs are chosen at the time of viewing (Television Audience Assessment, Inc., 1983). When viewers turn to television to see a specific, preselected program, the choice process specified here does not occur.

Orienting Search

There is evidence that some cable viewers attempt to become aware of program alternatives. Two studies reported greater guide use among cable households (Greenberg, D'Alessio, Heeter, & Sipes, 1983; Television Audience Assessment, Inc., 1983), although another study found no significant difference

(Sparkes, 1983). Guide use with cable was bimodal, with one third of viewers almost always checking a guide before watching television and one third almost never doing so (Heeter, 1984). Another means of becoming aware of program options is scanning the channels themselves. Cable viewers are more likely to scan. One third of noncable viewers, 47% of basic cable, 49% of single pay, and 52% of multipay subscribers reported almost always or often scanning channels before deciding what to watch (Television Audience Assessment, Inc., 1983). These efforts do not appear to be uniformly successful. Despite guide checking and channel scanning, two thirds of cable viewers were aware of few or no program alternatives at the time of viewing, and less than one third were aware of what was on all or most other channels (Television Audience Assessment, Inc., 1983).

Examination of the different methods of channel scanning suggest different impacts on awareness and channel repertoire, depending on the method used. Three dimensions of an orienting search have been identified: *processing mode* (automatic vs. controlled), *search repertoire* (elaborated vs. restricted set of channels checked), and *evaluation orientation* (exhaustive vs. terminating searches) (Heeter, 1984). These dimensions (see Table 10.1) appear to reflect consistent viewer approaches to the choice process. Shiffrin and Schneider (1977) define controlled processing as "temporary activation of a sequence of elements that can be set up quickly and easily, but requires attention, is capacity-limited (usually serial in nature), and is controlled by the subject" (p. 1). In contrast, automatic processing is "activation of a learned sequence of elements in long-term memory that is initiated by appropriate inputs and then proceeds automatically" (p. 1). Applied to channel scanning, an automatic search might be operationalized as scanning the channels in the order they appear, requiring little mental effort to scan every channel. A controlled search would be channel

TABLE 10.1
Orienting Search-Pattern Attributes

Ia.	Automatic Processing[a]	searching channels in numerical order
Ib.	Controlled Processing	searching channels in a purposive, regular order other than numerical
IIa.	Elaborated Search Repertoire[a]	a search pattern that includes all or most channels
IIb.	Restricted Search Repertoire	a search pattern that includes a limited number of channels
IIIa.	Exhaustive Evaluation[a]	searching *all* channels of an individual's search repertoire and returning to the best option
IIIb.	Terminating Evaluation	searching channels of an individual's search repertoire in order, only until the first acceptable option is located

[a]Indicates orienting search attributes most likely to lead to full awareness of program alternatives.

scanning in an order that moves from one selected channel to another selected channel, driven by some selectivity factor(s) other than channel order. Like automatic searchers, controlled searchers tend to use the same selected order each time they scan channels, but their search pattern is capacity limited, requiring more information-processing skills than automatic search to scan the same number of channels. The automatic search, because it hits each channel irrespective of familiarity with or interest in that channel, is likely to make the viewer more aware of cable's program options than a controlled search (Heeter, 1984).

Thirty-six percent of respondents reported scanning 26 to 35 channels in order (with a mode of 35, encompassing 20% of the respondents). These were classified as using the automatic processing mode. Fifty-three percent checked between 0 and 5 channels in order, suggesting a controlled search of specific channels in an order of their own design.

An orienting search can be elaborated, including most or all of the channels available on the system, or it can be restricted to a small number of options. Elaborated searches have better potential for viewer awareness and require more information-processing effort. Forty-two percent of cable viewers reported scanning 34–35 of 35 channels possible. Fifty-five percent checked 0 to 14 channels ($\bar{x} = 5.9$), evidencing restricted searches.

Shiffrin and Schneider (1977) also label different outcomes sought in the choice-evaluation process. A terminating search occurs when the viewer abandons the search as soon as the first option that meets some minimal standard is located (in economic terms, a "satisficing" approach). An exhaustive search includes the scanning of all channels that comprise the individual's search repertoire, followed by a return to the best alternative. An exhaustive search requires more information-processing activity, both in terms of sheer volume of input and in terms of weighing more alternatives, and the potential of being faced with an ambiguous or difficult choice. It also increases the likelihood that a viewer will become aware of cable program options. Half of the cable subscribers surveyed normally engaged in terminating searches, 46% used exhaustive searches, and 4% were not sure (Heeter, 1984).

Viewers were found to have consistent, habitual orienting search patterns. After describing their pattern, more than half the respondents claimed that they "almost always" used that same approach. Three fourths of them used the pattern they described at least 50% of the time.

Controlled searchers tended to check a restricted number of channels ($r = .97$) and more frequently used terminating searches ($r = .23$). Terminating searchers used their search pattern significantly less (66%) than did exhaustive searchers (77%). Elaborated searchers checked channels automatically and were most likely to use exhaustive searches ($r = .25$).

To summarize, the orienting search dimensions are highly related (Heeter, 1984). The search pattern likely to elicit the most viewer awareness would be the automatic, exhaustive, elaborated search. Viewers who are aware of all program options should be more likely to find one that best suits their needs if it exists on the cable system and should, therefore, most clearly evidence more correct predictions of selective-exposure research and program-preference models.

Reevaluation

One definition of an "active viewer" is a person who engages in demanding orienting searches to select programs. Once a program has been selected, that critical active processing may cease until the program ends, or frequent reevaluation of the chosen program can continue with the intent of changing to other alternatives if it does not meet expectations. Again, viewers who actively engage in reevaluation are likely to watch programs more consistent with their program preferences or need states.

Cable viewers change channels more often at commercials between and during programs than noncable viewers (Greenberg et al., 1983; Heeter, 1983; Television Audience Assessment, Inc., 1983). For both cable and noncable, channel changing occurs more often during shows that are watched once or occasionally than during viewers' regular shows (Heeter, 1983).

Cable viewers have been classified into four levels of channel-changing activity by Guttman scalogram analysis, each group comprising about 25% of the total viewers (Heeter, 1984). The least active group rarely changes channels; the second group does so primarily between programs; the third group changes when commercials come on during a show; and the most active group changes in the middle of a show, other than at commercials as well. All of the channel-changing measures were significantly related to each other. The passive viewers average perhaps one channel change every 90 minutes during regular shows and one change every 45 minutes during nonregular shows. They search for something to watch less than twice a day, and only 9% of their members ever watch more than one show at a time. The most active reevaluators change channels three out of every four commercial breaks, change two of every three periods between programs, and change during 44% of the shows they do watch (other than at commercials). Overall they report changing channels 10 times an hour during regular shows and 12 times during nonregular shows, and two thirds of them sometimes watch more than one show at a time.

Viewing Style

Half of the cable subscribers surveyed generally do not even consider changing channels until the program they originally selected has ended. They approach the viewing situation from what might be termed a "program orientation." The other 50% use commercial breaks as an opportunity to examine other program options, and half of them (24% of the total subscribers) will even change in the midst of program content, exhibiting the weakest program orientation and greatest activity level while viewing.

A viewing style analysis of interactive household viewing data tends to support these systematic differences in viewing style and program orientation. Three modes of viewing were identified and operationalized: channel sampling or scanning (watching a channel or a "string" of channels each for 4 minutes or less); extended sampling (watching channels 4–15 minutes—less than a full program, but more than a brief scan); and program or "stretch" viewing (conservatively defined as viewing a channel 15 minutes or longer to avoid underestimating program viewership). On the average, scanning comprised 8% of total viewing time, extended sampling 10%, and program viewing 82%. Scanning and extended sampling were consistent across days (average correlations $= .70$), were highly correlated with each other ($r = .92$), and exhibited strong individual differences across households.

The choice process variables described and proposed here have been found to be highly interrelated in ways consistent with information-processing expectations. There are viewers who engage in elaborated, exhaustive, automatic orienting searches. They also tend to be the ones engaging in more frequent reevaluation. They are familiar with more different channels on the cable system. They have larger channel repertoires, and they watch more cable channels. They tend to be younger adults, consistent with the information-processing literature which identifies young adults as possessing the best information-processing skills (Watt & Krull, 1974). These viewers are the most aware of programming options and presumably should exhibit the best fit between preferences and needs and program exposure.

The information-processing model suggests that viewers with different information-processing approaches will watch cable in different ways, and this is supported by the consistent interrelatonships. The wide individual differences further suggest that an individual information-processing variable may differentiate viewing styles.

VIEWING GROUP

Webster and Wakshlag (1983) point out that most models of program choice ignore the role of group viewership, despite the fact that most viewing occurs in groups and group composition affects the program selected. They detail the possible influences of group viewership on the choice process in general:

> First, an individual's specific program preferences may have to operate through the viewing group to determine a program selection. Second, a program choice, per-

haps the result of some intense viewer preference, may affect the group composition. Finally, the nature of the group itself, may be a cause of specific program preference. For instance, a parent wishing to view with children, might prefer a program that is suitable for the group, but is otherwise unappealing. (p. 441)

But what impact does cable have on group viewing? The choice process is much more complex with cable, as discussed throughout, because of so many different choices. Because some of the channels appeal to particular and specific content preferences (e.g., sports, news, Nickelodeon, Playboy Channel), more conflict over what to watch might be expected. There is a greater likelihood that each person in a viewing group would select a different optimal program if they were aware of all viewing alternatives and if they selected the best one for their own needs. But somewhat surprisingly, one study that compared cable and noncable group decisions found no significant differences in how often people in their households agreed on what to watch, in the infrequency with which they watched something other than what they would have watched alone, and in the infrequency with which they left the viewing situation rather than be exposed to disliked programming (Greenberg et al., 1983).

Cable viewing with a remote channel selector might be expected to increase the dominance of one individual (i.e., whoever holds the channel selector). Contrary to this expectation, there was no difference between cable and noncable channel selector dominance by the randomly selected respondents (Greenberg et al., 1983). Within cable homes, females were less likely to report that they controlled the channel selector and more likely to report that someone else changed channels when they wished they wouldn't (Heeter, 1984).

Cable viewing in a group might also be expected to evidence less channel changing than when viewing alone. When viewing alone, there are few constraints on changing channels as the viewer becomes bored, or at commercials, or in the middle of a show. When viewing in a group, there is the distinct possibility that others might object. Again, contrary to expectations, when viewers were asked separately about channel-changing behaviors while alone and in a group, more channel changing was reported in the group situation than when alone (Greenberg et al., 1983).

In fact, viewers in cable and noncable homes both reported on the average more guide checking while watching, more channel changing between shows, and more channel changing at commercials when in a group than while watching alone. One explanation is that there is more diversity in the group's viewing preferences, and the changes are to accommodate that. Another explanation is that individual differences in channel changing exist, but in a group, there is a tendency for the channel changer to dominate, with more resultant changes on the average in groups than across randomly selected individuals reporting on their own behavior when watching alone.

ACCESS TO CHANNELS

Cable also introduces various means of accessing its multiple channels, and these have different implications for influencing the program-choice process. Such channel-access factors do not fit well into any of Webster and Wakshlag's (1983) existing categories and should probably be added to their model.

Cable television typically provides viewers with a channel selector that is separate and different from the traditional built-in television set dials. Cable channel selectors range from small hand-held digital units, to bulky push-button units, to combinations of the built-in television set dial for channels 2–13 with a separate unit for additional channels, and so on. The subscriber may instead substitute some other commercially available unit (e.g., remote infrared selector or a cable-ready television set). Different attributes of these channel selectors may affect viewers' channel-selection patterns.

Remote Control

The most obvious factor is whether or not the channel selector can be comfortably accessed from some normal viewing position. Selectors with remote extension cords (or wireless selectors) greatly reduce the effort involved in changing channels. Increased ease of channel changing should presumably result in more channel changing with other elements held constant. Specifically, we would expect viewers with remote channel selectors to be more likely to engage in orienting searches that are exhaustive, extended, and automatic. They should be familiar with more channels, watch more different channels, and engage in more frequent reevaluation, zapping commercials, changing in the middle of a show if it fails to suit them, and watching more than one show at a time. In short, they should be more effective at locating the content available on cable that best fits their needs.

In 1982, the Federal Communications Commission commissioned a study of the impact of broadcast channel selector types on UHF viewership in noncable households. The comparisons included continuous versus discrete single and double built-in dials, as well as remote selectors. No significant difference was found in the number of quarter hours of UHF programming viewed across the different selectors. The study was based on diary data reported in 15-minute blocks, which may be too gross a measure to tap the increased channel sampling of UHF channels (and other channels) that the literature reviewed here would predict (Brenner & Levy, 1982).

A more recent comparison of remote and nonremote channel selectors examined orienting searches by cable and noncable viewers. No difference was found in noncable viewers: One third with and one third without remote selectors almost always or often scanned channels to decide what to watch. A difference in the predicted direction was found among cable viewers, where 54% with remote selectors and 47% without remote selectors scanned channels, although the difference was less pronounced than the researchers expected (Television Audience Assessment, Inc., 1983).

Two other studies considered the impact of remote selectors among cable viewers. One of the studies (Greenberg et al., 1983) characterized cable viewers with remote selectors as: (a) watching less afternoon television, prime time television, and less television overall; (b) less likely to say they watch too much television; (c) more likely to zap commercials during and between shows; (d) more likely to change channels during a show; (e) more likely to believe it's hard to decide what to watch; (f) more likely to report that others change channels when they wish they wouldn't.

Watching less television is consistent with the expectation of more selective viewing, assuming that selective viewers may turn the set off when nothing desired is on. Increased channel changing implies frequent reevaluation. Difficulty in deciding what to watch could be consistent with an extended, exhaustive orienting search, where the viewer seeks maximal information before selecting one alternative.

The second study (Heeter, 1984) specifically assessed the relationship of remote selectors with elements of the model proposed here. A remote selector was associated with significantly more reevaluation, a more extensive orienting search, and a larger channel repertoire in bivariate comparisons, as expected. However, contrary to hypotheses, no significant relationship was found between presence of a remote selector and channel familiarity and exhaustive versus terminating searches.

None of these studies were specifically designed to assess the impact of remote selectors. A universal problem with research on them is a self-selection bias: Noncable households and cable households in at least two of the sample cable systems had remote selectors because they were willing to pay for them. A further common weakness is the confounding of different types of remote and nonremote selectors. For example, in one of the cable systems studied, remote selectors were digital, hand-held units, whereas those who elected not to pay for the remote capability received push-button units on very short cords. A research design that controlled for self-selection (perhaps by identifying cable systems where all subscribers are provided with remote units and others where remote is not offered) and channel-selector type could better address this issue.

Type of Selector

More subtle and complex than the question of remote control is the effect of different types of channel selectors. To exemplify potential impacts, some of the major selector types can be described and their implications for the choice process explored.

Older cable systems with limited channel capacity often still use the discrete dial built into a television set for accessing channels. With a dial, channel order for orienting searches is essentially fixed. The viewer can choose whether to cycle clockwise or counterclockwise, but is forced to at least pass over every channel in order when changing. To the extent orienting searches are engaged in, they are likely to be elaborated (checking many channels) and automatic (following the numerical channel order). Given forced exposure to all channels in the rotation, channel familiarity might be expected to be greater. For reevaluation, however, changing channels at commercials or trying to watch more than one show at a time, with the specific intention of returning to the original channel shortly, can be quite cumbersome. Reevaluation might be expected to be reduced. Overall, the cumbersomeness of moving purposively from one channel to another, nonadjacent channel might inhibit selection processes and, therefore, viewer effectiveness at identifying content on cable that best suits their needs.

When older 12-channel cable systems add new channels, they frequently provide a unit separate from the television dial to access new channels but continue to use the set dial for the original channels. The necessity of moving between two modes of access for different groups of channels may encourage viewers to concentrate on one of the two groups, limiting channel familiarity, size of orienting search, and channel repertoire.

A common cable channel selector is the push button, normally consisting of one row of 12 buttons, and a three-position switch on the side, making available 36 channel positions. On push-button units, it is easiest to change channels either horizontally (i.e., within a row) or vertically (i.e., between rows), which may influence orienting search order. Where a channel is positioned and the popularity of vertically and horizontally adjacent channels may influence its use. With a push-button unit, channels are accessed spatially, rather than numerically. Pretesting of an instrument to assess channel familiarity using a list of channel numbers found the more industrious push-button selector respondents using their fingers to try to match their spatial memory of where the channel was with the number to which it should correspond (Heeter, 1984). There may be a tendency for viewers to specialize in one row. Channel changing is easy, from one specific channel to another or straight down a row or column. Channel familiarity as well as channel repertoire might be expected to be larger. Also, viewers with a strong spatial orientation may be more skillful and more frequent channel changers.

Digital channel selectors, on which channels are accessed by entering numbers on a keypad, probably encourage a different approach. Here, an orienting search is likely to occur either from known channel number to known channel number (controlled) or in numerical order (automatic). An extended automatic search in a 35-channel cable system would require entering 70 digits (2 digits per channel). Considerably more effort is required than with a push-button unit to scan all the channels, suggesting a restricted search, less channel familiarity (but knowledge of channels by channel number of those that are known), and perhaps a smaller channel repertoire with digital selectors. Reevaluation should be equivalent or enhanced due to the ease of moving from specific channel to specific channel. Viewers comfortable with numbers and calculators should change more often and be more skillful at locating desired content.

Many of the digital selectors include a built-in function for "preprogramming" 10 channels, such that the 10 programmed channels may be automatically scanned in the programmed order at the press of a single button. Pretesting results suggest that few cable viewers with these devices are even aware of the programmable function. Those who are aware and do use it are likely to have a very fixed orienting search pattern limited to 10 channels and always following the same order.

A comparison of digital remote selectors and short-cord push-button units found equivalent channel changing for the purpose of turning to specific shows and to see what else was on. Digital viewers changed more often when bored, to avoid commercials, for variety, and to watch more than one show (Heeter, 1984). These results are confounded with the impact of remote control. No systematic examination of the impact of cable channel-selector type has yet been undertaken.

CABLE AND PROGRAM SATISFACTION

Most of the premises set forth in this chapter have been based on the assumption that cable, by making available more and different programming, has the potential to enhance the correlation between viewer preferences and viewer needs and program exposure. Yet, most of the research conducted on cable has concentrated on viewership of channels and channel types rather than on programs and program types. A few studies have examined aggregated program-type viewership. Cable subscribers, on the average, perceive themselves as watching more movies, sports, weather, national news and news in general, and less local news, fewer talk shows, and fewer soap operas since they subscribed to cable (Heeter, 1983). The reported change in program-type viewership suggests that there may be some difference in program exposure due to cable.

A study of diary-reported viewing by cable and noncable respondents found fewer, and somewhat contradictory, differences. Television Audience Assessment (1983) measured program-type exposure over a 2-week period, finding that pay cable subscribers watched more movies and sports and less public affairs and news shows than basic cable or noncable viewers. All cable viewers watched more sports. The following program types were not differentiated by cable subscription: comedies, action adventure shows, dramas, variety entertainment, and miscellaneous. The availability of cable in homes altered the viewing of only a few program types.

News viewership has been studied in more detail. Henke, Donohue, Cook, and Cheung (1983) report less frequent news viewing among cable subscribers, particularly less network news. Baldwin, Heeter, Anokwa, and Stanley (1983) found that among cable viewers, 25% of their news viewing was on cable-only channels. Of the 20 minutes spent with cable news channels or programs, one fourth occurred in periods when no broadcast news was available (demonstrating greater exercise of program-type preference with cable). The remainder of news viewing occurred when broadcast news was also available (greater exercise of specific program preference within an already available program type). Similarly, Hill and Dyer (1981) report that 39% of cable subscribers watched local news on a broadcast channel, and an additional 16% watched local news on a distant broadcast channel available to them only with cable.

Implicit in the premise that cable offers and viewers avail themselves of more programs that satisfy their needs is the corollary that cable viewers will be more satisfied with the programs that they choose to watch. Television Audience Assessment (1983) used their qualitative audience appeal and audience impact scores to compare cable and noncable viewer ratings of the programs they watched over a 2-week period. Both groups rated news programs, entertainment shows, and movies at about the same level. Noncable viewers were neither more nor less satisfied with broadcast programs than were cable viewers. Cable respondents did rate the cable programs at the same appeal level as the broadcast programs they watched. Overall, satisfaction with television was significantly higher among cable respondents, but program satisfaction was not different. The researchers conclude that it is the individual program, not the means of delivery, that determines appeal and impact ratings.

The program appeal index measures "overall entertainment value" and provides an estimate of whether viewers will plan ahead to watch a show again. Program impact measures intellectual and emotional stimulation, involvement, and the likelihood of viewers watching commercials placed within a program. Thus, these two satisfaction indices are confounded by viewing style behaviors that differ between cable and noncable viewers. Studies that more clearly define and measure program satisfaction and viewer-need satisfaction are needed before concluding definitively that cable does not result in greater viewer-need satisfaction. Program-type loyalty and other need-based program-choice predictions should be assessed on an individual level, under more controlled comparisons, isolating the impacts of number of program options and consistent content structure.

DISCUSSION AND RESEARCH AGENDA

Cable television differs from traditional broadcast television along a number of fundamental dimensions that have implications for program choice. Some of these differences have the potential to improve predictions of selective exposure, whereas others further confound the issues. The most obvious change is that the number of channels increases, often dramatically, from a range of 1 to 10 channels available over the air, to as many as 108 or more channels over a cable system. Second, the structure of programming available over the three broadcast networks is highly variable by program type (movies, sports, talk shows, comedies, action adventures, etc., all at different times, but not all the time), but the time structure for broadcast programming tends to be fixed, with programs typically lasting 30, 60, 90, or 120 minutes. On cable, the situation is reversed. There are many channels specializing in a particular program type (e.g., country music or news) so that much of the programming content is fixed. But program length is highly variable, with some "programs" lasting a few minutes and others for hours. Third, access to cable is different. Cable offers remote extension cords and channel selectors other than the traditional dial. Finally, television programs have been considered a "free" public good. But with cable, some of the channels are available for a package price, and others are charged for individually.

This chapter has begun to explore the implications of these cable-broadcasting differences for program choice. Many of the propositions suggested here have yet to be tested or are based on limited research. The research agenda is extensive.

We have suggested that the expanded program options and more consistent content structure with cable will decrease the impact of viewer availability to watch television and of scheduling factors, with a result of improving program-choice predictions based on program-type preferences. Suggested also is the possibility of enhanced predictions for all need-based models of program choice. These expectations must be tested empirically.

It has been noted that cable channels have varying degrees of content specialization and program-length cycles, and that they are watched in different ways by varying numbers of cable subscribers. Channel loyalty may be an even stronger predictor of viewership with cable, perhaps confounded with program-type loyalty. How much of the variance in viewership does cable channel loyalty explain? Can channel-use profiles be created? Are there channel types, distinguishable on the basis of use? What factors (structural, content, placement) determine channel use?

Channel repertoire has been defined as the set of channels that a viewer regularly watches. What causes a large or small channel repertoire? How does a channel repertoire develop? How quickly? How stable is it? To what extent does a channel repertoire limit viewers from watching (or even knowing about) content on other channels? There has been some evidence that individuals in a household share the same or similar channel repertoires. To what extent? How well does an individual's channel repertoire reflect his or her individual preferences? How can channel repertoire be used to define audience fragmentation? How can channel repertoires be characterized to describe a viewer's television fare?

Viewer awareness has been proposed as a key link between viewer needs and selection of the best alternative program. This can be tested empirically by manipulating awareness. How are guides used? Can a more effective guide be developed that will alter awareness and program choice? What impact would educating cable subscribers about the channels on their system have on viewing? Will increased awareness alter viewing patterns? Does channel-selector type or remote capability influence awareness?

A model of program-choice process has been proposed which posits adoption of an indefinite goal, capable of being satisfied in different ways and to different extents by more than one program option, where selection of a program option is based on information generated within the problem-solving process as to what alternatives are available and which needs they best serve. Only one study has tested this model, and it defined and linked general channel familiarity, orienting search pattern, reevaluation tendencies, and channel repertoire size (Heeter, 1984). Laboratory study is needed to assess whether goal clarification actually occurs during an orienting search. Do viewers evaluate alternatives with an "accept/reject/consider and check others" framework? An inverted U-shaped relationship between uncertainty and the attractiveness of a situation is consistently found in research on information-processing abilities and preferences (e.g., Eckblad, 1963; Munsinger & Kesson, 1964). Does this same distribution occur for channel-selection processes? If so, the expectation that program choice is a function of information-processing abilities may be supported.

There appear to be systematic relationships among the various choice-process measures. An orienting search that uses exhaustive evaluation is also likely to include an elaborated search repertoire and an automatic processing approach. That composite behavior pattern is associated with ongoing reevaluation. The interrelationships need to be defined more clearly. A small set of viewer types differentiated by viewing style or program-choice style may exist, and that classification can be used in further research on selective exposure. Orienting search has been measured only by self-report thus far. How valid are those data? What is the relationship between choice process and outcome? In terms of channel repertoire? In terms of viewer satisfaction?

The choice-process model is based on one individual selecting a program. What happens in the group viewing situation? There has been evidence of more channel changing by a group than by an individual alone. Can the model be applied to group viewing? Do goal clarification and orienting searches occur in that setting? If so, it may be a good opportunity to study the process where it is more overt, perhaps even where verbal discussions take place. If not, how then is the group choice made? Do children engage in the same choice process as their parents? How do their viewing styles develop?

Many of the propositions advanced in this chapter can be linked to other bodies of research. For example, research on the need for arousal (e.g., Berlyne, 1960; Donohue, Palmgren, & Duncan, 1980; Zuckerman, 1979) may provide an explanation for differences in program-choice styles. Those with high needs for arousal may be the most active viewers. Cortical as well as limbic arousal research should be considered. Studies that have examined attention to the screen (e.g., Anderson, Alwitt, Lorch, & Levin, 1979; Anderson & Levin, 1976: Husson, 1982) in situations where viewers did not have the opportunity to change channels may be extended to cable channel-changing situations to determine how closely attention and channel changing are motivated by parallel program or attention attributes. Research on selective exposure, information processing, and decision making are also primary candidates for integrative efforts. What has been presented here is a beginning. Perhaps it merits further exploration.

REFERENCES

Anderson, D., Alwitt, L., Lorch, E., & Levin, S. (1979). Watching children watch television. In G. A. Hale & M. Lewis (Eds.), *Attention and cognitive development* (pp. 331–363). New York: Plenum Press.

Anderson, D., & Levin, S. (1976). Young children's attention to *Sesame Street*. *Child Development 47*, 806–811.

Arbitron Ratings. (1983). *Two-way cable diary test: A summary of findings.* Laurel, MD: Arbitron Ratings.

Atkin, C., Greenberg, B., Korzenny, F., & McDermott, S. (1979). Selective exposure to televised violence. *Journal of Broadcasting, 22*(1), 47–61.

Baldwin, T., Heeter, C., Anokwa, K., & Stanley, C. (1983). *Programming: The challenge to fill 100+ channels.* Paper presented at the convention of the Speech Communication Association, Washington DC.

Berlyne, D. E. (1960). *Conflict, arousal and curiosity.* New York: McGraw-Hill.

Bowman, G., & Farley, J. (1972). "TV viewing: Application of a formal choice model. *Applied Economics, 4*, 245–259.

Brenner, S., & Levy, J. (1982, February). *UHF viewing and television channel selector type.* (UHF Comparability Task Force Report). Washington, DC Office of Plans and Policy, Federal Communications Commission.

Bruno, A. (1973). The network factor in TV viewing. *Journal of Advertising and Marketing Research, 13*(5), 33–39.

Donohue, L., Palmgren, P., & Duncan, J. (1980). An activation model of information exposure. *Communication Monographs, 47*, 295–303.

Eckblad, G. (1963). The attractiveness of uncertainty *Scandinavian Journal of Psychology, 4*, 1–13.

Frank, R., Becknell, J., & Clokey, J. (1971). Television program types. *Journal of Marketing Research, 8*, 204–211.

Gensch, D., & Ranganathan, B. (1974). Evaluation of television program content for the purpose of promotional segmentation. *Journal of Marketing Research, 11*, 390–398.

Gensch, D., & Shaman, P. (1980). Models of competitive television ratings. *Journal of Marketing Research, 17*, 307–315.

Goodhart, G. J., Ehrenberg, A. S. C., & Collins, M. A. (1975). *The television audience: Patterns of viewing.* Lexington, MA: Lexington Books.

Greenberg, B., D'Alessio, D., Heeter, C., & Sipes, S. (1983). *The cableviewing process.* Paper presented at the Midwest Association of Public Opinion Research convention, Chicago.

Greeno, J. (1976). Indefinite goals in well-structured problems. *Psychological Review, 83*(6), 419–491.

Heeter, C. (1983). *Cable and noncable viewing styles.* Unpublished manuscript, Department of Telecommunication, Michigan State University.

Heeter, C. (1984). *Cable and program selection: The choice process.* Paper presented at the convention of the International Communication Association, San Francisco.

Heeter, C., D'Alessio, D., Greenberg, B., & McVoy, D. S. (1983). *Cableviewing.* Paper presented at the convention of the International Communication Association, Dallas.

Henke, L., Donohue, T., Cook, C., & Cheung, D. (1983). *The impact of cable on traditional television news viewing habits.* Paper presented at the convention of the International Communication Association, Dallas.

Hill, D., & Dyer, J. (1981, winter). Extent of diversion to newscasts from distant stations by cable viewers. *Journalism Quarterly,* pp. 552–555.

Husson, W. (1982). *ARIMA models of the attention patterns to television of 3- and 6-year old children.* Paper presented at the convention of the International Communication Association, Boston.

Lefkowitz, H., Eron, L., Walder, L., & Huesmann, L. R. (1972). Television violence and child aggression: A follow-up study. In G. A. Comstock, E. Rubinstein, & J. Murray (Eds.), *Television and social behavior: Vol. 3. Television and adolescent aggressiveness* (pp. 35–135). Washington, DC: U.S. Government Printing Office.

Munsinger, H., & Kesson, W. (1964). Uncertainty, structure and preference. *Psychological Monographs, 78* (Whole No. 9)

Nielsen Newscast. (1983). The outlook for electronic forms of delivery. Number 4, Nielsen Company, Northbrook, IL.

Shiffrin, R., & Schneider, W. (1977). Controlled and automatic human information processing: I. Detection, search and attention. *Psychological Review, 84*(1), 1–34.

Sparkes, V. (1983). Public perception of and reaction to multi-channel cable television service. *Journal of Broadcasting, 27*(2) 163–175.

Stein, A. H., & Friedrich, L. A. (1972). Television content and young children's behavior. In J. Murray, E. Rubinstein,& G. Comstock (Eds.), *Television and social behavior: Vol. 2. Television and social learning.* Washington DC: U.S. Government Printing Office.

Television Audience Assessment, Inc. (1983). *The multi-channel environment.* Cambridge, MA: Television Audience Assessment.

Wakshlag, J., Agostino, D., Terry, H., Driscoll, P., & Ramsey, B. (1983). Television news viewing and network affiliation change. *Journal of Broadcasting. 27*(1), 53–68.

Watt, J., & Krull, R. (1974). An information theory measure for television programming. *Communication Research, 1*(1), 44–68.

Webster, J. (1983). *The impact of cable and pay cable television on local station audiences.* Washington, DC: National Association of Broadcasters.

Webster, J., & Agostino, D. (1982). *Cable and pay cable subscribers' viewing of public television stations.* Athens, OH: Broadcast Research Center.

Webster, J., & Wakshlag, J. (1983). A theory of program choice. *Communication Research, 10*(4), 430–447.

Zillmann, D. (1982). Television viewing and arousal. In D. Pearl, L. Bouthilet & J. Lazar (Eds.), *Television and behavior: Ten years of scientific progress and implications for the eighties: Vol. 2. Technical reviews* (pp. 53–67). Washington, DC: U.S. Government Printing Office.

Zillmann, D., Hezel, R. T., & Medoff, N. J. (1980). The effect of affective states on selective exposure to televised entertainment fare. *Journal of Applied Social Psychology, 10,* 323–339.

Zuckerman, M. (1979). *Sensation seeking: Beyond the optimal level of arousal.* Hillsdale, NJ: Lawrence Erlbaum Associates.

11 "Play It Again, Sam": Repeated Exposure to Television Programs

Percy H. Tannenbaum
Graduate School of Public Policy and Survey Research Center
University of California Berkeley

Devoted Humphrey Bogart fans may argue about whether he actually muttered (through clenched teeth, of course) the now immortal words of the above title in *Casablanca*. They agree, however, that the film's protagonist wanted to hear the tune (titled coincidentally, given our topic, "As Time Goes By") time and again—just as they, the aficionados, return to see the film at every opportunity. Many can recite whole strings of dialogue, wax on about plot and character development, even camera angles in critical scenes, and so forth. Nevertheless, that intimate familiarity does not deter them in the least from going out of the way to view the film repeatedly in revivals or on television.

That, I suppose, is what being a devoted fan is all about: There is never too much of a good thing. Not only are repeated exposures not dully redundant, but they are apparently intrinsically rewarding and whet the appetite for more of the same. In this case, familiarity breeds renewed commitment rather than contempt.

Is this a unique phenomenon, or does it apply as well to other ordinary daily activity? At least, does it apply to other media activity, especially television fare? Are the followers of certain series and regular prime time programs equally "hooked" on their favorite shows? Do they become devotees of a program and watch it regularly, even religiously? Given the opportunity, will they choose to see the same episode of a favorite program repeatedly?

These may not be the most compelling questions to ask regarding the functions of the media in our social existence. However, they do take on more significance when we try to understand the role of entertainment and play in our individual and collective lives. These are critical components of contemporary popular culture, so much of which is conducted in terms of vicarious experiences delivered through the mass media, primarily through television. The role that the

225

repetition of popular programming plays in the television market—on the supply side, in terms of deliberate industry decisions on program content and scheduling, and on the demand side, representing a public preference for such material—is a subject worthy of exploration.

My effort to come to grips with this issue is grounded in my earlier work on entertainment (cf. Tannenbaum, 1980; Tannenbaum & Zillmann, 1975) and is best appreciated in that context. I address the issue from the standpoint of an observer and student, but not a connoisseur, of popular culture.

TELEVISION AUDIENCE BEHAVIOR

It is perhaps not surprising that the matter of repeated exposures has not come in for more of its share of attention before this. I came upon it quite by accident, and were I not involved in my work on entertainment, I probably would not have given it a second thought. But once the first surprising encounter took place, I started searching about for more examples and later proceeded to some experimental investigations.

Tuning in Sitcoms

A totally fortuitous circumstance brought me into contact with the phenomenon under consideration, particularly in regard to repeated viewing of the same episode of a program, some years ago when I became acquainted with the results of a television audience survey conducted in Toronto, Canada. At the time, the Canadian Broadcasting Corporation carried a relatively popular situation comedy series, *Rhoda*, on Thursday nights prior to the identical episode being shown the following Monday evening over CBS network stations in the United States. Toronto is close to the CBS Buffalo, NY, outlet and most homes in the Toronto area have cable television, so this meant that a given episode of the series was available twice within a 4-day period.

The survey (which was subsequently repeated with similar findings) indicated that over 40% of the Monday night audience for *Rhoda* had already seen the identical episode in the previous week, despite the fact that 10 other channels were available for viewing. At the time, this struck my colleagues and me as a surprising, even incredulous, phenomenon. To be sure, the program did not vary that much from week to week in terms of characters and plot, but to select to see the identical segments did seem a bit much—if not quite a case of gluttony for punishment, then certainly an invitation to redundancy and possible boredom.

In an effort to find out more about what is behind this behavior, open-ended interviews were conducted with a number of repeat viewers. Although we thought the behavior odd, most of them took it as a perfectly natural thing to do and thought us odd for inquiring about it. An example of one such exchange between interviewer (I) and respondent (R) helps to convey the gulf between our expectation and theirs:

I: Why do you like *Rhoda?*
R: Because it's a funny program.
I: How come you watch it a second time the same week?
R: Because it was funny the first time.
I: What was so funny?
R: You know, a crazy mix-up between Rhoda and her boyfriend, with her mother and the sister butting in all the time. Lots of good jokes, you just can't help laughing.
I: Yes, but you already knew the jokes, the mixed-up situation. So why go back for the same thing?
R (a bit exasperated): Like I told you. I knew it was a good show so I was sure it would be good again.
I: You're not bored by seeing it again just a few days later?
R: Of course not. It's funny each time I see it. Don't *you* like to hear a good story again or tell a good joke you heard to your friends? (At this point, the respondent reverses roles and becomes the inquirer, apparently trying to figure out why the interviewer is surprised at this choice.)

It was obvious from the different interviews that these fans knew the main characters well and found the situations, the one-liners, and the occasional visual pranks amusing, and they wanted more of the same. They were not at all bored by the rerun. If the laughs were not quite as hearty the second time around, they were still good enough. The element of familiarity appeared to underlie the appeal: It was a known and hence a "safe" form of entertainment, especially compared to other programs with unfamiliar plots, characters, and uncertain humor.

Related Incidents

It turns out that the *Rhoda* case is not an isolated one, although I have yet to come across another instance where the audience overlap was quite so pronounced. Deliberate repeated exposure is not limited to situation comedies, not to the peculiar Canadian border situation. The necessary condition for it to occur is some form of program replication within a limited time span in a given area. Examples from different segments of the broadcasting entertainment spectrum help establish the point further.

Cross-Border Replication. The incident in Canada served to remind me of a somewhat similar case I observed 1 or 2 years earlier on a visit to the middle East. Israel and Jordan were not exactly the friendliest of neighbors, then as now, with little if any economic and social intercourse between the two countries. But the nature of the television signal is such that it knows no international borders and is exempt from passing through customs controls and the like.

As a result, in part of Israel not too distant from the Jordan River border between the two nations (I actually observed this in Jerusalem) television signals from Amman can be received reasonably well and are selectively watched by a considerable number of Israelis. In the mid-1970s, a popular feature on both Israel and Jordanian television was the American detective series *Ironsides* (in both cases in English, with appropriate subtitles in Hebrew and Arabic), with the Jordanian sequence of episodes 1 or 2 weeks ahead of the Israeli sequence. More than once I observed or was told of Israelis regularly watching *Ironsides* on Jordanian television and then tuning in the same episodes a week or two later on their home channel. The same phenomenon in reverse may, of course, have happened in Amman, but I was not privy to any reports from that locale.

Multichannel Replication.   Among the several public broadcasting outlets in the San Francisco bay area, KQED operates on both a main VHF and a secondary UHF frequency. It has adopted a policy for a number of the more popular (for public broadcasting, that is) programs to be repeated during the same week, both on the main and on the auxiliary channels. The main reason is to allow interested members of its audience who could not tune in the main regular broadcast (usually in the evening) of such a program to do so at another hour (say, daytime) on another day. This is especially valuable in a continuing serial or miniseries, where missing one episode can considerably affect the enjoyment and appreciation of the whole series.

It turns out that in addition to such single-time viewers at different periods, there are a number of double-time viewers who take advantage of the repeat later in the week to catch another look at one of their favorites. Exact data are hard to come by here, but there have been requests from regular KQED viewers to continue the practice for just this reason. This was especially evident recently when the station management was considering dropping the auxiliary UHF channel in the interest of economy. It applies apparently to one-off specials as well as to continuing series and serials.

Same-Channel Replications.   The introduction of pay television on cable provides another opportunity for examining the replicated exposure issue. Services such as Home Box Office (HBO), Showtime, the Movie Channel, and others are purchased for a fixed monthly rate in exchange for a variety of motion pictures and some specials, each of which is available on a considerable number of occasions during the following weeks. HBO officials are reluctant to reveal the details of their coverage and the results of various surveys they have conducted for internal management and marketing purposes. But Arbitron ratings, which are available for all television services (including cable and pay TV), and other sources again offer evidence for replicated viewing of the same HBO films within the same household.

In some homes, the same film may be seen as many as five or six times within a 2-week period. Because these are household data, we cannot be sure if it is the same or different individuals engaging in this repetitious behavior, but with such frequencies, considerable individual overlap is very probable. An added incentive for some individuals in this case may be the justification offered by one such viewer, who stated, "Since we're paying for it [the HBO channel] anyways, we might as well get our money's worth."

Same-Day Replication. Perhaps the most extreme versions of the phenomenon are those cases in which a viewer may have exactly the same program available more than once within a period of a few hours. This is made possible by the fact that more than one channel, especially over multichannel cable television, may carry several outlets from the same network. Especially in the western areas of the country, where stations conventionally delay broadcasts for most network programming to suit local prime viewing hours, it is possible that the same program may be available more than once on different outlets within a 2-hour period.

I do not have any hard data on how many people may take advantage of such immediate delays. I would imagine the number is fairly small, perhaps negligible. But I do have reports from individuals who have tuned in the same network news broadcast twice in an hour's time, especially on a day when some special event took place (e.g., the attempted assassination of the president or pope, an election, etc.). There are also anecdotal accounts of persons taking advantage of the multiple offerings of a special program (a documentary and a concert are the two I have heard about) a few hours apart.

Delayed Replications. It is not uncommon for a series with a good run during the regular season to extend its presence on the network schedule into the off-season (usually the summer, but a growing segment of the year's offerings due to more compact schedules, strikes, etc.) with repeats of earlier programs from that same season. In fact, this applies to early failures as well as hit programs; more than once, a show that has not fared well in its introduction early in the regular season has done considerably better the second time around.

At times, this may be due to a more favorable slot in the schedule, with less competition, so that the program attracts a new audience on the repeat. But it is also evident that a good portion (20% and up) are repeat viewers, back for a second look at a program they liked well enough on the initial and local station offering. For repeats of successful shows, network sources estimate even larger overlapping audiences.

Long-Term Replications.   One of the staples of nonprime time programming for network affiliated stations and a feature of the counterprogramming by independent stations during peak viewing hours are reruns, often on a daily basis, of previous popular programs (e.g., the old favorite *I Love Lucy*, *M*A*S*H** and *All in the Family* more recently). Perhaps reruns should not be included in the present context because the time gap (usually several years) between successive showings far exceeds the hours, days, and even months in the cases cited heretofore. Nevertheless, the ubiquity of the rerun format is strong testimony to the popularity of the good old shows both with carry-over and new viewers. These programs generally get good audiences on their repeat showings (otherwise they would not be so common), with repeat viewers estimated to make up well over half of the audience they attract.

These reruns, it should be noted, form an important part of the cost–revenue flow calculation involved in the production and distribution of new programming. Mainly because the domestic market is oligopsonistic (i.e., a large number of independent producers peddling their wares to a small number of buyers, basically the three major networks), United States television production is largely characterized by initial deficit financing. Hence, it is increasingly dependent on secondary markets to make up the shortfalls and yield some profit (which is, after all, the name of the game). These off-network markets take different forms, but a main form is the pattern of reruns that producers can exploit through syndication. Because the gap between production costs and network license fees ranges from 25% upwards, a series of 13 episodes may be over $2 million in the red (and as much as $8 million for a successful series of 22 hour-long episodes) at the end of its first run. In the United States (and increasingly on the international level), the repeat market is expected to pick up the slack, and that, in turn, depends on a substantial carry-over of the old faithful audience from the past. (Control of such secondary markets is what the recent courtroom battle is all about between program producers, on the one hand, and the major networks, on the other. The latter have been denied access to such markets but have put up a spirited battle for a share in their lucrative revenues.)

NEW COMMUNICATION TECHNOLOGY

In the course of the foregoing coverage of the contemporary television audience in the United States, I have touched upon some of the new telecommunication systems along with the more conventional network-based programming. The recent renewal and growth of cable TV have already had an impact on American television as we have known it for more than 3 decades, and cable is bound to have greater effects in the immediate future. In addition to providing more abundant service, it has also introduced more specialized services—such as Ted Turner's superstation and all-day news channel, the separate channels dedicated to sports, and more such dedicated services for children, cultural programming, and so forth on the horizon—and, as we have seen, pay television.

There are other technological wonders in the immediate offing, some of which (e.g., direct satellite broadcasting) may render the recent cable revolution obsolete before it gets off to a proper head start. Two such fledgling products and their use are of direct concern to us here because their very raison d'être is to provide opportunities for endless replications of favorite audio-visual material, including current television fare. I refer, of course, to the video disc and video cassette.

Both of these services have been introduced into the market in the past few years and seem to be doing well enough for starters. For some reason, there has been more penetration in Britain and, to a somewhat lesser degree, in other western European countries than in the United States. Both involve substantial enough outlays of cash or credit to make many consumers wary about taking the plunge, but the anticipated economies of scale that come with a developing initial market are beginning to materialize. Although there are some important differences between the two systems, both are based on the premise that enough people will want to have prerecorded, personally selected program material on hand for multiple viewing at convenient moments for the individual or family.

Video Discs

Video discs belong most clearly in the multiple-use category. The video disc system consists of a special unit, akin to a turntable for playing records, connected to one's television set and the prerecorded discs, which can be purchased or rented. Both the main unit and the discs are too expensive to warrant their purchase for just single viewing of favorite movies, plays and television programs, teaching materials, or what is perhaps more likely in the future, specially edited material put together from previous programs to make for new coherent entities. Accordingly, its success is most intimately linked to the concept of repeated exposure to selected materials by one or more members of a household.

It is possible that some use of the video disc will be through single rather than multiple usage if a vigorous rental system is developed. Some signs of such a system are evident at the time of writing this chapter, but it is still unlikely that the cost and the effort for picking up and returning the rented discs are inexpensive enough to warrant just single usage.

As with the basic system itself, the marketplace will decide the ultimate success or failure of the rental issue. Even if economically viable, the large-scale development of such a system in the near future is deemed too prohibitive in terms of cost and bother to encourage single-use rentals, so again, a multiple-use system seems to be the best guess. Some sort of diversification of specialization between the two (e.g., long-term multiple use for entertainment purposes, short-term single use for instructional purposes) is also a distinct possibility.

Video Tapes and Cassettes

The video disc market may be considerably eclipsed by the video cassette before the former gets off the ground. Although they may lack the same degree of image fidelity, video cassettes seem to do everything video discs can and then some. Their main advantage lies in more flexibility, especially in their ability to record regular television offerings without much effort for later viewing at a more convenient time. They can also be coordinated with a video camera setup so that the equivalent of home-produced movies can be seen time and again by the participants and guests.

Here again, the marketplace will decide the initial chances for success. So far, the video cassette has outpaced the video disc market, and there are strong signs of reduced cost to make cassettes even more attractive. The growth of a suitable software market is a must to such systems, and one is in fact taking shape for video cassettes. The rules of supply and demand will prevail here as readily as in any other purchase market, but a reasonably vigorous rental market is already apparent.

The flexibility of the video cassette system makes it more feasible for single and multiple use by one or more members of a household. For the former, if a viewer cannot be present when a favorite program or event (e.g., a special sporting match) is on the air, it can be recorded at the time and watched later on. In addition, the tape can be erased and then reused for some other program. As the video tape falls in price (in absolute dollars, at least), such delayed one-time viewing may be expected to increase.

However, it is clear that at least the present developers and entrepreneurs anticipate a high level of repeated usage for the system to succeed economically. Again, factors such as initial investment costs point in this direction. Perhaps even more to the point is the development of a prepackaged software sales market. Just how this dual-use pattern sorts itself out will have to be seen—the market analyses I have seen vary too widely in their relative allocation to single and multiple use for any one to be taken as a reliable indicator. In any case, it is clear that replication is a significant part of the mix, and hence in keeping with the basic assumption of motivated multiple exposure at issue here.

EXPERIMENTAL STUDIES

The foregoing illustrations amply document an appetite among the public for repetition and redundancy for the familiar fare of popular culture and entertainment as represented on television. The many different ways in which this appetite could be, and apparently is being, satisfied prompts one to look for the breadth of the phenomenon in areas other than television per se and to explore its depth through some specific research. The latter assumed the form of a series of experimental studies.

Preference for Special Moments

Sports—with its elements of rules and ritual, competition between teams, cooperation within a team, physical action and movement, fierce loyalty to the home team, and so on—occupies a precious place on the American cultural scene. It is a prime feature on the television schedule, where real-time coverage of sporting matches is one of the few instances of live programming on the air. Technically, it also represents one of the medium's finest accomplishments, where the use of multiple cameras shooting from different angles on the field, split-screen images, zoom lens close-ups, instant replays, and slow motion combine to give sports fans a fuller, richer coverage of the game as such, than they could possibly get from the best seat in the stadium or arena.

To be a resident of the state of Wisconsin during the mid-1960s meant becoming a football fan, if not a fanatic. That was the era of the Green Bay Packer dynasty, and watching the Sunday afternoon television broadcasts of their games was a ritual across the state. The Pack had some remarkable victories during their heyday, but clearly, their highlight was the championship match of the 1967 season, played in subzero temperatures at Green Bay against the Dallas Cowboys. The Packers staged a last-gasp effort in the closing minutes to march down to the Dallas goal line and, as the clock ran out, scored the winning touchdown on a quarterback sneak over right guard. It was a precious moment for a dedicated Packer fan.

That scene, with Bart Starr sneaking his way over the line behind Ron Kramer's blocking, has been lovingly replayed dozens of times since those halcyon days. Some 10 years after the actual event, two groups were assembled in Wisconsin for purposes of investigating television viewer preferences for special moments. One consisted of football fans, all of whom were screened as remembering and having seen the game and the winning play countless times on television over the years; the other group was composed of individuals not interested in football or those who were not exposed to the original game. The groups assembled on the day of a live Green Bay football game, which was being televised, and both groups were given a choice of watching the live game, an edited (an shortened) replay of the 1967 championship game, or two other nonsports television programs available at that hour. All but one of the football fans chose to watch one of the football games, but only about one third (19 of 52) of the noninterested group chose to do so. What was more surprising (at least to me) was that better than two thirds (49 of 72) of the football fans chose to watch the live game on television. To be sure, the Packers were having a rather poor season, and the live game was against another poor team, so not much was at stake. Nevertheless, that so many preferred a partial reliving of that certain moment of glory over an uncertain inconsequential game was more than we had expected. As if to justify their choice, the fans cheered and slapped each others' backs with almost as much gusto during that replay as they did a decade earlier at the actual event.

Interestingly enough, when we later conducted a similar study in the Dallas area, the results were almost directly reversed. The fan group still preferred seeing football in any form over some other programming, but the vast majority (27 of 34) wanted to see the live game. Of course, the fact that the Cowboys were having one of their characteristic winning years may have had something to do with the choice. But undoubtedly, so did the fact that Dallas had ended up losing the 1967 classic.

Pedaling for Pleasure

The measurement of choice and preference among available television programs has been a problem that has bedeviled the industry and academic researchers alike. Verbal expressions, through survey questionnaires or rating scales, are suitable for some purposes but are of questionable validity as indices of what the individual would actually choose in a real situation. Actual behavioral measures are obviously superior, but other than the industry ratings services, these have been curiously absent in broadcasting research until recently (see, e.g., chap. 3 by Webster & Wakshlag in this volume).

Some years back, I happened on a means of getting such a behavioral index and have been using it off and on ever since. It originated in personal experience (as much of my research has) when I was given an exercycle as a gift. I dutifully placed it in my study and worked up to the requisite half-hour or so of daily pedaling under varying conditions. A boring practice for the likes of me under the best of conditions, this was all the more so when I did it facing a blank wall. I even turned to relieving the monotony by imagining that I was pedaling along a lane in a woody forest with a stream beside me; for such situations are hallucinations made. The problem was resolved when I placed the machine in front of a television set and pedaled away while Walter Cronkite did the evening news.

It was a short leap from that experience to my laboratory. There we rigged up a set of exercycles to a corresponding number of television sets so that either the audio signals, the visual signals, or both would fade away unless the cycle was pedaled beyond a preset (an adjustable) standard. Thus, in this system, choice could actually be assessed by the relative level of energy subjects were willing to expend to see (and, more important, to keep seeing) a given program. Some very detectable differences in pedaling activity were apparent for a given individual across different programs, and hence for collections of individuals. (It may be of some interest that in one test between this procedure and more conventional verbal ratings, the correlation between the two was rather lower than anticipated, although statistically significant, $r = .33$. Of course, this does not prove the superiority of one procedure over the other, just that they are different enough to warrant not being treated as alike.)

Again, a fortuitous circumstance in the laboratory led to another useful measure with this technique. The apparatus broke down one day in the middle of group testing. Literally not knowing how long it would take to repair (the apparatus was in the hands of a technician who first had to be located and then repair the damage), we allowed the subjects either to wait it out or leave; they would be paid the same nominal fee either way. To our surprise, quite a few waited upwards of 2 hours to see the ending of the detective program that was being shown at the time. Ever since, we have included staged breakdowns at preselected points in a program, and we then use relative waiting time as an index of sustained interest in the program.

Both types of measures—the effort expended and the waiting time—have been used in a variety of studies. One was specifically designed to address the question of repetitive exposures. It dealt with the then popular, now defunct (although still enjoying a brisk rerun record) detective adventure series *Kojak,* which was positively rated by the subjects involved (mostly senior citizens of the San Francisco bay area). All subjects were first shown a 50-minute episode of *Kojak* over a 10-day period using the exercycle technique. *Kojak's* drawing power, in terms of effort and duration of exposure, was significantly superior to two other detective programs for most subjects; the few for which this did not apply did not participate in the next phase of the study. That consisted of a second exposure to the identical episode within a 2–3 week period of the initial showings.

Participation Rate.   All subjects ($N = 37$) had a choice of participating in the repeat presentation. All but two (95%) chose to watch the program a second time—a figure I still find hard to believe, even considering the relative popularity of that particular episode the first time. This higher rate may have been partly due to the "demand characteristics" of the experiment, that is, participants had already come to the laboratory, expected to act as subjects in some experiment, perhaps had a desire to please the experimenter, and so forth. But inasmuch as they were paid for their effort anyway and were able to spend the hour or so reading magazines and sipping coffee, the participation rate is still impressive.

Effort Expended.   Not only did most subjects watch the program a second time, but all who did so stayed with it. This despite the fact that the level of effort necessary for proper reception had been set approximately 12.5% higher (i.e., it required one eighth additional pedaling output). Gluttons for punishment indeed—but apparently loving every minute of it!

Staying Power.   Approximately 11 minutes before the end of the episode, at the point judged to be the climax in the plot development, we staged the fake breakdown. Again, subjects could wait (more or less indefinitely in terms of the experiment) or leave as they saw fit. All subjects waited for some period of time. The range was from 18 minutes to over 3 hours, with a mean of 1 hour 21 minutes—this for the end of a program all subjects had seen within the preceding 2 or 3 weeks. Although we can again invoke the same externalities and subject expectations and though it may be true that some subjects had little else to do, this still strikes me as incredible for a repeat showing of a not particularly unusual episode of a familiar program. Subject certainly knew the plot and could be expected to remember the ending in general, if not in exact detail, but they stuck with it and waited it out nevertheless. Such viewers are trying to tell us something.

Choosing Television for Relaxation

We have recently completed another investigation which, although directed at another set of concerns, bears somewhat on the repetition issue. In this research, subjects give us the better part of a long 10-hour day during which we expose them to a variety of physically and/or mentally demanding activities. They are then fed briefly and are given a selection of different communication activities "in order to relax." The majority tend to watch television. In this particular study, they were then given a choice of six programs: new episodes of two of their favorite programs (determined by a previous questionnaire), two reruns of past episodes (almost 2 months old) of the same programs, and two new programs with which they were totally unfamiliar (actually, pilots for possible new programs).

Faced with this decision, the 30 subjects made the following choices: 4 (13%) selected one of the new unfamiliar programs, 21 (70%) chose one of the new episodes of a familiar favorite, and the remaining 5 (17%) chose one of the repeats. These numbers are fairly small for firm conclusions, and I am not sure just what we expected to find, but the fact that one in six persons opted to see a repeat of a familiar episode still draws my attention. Put another way, it is no surprise that 87% chose the familiar over the unfamiliar programs, but it is noteworthy that of these individuals, 20% picked a rerun to a fresh episode.

THEORETICAL SPECULATIONS

In a real sense, this is selective exposure indeed. But what do we make of it? Is it some extraordinary phenomenon that has been uncovered? Or is it something quite prosaic, an expected occurrence that has not been identified or dealt with merely because it was not regarded as being important enough? It may have been my personal naivete that got me started on this path to begin with (if so, it seems to be shared by many others), and I am quite willing to accept a judgment that this is more molehill than mountain.

Certainly, the preference, perhaps even the quest, for repetitive experiences is not unique to television programs. For one thing, it is most readily apparent with young children, who can do the same thing over and over again an endless number of times. For example, in most households, there is a rather fixed repertoire of bedtime stories. As many a suffering parent can attest, children want the same set of stories told exactly the same way, down to tone of voice, hand and facial gesture, and the like. It is like a fixed script, which if departed from in the slightest way will not be accepted; if a little variation is added to ease the sheer tedium of it all (e.g., have Goldilocks end up in the Mama Bear's bed for a change), children let out a howl. It is not that they don't know what is coming up, nor is faulty memory a factor. Just the opposite in fact: Pause at any point, and children can fill in the exact lines word for word. They know the script by heart; they enjoy it as it is, without frills and amendments; and they want it as it is. We tend to outgrow these childish fixations with what is narrow and familiar in time, just as we develop a wider choice of preferred foods beyond hot dogs, hamburgers, and peanut butter. But because there is a bit of the kid in all of us, similar behaviors persist throughout the life span. Adolescents have a wider range of things to do and topics to gossip about than do little tykes in kindergarten, but not by much if you trust the judgment of most parents. And one of the observed characteristics of old age is a renewed narrowing of focus of interest and preoccupation with the familiar past still available in long-term memory.

Even in mature early adulthood, at one's prime, there are still remnants of returning to old familiar faces and places. We noted the phenomenon for Bogart film buffs at the outset of the chapter, and similar cults exist for such film attractions as Marx Brothers flicks, a Woody Allen festival, or anything with Katherine Hepburn. Other people periodically reread favorite books, although that repeat activity appears to be less widespread and less intense than for film fans. For adults, it is most apparent in the area of music. Aficionados of one type of music or another have their own collections of records or tapes, which are played repeatedly according to one's mood. Individuals may add to their collection, but rarely if ever do they dump an old favorite, which remains something to fall back on when the conditions are right. (A personal confession may help clarify the point: I am far from a connoisseur of opera, but enforced listening to Saturday afternoon Metropolitan Opera radio broadcasts did leave me with a passing familiarity with the music and major arias of a number of classical operas. I am not terribly proud of it, but I stick to this limited repertoire, reluctant to venture into new territory. I am personally convinced that I derive my pleasure from the familiarity as such, possibly with some attendant appreciation for some of the nuances and the more difficult passages by which a particular performance may be judged.)

Despite such examples of repeated behavior, the findings in the audience and laboratory research—particularly the deliberate reexposure in the *Rhoda* and *Kojak* cases—still stand out and deserve considered attention. The point is not that the phenomenon exists, but the extent to which it is manifest; that is what gives it its public or mass character. Under the circumstances, it is motivated rather than imposed behavior, and as such, it testifies to a widespread segment of the television audience seeking out a relatively simple, preferred form of entertainment, that is, mild doses of amusement or involvement that are relatively effortless, reliable, and rewarding in and of themselves.

Emotional Arousal

That, in effect, is the basis of the model I have used to account for the popularity of television entertainment. Under such a formulation, the basic element of entertainment is some heightening of emotional arousal or excitation, usually in modest amounts, occasionally more deeply involving. But even mild emotion "jags" have a positive value for individuals beset with the many trials and travails of daily living. With little personal investment—a willingness to set aside concerns of the moment, to relax, suspend reality, and "get into" the fantasy of the situation (however inane it may appear on the surface)—the rewards can be dependable and titillating, if not deep and lasting.

Any emotional arousal induced through communication is viewed as having two components and stages, in keeping with the general Schachter (1964) theory of a two-stage model (Tannenbaum, 1980; Tannenbaum & Zillmann, 1975). The first is a set of physiological reactions (probably mediated by the release of adrenalin), which the organism becomes aware of generally, if not necessarily in the specific kind of physiological change. This leads to the second or cognitive stage where the individual searches his or her immediate environment for some likely explanation for the felt arousal. The model holds further that there can be behavioral consequences for both the emotional arousal per se (essentially, higher arousal, however induced, leads to more intense responses, whatever kind of behavior is called for) and the cognitive attribution (which shapes the direction and nature of the subsequent behavior).

Originally developed to deal with both causal and selective first-time exposure to television and other media content, the model can also be applied to subsequent motivated replications. The same incentives for an emotional reaction are there, perhaps somewhat reduced because it is the second time around, but by the same token, they are also certain, reliable, and familiar, thus requiring even less effort. The cost–benefit ratio, if you will, is still favorable enough compared to other, less reliable choices for diversion at the moment. The motivation is not in the reexposure but in the reexperiencing.

This formulation, tentative and inelegant as it may be, receives some empirical support from some past and recent research involving partial replications of previously arousing film and video messages. First, scenes for which relatively high degrees of physiological excitation were obtained on initial exposure were selected for each individual. Then, subjects were shown a small sample of the key scenes—either the first 20 seconds of film or a set of still photographs—while wired for physiological reaction recordings. In both cases, we found attenuated replications of the initial pattern of physiological reaction, rarely as high as in the original, but of the same locus, contour, and the like.

Associated Concepts

A variety of hypothetical concepts and constructs have been alluded to or hinted at in various segments of the foregoing account. Although I am not sure whether they overlap, fit together, or are disjoint—both in relation to one another and to the emotional arousal paradigm—they do merit more specific identification.

Familiarity.   Psychologists, information theorists, and aestheticians, among others, have tried for a long time to determine if people prefer novel stimuli to familiar ones (cf. Berlyne & Madsen, 1973). The answer seems to be that both are preferred, but by different people under different circumstances. Clearly, familiarity is a factor in choice for a lot of people much of the time, and the familiar-with variation may be optimal for most people most of the time.

Certainty.   This is closely related to, but not identical with, the familiarity notion. The assumption (and it is only that) here is that the sure and certain are generally preferred to the unknown and uncertain. Certainty and familiarity make for more *reliability,* which is assumed to have positive valence and hence guides selection.

Memory.   Clearly, some kind of memory trace—whether for the content, the arousal itself, or merely for the associated positive reward—is involved in the aforementioned studies of replicated physiological arousal. Memory can also be invoked in many of the other illustrations, at least as a mediating factor. Indeed, it is difficult to consider voluntary repeated exposure without memory being intimately involved.

Nostalgia.   Selective memory for positive experiences can obviously be an important motivator. This is the basis for that yearn to return to what we identify as nostalgia, at least in the way it is developed and treated in Davis' (1979) astute and insightful sociological study of that topic. In keeping with the foregoing formulation, the emphasis is how positive artifacts and experiences from the past are incorporated into current experience so that they have value in and of themselves in the here and now.

Fantasy.   Although they have not been alluded to directly, I personally believe imagination and fantasy play powerful roles in vicarious emotional arousal through communication messages. The nostaligc component for replicated exposure may in fact be as much for the fantasized associations as for elements actually present.

Ritual. There are times when the seeking or preference for repeated experience by individuals takes on the characteristics of social rituals. The cultural role of ritual perhaps has its parallel in the psychological functions of repeated media (and other) exposure, a topic I gladly leave to others more knowledgeable to explore.

An Industrial Perspective

So far, this discussion has dealt solely with the consumer's approach to repeated offerings. But there is a market involved here, and the suppliers have a vital interest in it. Television producers and network programmers may be unsophisticated in terms of the nuances and niceties of social science theory, but they play in a high-stakes game, and their programming and scheduling tend to reflect— and given the cyclical nature of the television market, may also partially determine—public wants. At least within the considerable constraints under which such a competitive industry operates, they have tried out various program combinations and have data, in the form of ratings, on what choices are exercised.

As in any economic enterprise, the key factor is bottom-line profit for each of the parties along the supply chain. Earlier in this paper, certain economic realities that contribute a market for rerun offerings were identified. The factors making for deficit financing at the initial production stage for network prime time programming (serials, movies made for television, and one-off specials) lead to the need for a considerable off-network market, of which reruns constitute a considerable part. Increasingly, production houses with large amounts of capital investment at stake have to engage in advance up-front calculations (and negotiations) for such secondary distribution markets. An example of how important this market is for producers is represented in Norman Lear's court challenge to the so-called "family hour" concept. This was a result of behind-the-scenes negotiations between the FCC and the three networks to exclude certain content (e.g., violence, sexual innuendo, etc.) from the pre-9 p.m. programming, thus tending to concentrate any such material in the post-9 p.m. period. Lear successfully argued that this constituted a restraint of trade in that the resale potential of his shows on the rerun market would be impaired.

For networks and local stations (not to mention foreign broadcast systems), such repeats can be a bonanza because they are often available at substantially reduced costs. With a reasonable audience for such programs, advertising revenue can be accrued so that the net profit is at or above the average level. As long as this three-way producer-broadcaster-audience symbiosis is maintained, the repeat market should continue to flourish for some time to come. That the networks seek to take over some or all of the rerun revenue from the producers is merely added testimony to the economic stakes involved.

ACKNOWLEDGMENT

A version of this paper was presented as an address to the Seminar on Media Mythology in February, 1981, chaired by Mary Douglas, at the New York Institute for the Humanities. Support for some of the research reported here came from the Committee of Research at Berkeley, the John and Mary Markle Foundation, and the National Institute of Mental Health.

REFERENCES

Berlyne, D. E., & Madsen, K. B. (Eds.). (1973). *Pleasure, reward, preference: Their nature, determinants, and role in behavior.* New York: Academic Press.

Davis, F. (1979). *Yearning for yesterday: A sociology of nostalgia.* New York: Free Press.

Schachter, S. (1964). The interaction of cognitive and physiological determinants of emotional state. In L. Berkowitz (Ed.), *Advances in experimental social psychology* (Vol. 1, pp. 49–80). New York: Academic Press.

Tannenbaum, P. H. (1980). Entertainment as vicarious emotional experience. In P. H. Tannenbaum (Ed.), *The entertainment functions of television* (pp. 107–131). Hillsdale, NJ: Lawrence Erlbaum Associates.

Tannenbaum, P. H., & Zillmann, D. (1975). Emotional arousal in the facilitation of aggression through communication. In L. Berkowitz (Ed.), *Advances in experimental social psychology* (Vol. 8, pp. 150–192). New York: Academic Press.

Author Index

Page numbers in *italics* show where complete bibliographic references are given.

Subject Index